The Grasping Imagination

Peter Buitenhuis

❧⸻❧

UNIVERSITY OF TORONTO PRESS

The Grasping Imagination

❖

THE AMERICAN WRITINGS OF HENRY JAMES

©
University of Toronto Press 1970
Printed in Canada by
University of Toronto Press, Toronto and Buffalo
ISBN 0-8020-5244-4

Quotations from James's Tales are from
The Complete Tales of Henry James
Vols. 1–5, edited by Leon Edel
Volume 1 copyright © 1961, 1962 by Leon Edel
Volume 2 copyright © 1962 by Leon Edel
Volume 3 copyright © 1962 by Leon Edel
Volume 4 copyright © 1962 by Leon Edel
Volume 5 copyright © 1963 by Leon Edel
Reprinted by permission of J. B. Lippincott Company

For Elspeth

Contents

Contents

Contents

ix

Acknowledgments

The origins of this study lie in a thesis done under the supervision of the late Stanley T. Williams at Yale. I should like to acknowledge here both his pioneering work in American studies and his great kindness to myself. Some of my ideas were derived from seminars on Henry James conducted over a four-year period at the University of Toronto. I cannot thank this international group of graduate students by name, but should like to acknowledge their collective help. This book has been published with the help of a grant from the Humanities Research Council of Canada, using funds provided by the Canada Council. Funds have come also from the Canada Council, the University of Toronto, and McGill University for research, to all of whom I owe a debt of gratitude. I should like also to thank Leon Edel for his advice and corrections of my copies of manuscript material, Kenneth MacLean for his reading of the manuscript, and the editors of University of Toronto Press for their exacting scrutiny of my work.

In the rich collection of materials that Alvin Langdon Coburn left to the George Eastman House archive on his death in 1966, there is a bound collection of the photographs that Coburn made for the New York Edition of *The Novels and Tales of Henry James*. Inside the front cover appears this inscription:

> For remembrance of all our pleasant pursuit or capture of the
> charming and interesting impressions here recorded,
> as well as of others not gathered in.
> Henry James to A. L. Coburn/Lamb House Dec. 27, 1909

Acknowledgments

The impressions gathered together for this book are all from the Coburn Collection and were made on trips that Coburn, an expatriate like James, made to his native land in 1907 and 1910–11. The combination of words and images presented here show some of the similarities of perception and taste that the two friends shared.

Hitherto unpublished notes on *The Ivory Tower* and unpublished letters by Henry James are printed here with the kind permission of the literary executor, Mr. Alexander R. James. Copyright/1970/ Alexander R. James. I am also grateful for Mr. James's permission to use material still in copyright in *Notes on Novelists*, 1914.

Professor Leon Edel has generously allowed me to use letters to which he has prior claims.

The letters of John Morley and the letters and manuscripts of Henry James in the Houghton Library at Harvard are quoted by permission of the Harvard College Library. I wish to thank the Yale University Library and the Library of Congress for permission to quote from letters of Henry James in their collections.

Thanks are due to the following publishers: the Oxford University Press, New York, for permission to quote from *The Notebooks of Henry James*, edited by F. O. Matthiessen and Kenneth B. Murdock, and to Charles Scribner's Sons for permission to quote from *The Letters of Henry James* edited by Percy Lubbock, from *Henry James Autobiography*, edited by F. W. Dupee, from the Prefaces to the New York Edition of *The Novels and Tales of Henry James*, and from material in *The American Novels and Stories of Henry James*, edited by F. O. Matthiessen.

Mr. John Fowles willingly gave his permission to use the quotation from *The French Lieutenant's Woman* (Jonathan Cape), which appears as an epigraph.

I wish to thank the editors of the *University of Toronto Quarterly*, the *American Quarterly*, the *Humanities Association of Canada Bulletin*, and the *Canadian Association for American Studies Bulletin* for their permission to use articles or parts of articles which have already appeared in their journals.

Montreal, February 1970

The Grasping Imagination

The artist ...
has but to have his honest sense of life
to find it fed at every pore
even as the birds of the air are fed ...

FROM THE PREFACE TO VOLUME XIV OF
The Novels and Tales of Henry James
1908

The novelist is still a god,
since he creates
(and not even the most aleatory
avant-garde modern novel
has managed to extirpate its author completely);
what has changed is that we are no longer
the gods of the Victorian image,
omniscient and decreeing;
but in the new theological image,
with freedom our first principle,
not authority.

JOHN FOWLES
The French Lieutenant's Woman
1969

Introduction

The use of the term 'American' in the subtitle of this study is of course an arbitrary one. In a sense all of James's work is American, since, as has often been pointed out, he never lost that orientation even after many years of residence in England. On the other hand, the limited sense of 'American' as applied to a section of his work seems to have been sanctioned by James himself when he expressed the desire to write 'a very *American* story' in outlining *The Bostonians*. The term was taken up by F. O. Matthiessen when he collected *The American Novels and Stories of Henry James* and later by Leon Edel for his edition of *The American Essays of Henry James*.

This study concentrates on the fiction that is set entirely in the United States. I have also written extensively on the non-fiction, both the critical essays and the travel notes, particularly *The American Scene*. Some of the stories set partly in the United States, such as *An International Episode* have also been used. For reasons of length and unity, I have discussed the 'non-American' fiction – for example, *A Passionate Pilgrim* and *The Portrait of a Lady* – only when it has been necessary for the development of my central theme.

Most of the characters in these American stories are natives of the country, a good many are expatriates back on a visit; a much smaller number are Europeans visiting or residing in the United

States. Henry James used all their view-points to give a spectrum of opinion about America that amounts to one of the most comprehensive criticisms that any writer has made of his own country. My main intention is thus to provide an extended refutation of those critics, like Van Wyck Brooks and Maxwell Geismar, who have maintained that James abandoned his native land imaginatively as well as physically in favour of Europe and ultimately in favour of fiction that bears resemblance to no existing reality.

I have tried to avoid the large generalizations that have so often dogged Jamesian criticism in this area and have made as close a textual analysis of the relevant fiction and non-fiction as a reasonable length allows. In this manner I have hoped to follow the trail pointed out by F. O. Matthiessen in the excellent introduction to his collection of the American fiction. 'Confronted with so voluminous a writer as Henry James,' he wrote, 'we may always gain fresh insight into his work by following a single phase of it from first to last.' The American aspect is a phase that has come in for surprisingly little comment in comparison with the 'international' aspect of his fiction. Such neglect is understandable, to a degree, in the light of James's pre-eminence in his chosen major theme. The overshadowing of the American aspect has, however, been even more marked than this pre-eminence warrants. One reason for this may be that James chose to present himself to posterity, particularly in his selection for the New York Edition, as the international novelist *tout court*. He said of himself in the preface to Volume XIV of that edition that he 'might even ... be represented as scarce aware, before the human scene, of any other sharp antithesis at all.' Such representation, as James's own irony reveals, would be quite misleading. The posthumous publication of collections of his essays and reviews on the theatre, painting, and travel, as well as little-known fiction, has demonstrated that James was always aware of multitudinous subjects and antitheses beyond the range of the international contrast.

The American aspect spans the whole length of James's career and thus provides an opportunity for the critic to come to grips with ideas and themes which he developed through a creative lifetime of over fifty years. In a well-known letter to Charles Eliot Norton in 1871, he claimed: 'Looking about for myself, I conclude that the face of nature and civilization in this our country is to a certain point a very sufficient literary field. But it will yield its secrets only to a really *grasping* imagination.' It is my main contention that in this phrase Henry James had defined the essence of his problem, although he had at that time little idea how to solve it. Before he could find successful artistic forms for his themes, he had to overcome many barriers in his own ways of perceiving reality. Growing up with a vision conditioned by images from English literature, devoted later to techniques drawn from French literature and art, he had to go through an abnormally long period of experimentation and trial and error before he could arrive at the strikingly original method of perception that finds unique form in the late style. To discover the secrets 'of nature and civilization' in America took all the unremitting efforts and the sustained growth of an imagination whose grasp eventually became as great as its reach.

Something should be said here of the method used in the study to elucidate this theme. While my major technique has been a detailed analysis of the main texts, I have tried to trace the development of James's perception in terms of the method used by the art historian, E. H. Gombrich. In an essay on 'Imagery and Art in the Romantic Period' (collected in *Meditations on a Hobby Horse,* London, 1963), he wrote: 'Even the greatest artist – and he more than others – needs an idiom to work in. Only tradition, such as he finds it, can provide him with the raw material of imagery which he needs to represent an event of a "fragment of nature." He can re-fashion this imagery, adapt it to its task, assimilate it to his needs and change it beyond recognition, but he can no more represent what is in front of his eyes without a pre-existing stock of acquired images than he can paint it without the pre-existing set of colours which he must have on his palette.'

Professor Gombrich develops this insight into the creative process in his brilliant study *Art and Illusion* (London, 1960). There he analyzes closely in painters of all eras the process of perception in relation to the techniques of rendering. He shows how, in all cases, the painters used existing models on which to base their work and developed according to a process which he calls 'matching and making.' The term that Gombrich uses for the received image or form is schema (plural schemata). As he notes in the introduction to *Art and Illusion*, he derived this term from the philosophy of Kant, in which it plays a role of major importance. Kant claimed in *The Critique of Pure Reason* that 'the schemata of the pure concepts of the understanding are the true and sole conditions that make possible any relationship of the concepts to objects, and consequently the conditions of their having any meaning.' This generalization applies with particular force to the realm of art, as Gombrich has shown. Without his schemata, the artist cannot begin to create, for he cannot organize his sense perceptions, *ex nihilo*, into a meaningful form.

In using schema and schemata as terms of literary criticism I am implying both Kant's general and Gombrich's specific use of the terms. The writer matches and makes as a painter does, but he also derives concepts from other writers. These may include attitudes, moods, and tones as well as images and symbols. By gradually learning to select from other writers the concepts most suitable to his own talents, the writer can begin to develop and refine his perceptions and finally make his own unique style.

Gombrich's insights have, I believe, a particular relevance to this study, as they were anticipated by Henry James himself in his fiction, and foreshadowed more precisely by William James in his *Principles of Psychology*. William wrote: 'Whilst part of what we perceive comes through our senses from the object before us, another part (and it may be the larger part) always comes ... out of our own head.' The part from one's own head is of course the schema derived from received forms of perceiving reality. Henry James's artistic awareness of his brother's philosophical speculation is discussed in chapter eight, below.

Matthiessen's collection, *The American Novels and Stories of Henry James*, has been used as the main text for this study. For the many American short stories that Matthiessen did not collect in that edition I have used Professor Leon Edel's *The Complete Tales of Henry James*, except where there were significant variations from earlier printings of these stories. My critical analyses of James's work have been set in the context of that part of his life which was spent in the United States. In the first part of the study I have drawn extensively from James's autobiography and from the first four volumes of Leon

Edel's rich biography. For the later chapters, in years that Professor Edel has not yet reached, I have gone mostly to James's own letters, a number of which are quoted here for the first time. Although Henry James did not rely as heavily as most American writers on his own biography as a direct source of his fiction, he did create through his characters a wide range of attitudes and points of view on the basis of his experience. It has been my endeavour to locate these points of view in the framework of his life in the United States.

⁕ 1 ⁕

The Civil War

and

Harvard's Tented Field

On New Year's Day, 1863, a huge crowd filled the Boston Music Hall. It had gathered to celebrate Abraham Lincoln's Emancipation Proclamation, the text of which was expected by telegraph from Washington at any moment. Many of the great abolitionists and other Boston notables were there. Most of them made speeches. Between the drumrolls of rhetoric an orchestra played Beethoven's *Egmont* overture and the 'Hymn of Praise' from the Ninth Symphony. During an interval, it was announced to roars of applause that the president's proclamation was in process of transmission.[1]

In the audience was nineteen-year-old Henry James who recalled the occasion nearly a quarter of a century later in an essay on Ralph Waldo Emerson. Prominent on the programme had been a reading by Emerson of his own poem 'The Boston Hymn.' 'I well remember,' James wrote, 'the immense effect with which his beautiful voice pronounced the lines –

> Pay ransom to the owner
> And fill the bag to the brim.
> Who is the owner? The slave is owner,
> And ever was. Pay *him!*'

Still vivid to James as he wrote the essay was his sense of 'the momentousness of the occasion, the vast excited multitude, the crowded platform, and the tall, spare figure of Emerson, in the midst ...'[2]

8

To many present it must have seemed like the dawn of a new era. The cause to which so many idealistic Bostonians had devoted themselves, and for which so much blood had already been shed, had at last been made national policy. The war was now on the turn towards victory and the North was united as it had never been before. Henry James, Sr., had written to Emerson in 1862: 'What a world, what a world! But once we get rid of Slavery the new heavens and new earth will swim into reality.'³ The pages of the autobiographical *Notes of a Son and Brother* indicate that Henry, Jr., shared this enthusiasm, if not this much faith. Who could, after all, have imagined that this New Year's Day vision of harmony, unity, and equality would so quickly perish as the war dragged on to its bloody end, only to give way to the bitterness of the Reconstruction period?

The James family itself was too much caught up with the passion and excitement of the war to have any doubt about its outcome. The two younger brothers, Wilky and Bob, had enlisted as soon as they could. Both saw a great deal of action. Wilky served in the most famous northern regiment of the war, the 54th Massachusetts. This was the first Negro unit to be raised and was commanded by the energetic and colourful Robert Gould Shaw. To Henry, made a spectator by a back injury, which he called 'a horrid even if an obscure hurt,' sustained in fighting a fire,⁴ his brothers were figures of romance and valour. From the first, however, spectatorship was a role that he was admirably qualified to play, and in a sense it remained his most characteristic stance throughout his life. As an older man, he remembered how, in his early childhood, he used to gaze through the railings of a country estate that then remained on the northeast corner of Eighteenth Street and Broadway in New York. 'There,' he wrote in *A Small Boy and Others,* 'was the very pattern and measure of all he was to demand: just to *be* somewhere – almost anywhere would do – and somehow receive an impression or an accession, feel a relation or a vibration.'⁵

After spending his most impressionable years in travel and rootless residence in Europe, he was in a position to be profoundly influenced by the sudden onset of the Civil War. It quickly catalyzed his deep yearnings for a spiritual homeland. The war came to him in an 'indirect and muffled fashion,' he wrote in *Notes of a Son and*

Brother; but this did not 'prevent the whole quite indescribably intensified time – intensified through all lapses of occasion and frustrations of contact – from remaining with me as a more constituted and sustained act of living, in proportion to my powers and opportunities, than any other homogeneous stretch of experience that my memory now recovers.'[6]

During the second year of the war, in the fall of 1862, Henry had gone up from Newport, where the family was then living, to the Harvard Law School. There he felt associated for the first time with 'matters normally, entirely, consistently American ...' Newport was 'adulterated' and 'incurably cosmopolite,' but in Cambridge, he believed, American data would be given 'as with absolute authority.' The Harvard campus was his 'tented field,' since the 'bristling horde' of his law school comrades 'fairly produced the illusion of a mustered army.'[7] These metaphors of war service are retrospective, of course, in *Notes of a Son and Brother*, but it is likely that he thought in these terms at the time to ease a sense of guilt about his absence from the ranks of the Union army. For a brief period, at least, his enrolment in the law school, incongruous as it turned out to be, gave him a needed sense of identification, of Americanization, as it were, which he had felt his cosmopolitan upbringing had hitherto denied him. As he had written to T. S. Perry from Bonn in July 1860, shortly before returning to the United States, 'I think that if we are to live in America it is about time we boys should take up our abode there; the more I see of this estrangement of American youngsters from the land of their birth, the less I believe in it. It should also be the land of their breeding.'[8] At Harvard, for the first time in his life, he felt fully immersed in the current of American experience.

It was while he was still formally enrolled in the law school that he realized his long-felt dream of becoming a writer. No matter how much he deplored his estrangement from his native land, it had prepared him in many ways admirably for his chosen career. He was now a cosmopolitan young man with an unusually deep, if narrow, range of knowledge of Europe and European – particularly English and French – literature. While he was young, he was probably not really aware of how much his early travel and reading had not only formed his critical standards but also conditioned his perceptions. As an older man, with his remarkably developed sensitivity, he could look back and see how cosmopolitanism – even that of his childhood home in New York – had obscured his vision of American life. *A Small Boy and Others* and *Notes of a Son and Brother* are, like *The Prelude*, records of the growth of an imagination. But James grew up not so much in a natural world as in the realms of gold of foreign authors.

The autobiographies make abundantly plain how, from his earliest childhood, James learned to see life through the spectacles of English books. His father was an intensely bookish man, who when not living in England, was constantly importing books from there. The very smell of paper and printer's ink was known in the James household as 'the English smell.' 'All our books ... were English ...,' he recalled, 'and I take the perception of that quality in them to have associated itself with more fond dreams and glimmering pictures than any other one principle of growth.'[9] He was, as he phrased it, prematurely poisoned by the English infusion. Smollett, Fielding, Trollope, Thackeray, the Brontë sisters, George Eliot, all supplied him with pervasive images of life. Above all, the force of the Dickens imprint, as James called it, was immense.

One of the supreme moments of his young life came when, at twenty-four, he was invited to meet Dickens following a dinner given in his honour by Charles Eliot Norton after a reading in Boston in 1867. 'I saw the master,' James recalled, '... in the light of an intense emotion, and I trembled, I remember, in every limb, while at the same time, by a blest fortune, emotion produced no luminous blur, but left him shining indeed, only shining with august particulars.'[10] The sight of the master seems to have been for James a kind of consecration to a literary career. 'He laid his hand on us,' he wrote, 'in a way to undermine as in no other case the power of detached appraisement.'[11]

This is another of Henry James's retrospective impressions. It must be said on the other side that as a young writer he by no means abandoned 'detached appraisement' in the face of Dickens' work. Two years before this meeting, he had reviewed *Our Mutual Friend* in the *Nation* (December 1865) and shown a sharp discontent with the novel's limitations and with Dickens as an artist in general. 'Mr. Dickens,' he wrote, 'is a great observer and a great humorist, but is nothing of a philosopher.'[12]

By 1865, James had already realized some of the limitations of the

11

English tradition of fiction. His awakening on this score probably came in 1860 in Newport where the James family had settled after an extensive tour of Europe. There William attended the studio classes of the American painter William Morris Hunt, and Henry would hang around, vaguely sketching, in an outer studio. Among the other students was the sophisticated, travelled, and knowledgeable John La Farge. La Farge painted Henry's portrait and, as was his custom, talked volubly about life and literature to his young sitter. He introduced him to the work of Balzac, one of the determining and continuing influences on James's art, and also to the short fiction of Prosper Mérimée, whose influence, though far less important, was immediate and dazzling. Reading Mérimée led James to his first literary work, a translation of *La Vénus d'Ille*. He sent it around to some magazine editors who, however, blandly ignored it.

La Vénus d'Ille contains a theme which obviously chimed with one of James's most deeply held beliefs, or fears. The basis of the story, as myth, is rooted in classical literature, but it was probably Mérimée's sardonic and realistic treatment of its fantasy that first attracted James to rendering it into English. *La Vénus d'Ille* thus became James's first schema, and gave him a starting point, in its theme and tone, for many subsequent fictions. The narrator is a Parisian scholar who visits an aristocratic dilettante in the south of France. Among other things, the aristocrat is an amateur archaeologist, and he is greatly excited by his recent find of a magnificent statue of Venus, in bronze, dating from Roman times, which he has set up in his garden. He has a son, a selfish and grasping young man, who is on the eve of marriage to an innocent and beautiful girl of the neighbourhood. The son is indifferent to the girl's charms, being interested only in her money. On the day of the wedding, already dressed for the ceremony, he is drawn into a keen game of tennis with some travelling Spaniards. Heated by the sport, he takes off his coat and betrothal ring, slipping the latter on the ring finger of the statue of Venus, which stands near the court. When the game is over, he tries to take the ring back before rushing off to the ceremony, but he finds that the statue appears to have crooked its finger, making the ring immoveable. He has to leave without it. That night, while the groom is still carousing, the bride, in bed, hears heavy footsteps approaching the room. Then, to her terror, she is aware of a large, cold figure getting into the bed beside her. Later, when the groom comes to bed, she hears the sounds of an agonizing struggle. In the morning the crushed body of the groom is found in bed beside his insane wife. By the bedside is the betrothal ring.

Henry James's first published work, which appeared anonymously in an abolitionist paper in February 1864, shows strong traces of Mérimée's influence. *A Tragedy of Error* is set in a French coastal town and all its characters appear to be French. Its triangle situation, its sardonic tone, its violent dénouement are all typical of Mérimée. Moreover, there is a strong hint of Mérimée's sinister Venus in James's portrayal of a woman who does not scruple to hire an assassin to murder her husband so that she may have her lover. The plan ironically miscarries when the assassin murders the lover by mistake, a touch that would have pleased Mérimée. America only figures in the story as the promised land offered by the woman as a bribe to the assassin for killing her husband.

After publication of this story, James turned to reviewing books for a time. Two editors, both known to his family, were ready to welcome his work: Charles Eliot Norton, in charge of the recently enlivened *The North American Review*, and E. L. Godkin, who started the *Nation* in 1865. James's earliest reviews showed all the definiteness, not to say arrogance, of a young writer who knows what he wants and is writing according to firm critical standards. His second notice, published in *The North American Review* in January 1865, consisted of an attack on two popular, now forgotten, American women novelists. He lectured them with all the confidence of his twenty-one years. If they wanted to write better novels than the elaborate and extravagant ones under review, he recommended that they follow the example of Mérimée, who 'seldom or never describes; he conveys.' Better yet, they should imitate Balzac, who 'represents objects as they are ... with the fidelity of a photograph.' James went on to discuss the accurate realism of the house of Eugénie Grandet and the relationship of that setting to the novel's action. 'Each separate part,' he maintained, 'is conducive to the general effect, and this general effect has been studied, pondered, analyzed: in the end it is produced. Balzac lays his stage, sets his scene, and introduces his puppets. He describes them once for all; this done, the story marches.'[13]

With these two French writers as his most important guides, James formulated his philosophy of realism. He advocated it strongly in the reviews he published as the Civil War drew to its close. The war itself seemed to him a time in which the American people had been tested and proved. He believed that the peace would reveal a public ready for mature works of literature. This conviction is the basis of his scornful condemnation of Walt Whitman in his famous review of *Drum Taps*, published in the *Nation* in November 1865. The crudity, the egotism, and the lack of style in Whitman's poetry, he felt, were unworthy of this 'great civilizer,' James wrote, 'this democratic, liberty-loving, American populace, this stern and war-tried people ...' Whitman's attempts to create a new style appeared ludicrous to James. 'As a general principle,' he wrote, 'we know of no circumstance more likely to impugn a writer's earnestness than the adoption of an anomalous style. He must have something very original to say if none of the old vehicles will carry his thoughts.' Instead of originality, James thought, Whitman provided only 'extravagant commonplaces' and 'flashy imitations of ideas.' Battles and tragic deaths of young men made fine subjects for the poet, but merely to shout about these events was not to make literature. 'Art requires, above all things,' he lectured Whitman, 'a suppression of one's self, a subordination of one's self to an idea ... You must respect the public which you address; for it has taste, if you have not. It delights in the grand, the heroic, and the masculine; but it delights to see these conceptions cast into worthy form.'[14]

This attack clearly reveals the aesthetic standards that James had already formed. The artist must escape from the prison of the self into the freedom of his idea and his form. He must be 'possessed' by these, and under their stimulus might break into 'divine eloquence.' James's preconceptions blinded him to the effective rhythms and diction of Whitman's poetry, as well as to the subtleties of his first-person usage. In *Drum Taps* the 'I' of the poem becomes the surrogate for the reader, who is meant to participate and suffer in the battles and hospital scenes which Whitman graphically depicts. There is, too, the dramatic modulation from the excited, jingoistic, rabble-rousing 'I' of the earlier poems in the sequence to the sombre, reflective 'I' who watches over the mortally wounded and dead, and then to the subdued but hopeful 'I' who looks forward to the reconciliation of North and South in the final poems. The 'I' of *Drum Taps* emerges, then, not only as the persona of Walt Whitman but also as the democratic self changing from a sense of diversity and disunity into an awareness of harmony and national unity. The loose rhythms of Whitman's verse are flexible enough to encompass these changes of tone and idea; the colloquialisms and uneven syntax express the writer's identification with the soldiers who are fighting the war. It is evident to the modern reader that none of 'the old vehicles' would have been suitable for carrying Whitman's thoughts and images. Only by breaking these down and creating his own style could Whitman open up realms of expression unknown before. James's perceptions could not accommodate this new vision; his use of the word 'extravagant' to describe Whitman's poetry quite literally expresses his sense of how Whitman had strayed away from the traditional paths of expression which he himself was following. It was not until he had been able, much later, to arrive at his own, original vision that he was able to comprehend and appreciate what Whitman had done.

On the other hand, James's elevated notions of the artist's duty to his audience in the post-Civil War period did not delude him into thinking only of the promises that America offered. In *Notes of a Son and Brother*, he recalls the blighted spring of 1865. He knew that Lincoln's assassination meant the end of a statesman's vision for a reunited country. The President's death was coupled in James's mind with the death of Hawthorne, which occurred shortly afterwards. The New England romancer was to remain to James a symbol of the 'Eden-like consciousness' of America. Hawthorne seemed to him to be the true chronicler of American life before the Fall, the Civil War. The accession of Andrew Johnson to the presidency was, on the other hand, for James, emblematic of all the coming changes in American life. He recoiled in dismay from the sight of this man 'perched on the stricken scene ...' What had the Americans been guilty of as a people to deserve 'the infliction of that form? ... No countenance, no salience of aspect nor composed symbol, could superficially have referred itself less than Lincoln's mould-smashing mask to any mere matter-of-course type of propriety ...' The head of Lincoln had made 'for commanding Style.' 'Before the image now substituted representation veiled her head in silence and the element of the suggested was exactly the direst.'[15]

The gap between promise and fulfilment, ideal and reality must have been well symbolized for James by the difference between Lincoln's Emancipation Proclamation, on New Year's Day, 1863, and Johnson's succession in April 1865. The gap widened continually in the subsequent years of Grant's administration. Wilky and Bob James, after their demobilization from the army, took a plantation in Florida to give employment to freed slaves. This project failed miserably and both, in subsequent years, went from one profitless occupation to another. In common with many of their generation they felt a powerful sense of disillusionment with post-war American developments, a disillusionment that was later to be given its most succinct expression in *The Education of Henry Adams*. Henry James did not escape the emotion, as the tone of many of his early stories reveals, yet his more detached mind could deal with events in a way that many of his contemporaries, too deeply hurt by them, could never do. In some of his later references to the war, he even suggests that it was a sort of 'felix culpa.' As he observed in his study of Hawthorne (1879), the war 'marks an era in the history of the American mind ... The good American, in days to come, will be a more critical person than his complacent and confident grandfather. He has eaten of the tree of knowledge.'[16]

Significantly, when James wrote his first American story its subject was the war. Later on he wrote two others. All three are among the best of his early work. Although he had no first-hand experience or even the vicarious experience of Walt Whitman to bring to his Civil War stories, he obviously believed that his own emotions of the time were susceptible to transformation into the worthy form of art. As it turned out, the Civil War stories were to set the pattern of all his fiction about American life. He was always to feel that he was a non-combatant, an observer of, rather than a participant in, its most significant processes.

⅔ 2 ⅔

Literary Influences –
All the Breezes
of the West

After the prophetic venture onto the future ground of his fiction in
A Tragedy of Error, the young Henry James returned to the United
States for the settings and characters for his next twelve stories, written
between 1865 and 1869. A discussion of the more significant of these
stories should elucidate his main preoccupation during this period.
His second tale, *The Story of a Year*, printed in *The Atlantic Monthly*
a few weeks before the end of the war, is among the best of his early
work. It brings to a focus some of the strong emotions that the war
had aroused in his mind and reveals some of the fear that he had
already begun to feel about its consequences. 'My story begins,' he
wrote, 'as a great many stories have begun within the last three years,
and indeed as a great many have ended; for, when the hero is des-
patched does not the romance come to a stop?' (ANS, 3). It is a warning to his readers not to expect the romantic slop of the typical magazine story and also an ironic foreshadowing of the conclusion. The
hero is John Ford, a freshly-made lieutenant in the Union army, who
becomes engaged to Lizzie Crowe before he goes off to join the Army
of the Potomac. Lizzie's guardian is also Ford's mother. The latter
disapproves of the engagement as she believes Lizzie to be a shallow
girl. Her perception is shown to be accurate. While Ford becomes a
veteran down in Virginia, Lizzie becomes a veteran of love at home
and starts to see another suitor. She is shamed, however, by the news
that Ford has been severely wounded. His mother, after refusing

Lizzie's offer of help, goes down to Virginia to nurse him, since he is too ill to be moved. Later she sends word that he is dying. Lizzie, without delay, accepts the proposal of her other suitor. But John then takes a turn for the better and is brought home on a stretcher, still very weak and wasted. His mother learns that Lizzie has made promises to another man and relates this news to Ford. He asks to see Lizzie and holds her hand until, soon afterwards, he dies.

The account of the wounded man's return from the front is based on the return of Henry's younger brother, Wilky, in the same condition in the summer of 1863. There is a drawing of Wilky, reproduced in *Notes of a Son and Brother*, that William James made while the young soldier lay on a stretcher just inside the door where he had been placed, too badly wounded to be moved further. William's drawing closely resembles James's description of his hero: 'It was, indeed, almost a question, whether Jack was not dead. Death is not thinner, paler, stiller' (ANS, 31).

Taking this thread of personal experience, as he was so often to do in his writing career, James wove a fictional pattern with characters who also represent aspects of his vision of life. Lizzie, selfish and impulsive, is the first of his long line of American women whose behaviour makes them at least as potentially destructive as the Vénus d'Ille. The mother is a dominant, wise figure, whose motives are, nonetheless, slightly sinister. The hero, on the other hand, is the invalid figure, common to James's early and latest work, who renounces, declines, and, not infrequently, dies as a result of love. The most interesting aspects of the story are James's concern with the psychology of his characters' behaviour, and his concern about properly representing it. When Ford goes to join his regiment, James announces that he will not follow him to the battle lines. 'My own taste,' he adds, speaking as the narrator, 'has always been for unwritten history, and my present business is with the reverse of the picture' (ANS, 12). Unwritten history might be said in this context to be the analysis of character, and the reverse of the picture is not only the home front but the drama of consciousness rather than that of action.

Aware of the limitations of his knowledge for a story about the Civil War, James attempted to extend its scope by the use of allegory, something which he was rarely to do again. At the beginning of the story, as Ford and Lizzie make their way home after becoming engaged, they stop to watch the sunset. Looking at the clouds 'in the great splendor of the west,' Ford sees in them the imagery of war, 'a rolling canopy of cannon-smoke and fire and blood.' Then, in imagery strangely prophetic of Stephen Crane's *The Red Badge of Courage*, James goes on, 'You might have fancied them an army of gigantic souls playing at football with the sun. They seemed to sway in confused splendor; the opposing squadrons bore each other down; and then suddenly they scattered, bowling with equal velocity towards north and south, and gradually fading into the pale evening sky. The purple pennons sailed away and sank out of sight, caught, doubtless, upon the brambles of the intervening plain. Day contracted itself into a fiery ball and vanished.' Ford interprets this display as a prophecy about the end of the war. 'The forces on both sides are withdrawn,' he says. 'The blood that has been shed gathers itself into a vast globule and drops into the ocean.' Lizzie, however, interprets the display differently. 'I'm afraid it means a shabby compromise,' she says. 'Light disappears, too, and the land is in darkness.' Ford refuses to be discouraged. 'Only for a season,' he replies. 'We mourn our dead. Then light comes again, stronger and brighter than ever' (ANS, 4).

The symbolism foreshadows the outcome of the story, comments on the minds of the characters and also, it might be added, seems to reveal James's own fears about the outcome of the war. In addition, it looks forward to the technique by which he would later, without the purple prose, employ metaphor and symbol to represent psychological states. He uses more sophisticated techniques than allegory even in this early story. The girl's surname, Crowe, is gruesomely apt. Its symbolism is made clear enough when, later in the story, after Ford has been wounded, she has a dream, which may also indicate James's own suppressed guilt from his non-involvement in the war. She and her new lover are walking in a lonely place when they come across an unburied corpse. They dig a hole in which to bury it, but when they lift the corpse, it opens its eyes. They notice then that the body is covered with wounds. The corpse looks at them, at last solemnly says 'Amen,' and closes its eyes. They put it in the grave, fill it with earth, and stamp it down. The symbolism is given a further sinister development near the end of the story when James compares Ford staring at Lizzie to a Greek warrior who has crawled into the temple to die 'steeping the last dull interval in idle admiration of sculptured Artemis.' This mythic reference – analogous to the Vénus d'Ille story – is supported by James's conscious use of the time scheme of a year. The lovers plight their troth in May; Ford is wounded in the dead of winter in the next year. He dies, after his betrayal by Lizzie, at the end of the winter. Then she takes her new suitor.

James had more material than he could comfortably handle in a story of this length and it is full of Victorian editorial asides of the 'gentle reader' variety. His point of view is omniscient, in the manner of Balzac or Dickens, but he dramatizes much of the action through conversation and then later in the story centres it almost entirely within Lizzie's consciousness. The setting of the story is somewhere in New England, in the village of 'Glenham,' and in 'Leatherborough,' a 'great manufacturing town ... at the mouth of the great river Tan.' These fictional places are given no specific treatment, just as the physical details of the houses and the manners of the people are largely ignored. James was a long way away from the concrete world of his master, Balzac, in *The Story of a Year*. Apart from brief references to a sleigh ride and several to the war itself, the American data are very meagre. The success of the story stems from its grim sense of loss and waste and the subtle exploration and presentation of the heroine's mind.

Henry James's third story, published in the *Atlantic* almost a year later, shows more clearly than the first his problems in dealing with American material. *A Landscape-Painter* is the first of a long series of tales about artists. As in *A Tragedy of Error*, James derived the theme from Mérimée's tale *La Vénus d'Ille*. The painter, Locksley, is a rich young man who has escaped from an unfortunate love affair to the obscurity of a New England Coastal village. James named it 'Cragthorpe' in the first publication and revised it to the more obviously American 'Chowderville' in later printings. According to the narrator, who introduces the story, Locksley liked to refer to Miss Leary, the girl from whom he fled, as the Venus de Milo. He left her when he discovered that she had a mercenary spirit. The narrator has inherited Locksley's personal effects after his early death and among them is the diary from which comes the story. Introducing the diary entries, the narrator comments: 'I will place before you the last hundred pages of his diary, as an answer to your query regarding the ultimate view taken by the great Nemesis of his treatment of Miss Leary – his scorn of the magnificent Venus Victrix. The recent passing away of the one person who had a voice paramount to mine in the disposal of Locksley's effects enables me to act without reserve' (CT, I, 101).

The diary entries, which follow, chronicle the growth of Locksley's passion for the daughter of the retired sea captain with whom he finds lodgings, Miriam, a girl whom he takes to be as honest as she is natural. He courts her in the guise of a poor painter, but, after they have become engaged, finds out to his chagrin that she had early in their acquaintance discovered by reading his diary that he was a rich man. 'It was the act of a false woman,' he tells her. She replies 'A false woman? No, it was the act of any woman – placed as I was placed' (CT, I, 138).

What happens after the end of the story is central to James's theme, and it has been subtly introduced through the narrator's preface in which he tells us that Locksley honoured the engagement and married Miriam. Miriam seems to have been the 'Nemesis of his treatment of Miss Leary,' another Vénus d'Ille figure. Locksley dies 'an early death' – obviously very soon after his marriage. The narrator's preface also reveals that only now that Miriam is dead can he reveal the truth about her. The women in James's early tales, as in those of Mérimée, are to be neither trusted nor trifled with.

Even more significant in this story than the influence of the French writer, however, is the power exercised over James's imagination by European landscape painting and English romantic fiction. As he later recalled in *Notes of a Son and Brother*, he began 'to woo the muse of prose fiction' while still enrolled in the law school, an enrolment which had become nominal only, after a disastrous appearance in a moot court. He was living in a colonial house on Winthrop Square, Cambridge. On one side was an alcove with a large window looking out towards the Brighton Hills. 'Over the intervening marshes of the Charles ...' he wrote, 'there was all the fine complicated cloud-scenery I could wish – so extravagantly did I then conceive more or less associational cloud-scenery, after the fashion, I mean, of that feature of remembered English and Boulognese water-colours, to promote the atmosphere of literary composition as the act had begun to glimmer for me.'[1]

It would seem probable that James composed *A Landscape-Painter* while living on Winthrop Square, since it is saturated, not with the American scene which it purports to represent, but with references to European and English landscapes. Locksley prospects for sketchable views along the coast. He finds a ruined fort on a picturesque island. The sky and sea look to him 'like a clever English water-colour.' Sheep browse upon the marsh, 'as they might upon a Highland moor' (CT, I, 110–11). The name of the heroine in the first publication of the story was the Dickensian one of Esther Blunt. For later publication James changed it to the Hawthornesque and slightly sinister Miriam, just as he had changed the incongruous Cragthorpe to Chowderville. When Miriam goes out for a walk with her New-foundland dog, she still looks to Locksley 'like one of Miss Brontë's heroines.' Later on, Locksley takes Miriam out for a trot in a dog-cart. As they ride over the hard sand of the beach, they gaze at 'one of those gorgeous vertical sunsets that Turner sometimes painted' (CT, I, 125).

Turner was one of James's earliest passions in painting. It is possible to see how close he was to idolatry from a review he wrote of a group of Turner's water-colours in the Wallace Collection in London in 1873. 'Magic,' he wrote, 'is the only word for his rendering of space, light, and atmosphere.' Of a little picture of a rain-washed moor called 'Grouse shooting,' he wrote: 'When Art can say so much in so light a whisper, she has certainly obtained absolute command of her organ.' Of another, 'Richmond, Yorkshire,' he observed: 'The way in which the luminous haze invests and caresses the castle-crowned woody slope which forms the background of this composition is something for the connoisseur to analyse, if he can, but for the uninitiated mind simply to wonder at.'[2]

The early fiction of James amply confirms the testimony in the autobiography and the art criticism that he was schooled to see his American environment mainly in terms of English forms like those of Turner. As E. H. Gombrich has demonstrated in his study, *Art and Illusion,* the artist can paint what he sees only in terms of previously learned schemata. It is psychologically impossible for him to follow Pope's maxim and 'copy nature.' He can evolve original means of perception only through learning to adapt schemata already invented by other artists. The painter, he observes, 'begins not with his visual impression but with his idea or concept ...'[3] The camera eye's record of a landscape often completely differs from an artist's rendering because the painter's eye is reading into the scene images, colours, and forms which he believes should be there through his knowledge of previous applicable schemata. What Gombrich most effectively does in his study is to abolish the idea of the 'innocent eye.' He incidentally opens up a fruitful field for the critic of literature.

This is particularly true in the criticism of the work of Henry James, who was from his earliest years influenced by art and was for some time, indeed, a professional critic of painting. For James, in his early years, the European, and particularly the English, romantic tradition of landscape painting had an unshakeable authority, an authority no doubt bolstered by James's knowledge of Ruskin's work and by his time as an acolyte in the studio of the academic American painter, William Morris Hunt. It is possible to see the extent of Ruskin's authority by reading James's review of a show of Winslow Homer's paintings in New York in 1875. Homer thought of himself, with some justice, as the Walt Whitman of painters and was trying to capture on canvas the same kind of images of American life that Whitman had done in poetry. James attacked Homer with the same ferocity he had shown towards Whitman ten years earlier. After admitting that he was 'a genuine painter' whose only care was 'to see, and to reproduce what he sees' he went on to say that he had 'no imagination,' and that his work was 'barbarously simple' and 'horribly ugly.' James frankly confessed that he detested Homer's subjects, 'his barren plank fences, his glaring, bald, blue skies, his big, dreary, vacant lots of meadows, his freckled, straight-haired Yankee urchins, his flat-breasted maidens, suggestive of a dish of rural doughnuts and pie, his calico sun-bonnets, his flannel shirts, his cowhide boots.' The review would be an unredeemed mass of prejudice but for a noble doubt that shines through this condemnation. In spite of his better judgment, James could not help liking Homer's boldness in treating his American

23

subjects 'as if they *were* pictorial, as if they were every inch as good as Capri or Tangier.' He concluded wistfully, 'If his masses were only sometimes a trifle more broken, and his brush a good deal richer – if it had a good many more secrets and mysteries and coquetries, he would be, with his vigorous way of looking and seeing ... an almost distinguished painter.'

The review reveals the limits of James's belief in realism as a viable artistic method as late as 1875. The main trouble with Homer's work, as seen by James, is that he refused to see 'the distinction between beauty and ugliness.' Reality still had to be dressed in 'mysteries and coquetries' in order to make it palatable. He failed to see how Homer's 'vigorous way of looking and seeing' had performed the office of the 'grasping imagination' in seizing on the salient details of the American scene.[4]

For James as a beginning writer of fiction, there was an even greater problem in using American material. In *Notes of a Son and Brother*, he writes at some length on the absence of variety of type in the faces and manners of his fellow students at the Harvard Law School. 'It was to differentiation exactly,' he wrote, 'that I was then, in my innocence, most prompted; not dreaming of the stiff law by which, on the whole American ground, division of *type*, in the light of opposition and contrast, was more and more to break down for me and fail ...'[5] He described the two or three 'characters' among the Law Faculty and a monocled dandy among the students who came from New York City, but the New Englanders presented a complete facial and physical monotony to his vision. 'The difficulty with the type about me was that, in its monotony, beginning and ending with itself, it *had* no connections and suggested none ...' Whether this monotony was real or existed only because the type did not match any of the characters of English or French fiction, it is impossible now to know. James himself, however, did realize why it was that he was searching for division of types. 'Young as I was,' he wrote, 'I myself clearly recognized that ground of reference, saw it even to some extent in the light of experience [and here James is referring to his experience of European countries] – so could I stretch any scrap of contact; kept hold of it by fifty clues, recalls and reminders that dangled for me mainly out of books and magazines and heard talk, things of picture and story, things of prose and verse and anecdotal vividness in fine, and, as I have elsewhere allowed, for the most part hoardedly English and French.'⁶ Characteristically, James converted the boarding house in which he ate in Cambridge into an imagined facsimile of the Maison Vauquer of Balzac's *Père Goriot*, even while recognizing the absurd differences. To an imagination nourished and formed by the images derived from Balzac's vast, varied, and possibly exaggerated gallery, not to mention the range of character and classes exhibited by Dickens, Smollett, Thackeray, and the rest, the social mixture of Cambridge seemed painfully thin. At this time, James was unable to penetrate below the apparent monotony to the qualities of difference that existed in American, as in all, societies.

The early stories, at any rate, exhibit the apparent poverty of choice of characters that he found and also show how greatly James was influenced by the class basis of the English novel. His fourth story, *A Day of Days*, a rather slight anecdote, hinges on the relation between a lady of means and a man who 'isn't a gentleman.' It is entirely possible that Adela Moore, James's lady, might have felt this, but it is hardly likely, given the nature of American society in the 1860s, that the man, Thomas Ludlow, would also have admitted as much and added besides that he was 'a very common creature.' Adela Moore lives with her brother, a scientist, in the countryside of New England. Ludlow comes to see her brother to get letters of introduction to scientists in Germany where he is just about to go. But the brother is away for the day and Adela plays hostess instead. They spend the day together in the woods and fields. In spite of the 'difference in rank' she falls in love with him and, before he goes, indirectly makes it plain that it would be worth his while to miss his boat to Europe. But Ludlow says to himself: 'It's a very pretty little romance as it is ... Why spoil it?' and he leaves at once (CT, I, 164).

There is some pleasant description in the story of what James calls 'the unsophisticated beauties of a casual New England landscape.' Adela has to say, however, that a certain circle of trees against the blue sky reminds her of the 'stone-pipes of the Villa Borghese' (CT, I, 154). This 'sudden pastoral,' as Ludlow calls it, is only superficially developed and the reader gets very little knowledge of the reasons for Adela's quickly grown passion. Ludlow is a typical Jamesian hero in his coldness to this beautiful as well as rich woman. He feels no hesitation in rejecting all her attractions in favour of Europe. His common origins are, however, quite untypical of James's work. Although the author supplies a brief account of Ludlow's poverty-stricken childhood in New York, he fails to make it sound convincing. Ludlow's motivation in refusing Adela's veiled invitation is not made plain, except that he appears to feel that Europe is necessary to his development as a student and a man. As usual in these early stories, the woman represents a threat to a man's growth – if not to his happiness – which he must resist.

The question of class distinctions appears once again in the next published story, *My Friend Bingham* (1867). Bingham is one of the rich, unoccupied men whom James chose as heroes more and more in this early period as other sources of American types and professions seemed to be lacking. Bingham, jilted in love, takes a vacation with the narrator in a deserted unnamed resort that looks in some respects suspiciously like Newport. The two men one day go out duck-shooting. Bingham, aiming for sport at a sea-gull (as the narrator quotes the appropriate passage from *The Ancient Mariner*), shoots and kills a young boy who had been concealed behind the bird. The boy's mother is the widow of a Baptist minister. From the time of the shooting on, the death hangs like an albatross around Bingham's neck until, at the end of the story, he marries the young widow, who comes of poor parentage and background. But this apparent misalliance is remedied by the change in her. As in Hawthorne's fiction, suffering brings about refinement of feeling and access of knowledge, so that the narrator believes that she has become 'potentially at least, a woman of the world' (CT, I, 187).

Although quite slight, the story is a significant development of the theme of the intimate association of love and death in James's fiction. Fulfilled love seems to demand in much of his work some human sacrifice. In this case a substitute or scapegoat pays the price so that, for once in a great while, the outcome of the story can be happy. The marriage, the narrator concludes, 'has been a truly happy one,' although, through some principle of equity, the couple has remained childless. Here again James insists upon a kind of moral retribution as a principle of his fiction. It is notable also that, for the second time in his first five stories, James makes use of a narrator involved in the action to present and dramatize his story. He was already aware that this technique gave him more control over his material than the omniscient method which he used in the earlier stories. Even at this early point in his career he seems to have been groping for the right point of view through which to present and colour his materials. The early narrators, however, tend to remain anonymous and passive figures.

Throughout this period of fiction writing, James kept broadening the scope of his reviewing activities. As Miss Cornelia Kelley has shown, probably the most important author, outside the English and French novelists, who influenced James at this time was Goëthe. He reviewed *Wilhelm Meister* in the Carlyle translation for *The North American Review* in July 1865. Although he found it 'anything but a novel,' he was deeply impressed by the reach of Goëthe's mind and the depth of his psychology. James seems to have realized after reading *Wilhelm Meister* that the boundaries of the novel could be extended to include philosophical speculation. Goëthe probably enabled him to discern more clearly the limitations of English writers like Dickens and Trollope.

It took another English novelist, however, to bring James to the awareness of how the novel could combine the detailed observation of Balzac and Dickens with the philosophical depth of Goëthe. This was George Eliot, whose novel, *Felix Holt*, James reviewed in the *Nation* in August 1866. He had read her earlier work but, as Miss Kelley points out, he does not seem to have been ready before this to profit from her example. *Felix Holt* showed James how a novelist could, through understanding and sympathy and 'the firm and elaborate delineation of individual character,' represent man as well as men.[7] He turned to the other novels she had written to date and, greatly excited, wrote the first long critical article of his career. It appeared in *The Atlantic Monthly* in October 1866. In essence, he asserted, George Eliot not only observed closely, she also reflected and felt deeply about the lives of her characters. Although her plots were frequently weak and she was occasionally tedious, she never forgot the importance of character. She knew the members of her own class, the people among whom she had been brought up, extremely well, and made their lives the basis of her vision.

Since Miss Kelley published her study, Professor Edel has discovered that James also wrote a long, anonymous review of *Middlemarch* in *Galaxy Magazine* in March 1873. Although to discuss this review at this point is to anticipate a little, it does reveal how George Eliot continued to exert a powerful influence on James's mind and also how he came to grasp her limitations as time went on. 'We can well remember,' James wrote, 'how keenly we wondered, while its earlier chapters unfolded themselves, what turn in the way of form the story would take – that of an organized, molded, balanced composition, gratifying the reader with a sense of design and construction, or a mere chain of episodes, broken into accidental lengths and unconscious of the influence of a plan.' He anticipated the result. *Middlemarch*, he found, was episodic, not closely organized. If it had been well-designed, James would have called it 'the first of English novels.' The strengths of the novel, he found once again, were in its characterization, its 'rare psychological penetration,' and its intelligence. George Eliot demonstrates, James observed, 'perception charged with feeling.' English readers might enjoy *Middlemarch*, James went on, but really to 'relish its inner essence' one must be an American. For him, she stood alone among English romancers (an unusual application of the term, surely), surpassing even Fielding, who was didactic where George Eliot was philosophic. He thought that while her native tendency was to be an idealist, she had commissioned herself to be real. The result was 'a very fertilizing mixture.' *Middlemarch*, James concluded, 'sets a limit, we think, to the development of the old-fashioned English novel.' Its main trouble was that it was too copious. 'If we write novels so,' James asked, 'how shall we write History?'[8]

The influence of Goëthe and more particularly that of George Eliot led James toward an increasingly analytic mode in his fiction, particularly in those stories that have a narrator. The analysis tended to slow the forward march of the narrative and his work tended to lose the pace that he had achieved from imitating Mérimée and Balzac. In fact, the stories written between 1866 and 1869 often betray a confusion in method and purpose. His successive enthusiasms for European writers, coming on top of a bewilderment about how he should represent American life, exacerbated the difficulties that he was facing as a writer. Which way should he turn? His uncertainty seems to have been not only an aspect of his own development but also of the problems faced by many American writers in the period immediately following the Civil War.

The question of how American literature should develop, a recurrent one in the nation's life ever since 1776, cropped up again even more insistently to James and his contemporaries. He was fortunate to find at the beginning a sympathetic spirit with which to discuss the problem in W. D. Howells, who joined the staff of the *Atlantic* in 1866. Not long after the two aspiring novelists had first met, Howells wrote to the businessman-poet, E. C. Stedman: 'Young Henry James and I had a famous [talk] last evening, two or three hours long, in which we settled the true principles of literary art. He is a very earnest fellow, and I think extremely gifted – gifted enough to do better than anyone has yet done toward making us a real American novel.'[9] The touch of irony in this note indicates that the two young men would not have had much interest in issuing the kind of manifestoes that Emerson, Poe, Melville, and many others had written earlier in the century about the necessity of throwing off the chains of European domination in the arts.

The problem of the European influence could never again be as simple as it had been to the pre-Civil War writers, as James well knew. Walt Whitman's buoyant optimism about the future of American literature in *Democratic Vistas* (1871) rested on the belief that the ground had been cleared and the national purpose forged by the war. The oncoming 'native literatuses,' as he called them, were not, however, exhilarated by the prospect before them. The militant nationalism characteristic of the 1840s and 50s is replaced in the 1860s and 70s not with confidence but with a sense of loss, of exclusion, of nostalgia for a richer order. This manifested itself not merely in the increasing tide of expatriation but also in the choice of themes by those who stayed in the United States. Even Mark Twain turned constantly towards the history and colour of Europe for his subject matter, as in *Innocents Abroad* and *A Connecticut Yankee in King Arthur's Court*.

James, always a highly self-conscious artist, had begun as a very young man to theorize about the situation of the American writer *vis à vis* Europe. He attempted to define a satisfactory stance for himself in a letter he wrote to T. S. Perry from Cambridge, Massachusetts, in 1867. 'I feel that my only chance for success as a critic,' he wrote, 'is to let all the breezes of the west blow through me at their will. We are Americans born – *il faut en prendre son parti*. I look upon it as a great blessing; and I think that to be an American is an excellent preparation for culture. We have exquisite qualities as a race, and it seems to me that we are ahead of the European races in the fact that more than either of them we can deal freely with forms of civilization not our own, can pick and choose and assimilate and in short (aesthetically etc.) claim our property wherever we find it.'

American culture had, he went on to say, no 'national stamp,' but this was less cause for regret to him than of hope that American writers could achieve 'a vast intellectual fusion and synthesis of the various National tendencies of the world.' He looked forward to 'something of our own – something distinctive and homogeneous' in the future, and predicted that this would be found in 'our moral consciousness, our unprecedented spiritual lightness and vigour.'[10] On the other hand, he expected that nothing great would emerge during the span of his own lifetime. The conservatism, not to say pessimism, of this prediction, contrasts dramatically with the chauvinistic confidence of many American writers before the Civil War, but it is in tune with the more decorous cosmopolitanism of the contemporary New England writers. The main risk that James ran as a young writer was in slipping into the desiccated urbanity of what Roy Harvey Pearce has aptly called 'the fireside poets.' In his study of American poetry, Professor Pearce quotes some remarks of Longfellow that are very similar to those of James in his letter to Perry. Longfellow wrote: 'We shall draw from the Germans, tenderness; from the Spaniards, passion; from the French, vivacity, – to mingle more and more with our English solid sense. And this will give us universality, so much to be desired.' As Pearce points out, however, Longfellow 'conceived of universality as being defined as a lack of particularity.'[11] His verse dwindled, for the most part, into the genial vagueness or anecdotal sentimentality that were the chief snares of so much of late nineteenth-century American writing. James shared the fireside poets' dislike of the grossness, restlessness, and raw power characteristic of much American life, but he came to realize in time that the essentially genteel literary vision of his New England contemporaries falsified life in its own way. He expressed this realization tactfully, but clearly enough, in discussing, in an essay of 1892, the poetry of James Russell Lowell. Of *The Biglow Papers*, Lowell's most 'folksy' work, he wrote: 'If they had no other distinction, they would have that of one of the acutest of all studies in linguistics. They are more literary, in short, than they at first appear; which is at once the strength and weakness of his poetry in general, literary indeed as most of it is at sight.'[12]

Attractive as it must have been, James never fell into the smooth groove of academic cosmopolitanism. For one thing he read more closely, if not as widely, in European authors than his Harvard friends, and was able to see more clearly what some of them, particularly the French, were trying to do. For another, he continually strove to bring his own experience to bear in his fiction, to adapt the new areas of awareness that the French in particular had opened up in writing to the facts and conditions of American life. An instructive example of this process can be seen in the second story that he wrote with a Civil War background, called *Poor Richard* (1867).

Leon Edel has described how this story had its origins in James's experience in the summer of 1865 when he went on a visit with Oliver Wendell Holmes and John Gray, later a distinguished jurist and professor of law at Harvard, to North Conway in New Hampshire's White Mountains. Also staying there were his cousins, the Temples, including particularly the beautiful, brilliant, and doomed Minny, whose image was to play such an important part in James's fiction. Holmes and Gray, recently demobilized, were apparently still in their Union officers' uniforms; the two soldiers and the one civilian revolved around the heroine of the drama, as he was later to recall her in *Notes of a Son and Brother*. Beside the bronzed, vigorous, and articulate veterans and the brilliant Minny, Henry felt shy and awkward. This sense of frustration he expressed in *Poor Richard*, which has an heiress, two Union officers, and a young civilian as its cast of characters. The story, however, was substantially different from the incident he himself had silently endured, for it was written under the guiding genius of George Sand.

The literary schema quite made over the life experience into its own image. The poor Richard of the title, the civilian, has no more of the Ben Franklin hero about him than he has of the young Henry James; he is instead the young man of uncontrollable passions common to George Sand's stories. He proposes to the rich, cool, sensible Gertrude, who has been educating him out of his former dissolute ways, and flies into a passion when she refuses him. Two other suitors then make their appearance. Captain Severn is the one that Gertrude prefers; the other is Major Luttrell. Severn, recovering from a wound, feels that he must return to his regiment when news comes of the beginning of a great battle. He comes to say goodbye to her, but before he can reach the house encounters Richard and the major who have both been paying calls on Gertrude. In a fit of passionate jealousy, Richard tells Severn that she is not at home and Major Luttrell tacitly accedes to the lie. Thus the interview which probably would have resulted in their engagement is prevented. The guilt-ridden Richard returns to the drink that he had given up under Gertrude's guidance, and then falls ill of a fever. In the meantime, Major Luttrell takes advantage of the absence of the other two to court Gertrude, particularly after he hears of the death of Severn in battle – another Jamesian instance of love leading to death. In despair, Gertrude consents to marry the major. Before the marriage can take place, however, the recovered Richard appears and confesses his treachery to Gertrude. She then refuses the major, but paradoxically forgives Richard and is indeed ready to marry him, but his passion has 'perished in the tumult.' Richard himself goes off to the war, from which he emerges un-scathed, but he is unable to settle down in his old neighbourhood and is thinking, as the story ends, of going out west. Gertrude goes to Europe and settles in Florence, where she passes for 'a very independent, but a very contented woman ...' (CT, I, 258).

To suit American magazine requirements, the story has, of course, none of the illicit passion that was *de rigueur* in George Sand, but all the same the behaviour of the Yankee Richard, with his passionate outpourings and extravagant gestures could hardly have been typical of those undemonstrative Yankees that James had complained of at the Harvard Law School. The scene, once again, is only briefly sketched in, except for one at Richard's farm, in which the sunburnt

Richard leading in a farm cart is more reminiscent of one of Constable's oils than of rural New England. Although the Civil War background does give a certain warrant to the violence of the dialogue, that is not sufficient to make *Poor Richard* fit convincingly into an American context. In the first publication of the story, Richard's second name was Clare. In the revision, James, apparently once more seeking to strike the American note more firmly, changed it to Maule, perhaps in order to recall the curse placed on the Pyncheon family in Hawthorne's *The House of the Seven Gables* as an analogy of Richard's betrayal of Severn.

Goëthe's influence is also visible in *Poor Richard* in the hero's habit of analyzing his sorrows and arriving at philosophical conclusions in the manner of young Werther. On the other hand, this philosophical strain does not match the passionate impulsiveness that he shows again later in the story. With the character of Gertrude, James seems to be experimenting in the manner of the intellectual heroines of George Eliot, foreshadowing, incidentally, the type that he was to develop into Isabel Archer of *The Portrait of a Lady*. Many of these elements seem to be unassimilated into the narrative theme. In spite of this, however, *Poor Richard* is curiously effective, perhaps because of the latent drama that James had discerned in the incident in New Hampshire's White Mountains.

The Civil War appears for the third and last time as background for a Jamesian story in *A Most Extraordinary Case*, published almost a year after *Poor Richard* in the *Atlantic* of April 1868. Once again, the story appears to have had its beginnings in James's own experience – his feelings of frustrated inaction as his back ailment plagued him during and immediately after the Civil War. Ferdinand Mason, lately a colonel in the Union army, is lying prostrate from exhaustion from his war service in a small hotel room in New York. The war is over and Mason has no idea what he can do. He is discovered by a rich aunt who takes him up to her Hudson Valley home. There he finds supreme comfort, a servant who 'looks as if he had come out of an English novel,' and a beautiful girl who, according to another character, 'looks as if she had come out of an American novel.' 'I don't know that that's great praise,' he adds, 'but, at all events, I make her come out of it' (CT, I, 330). Mason falls in love with the girl, Caroline Hofmann, who appears, in fact, to have come out of Mérimée, for she turns out to be another deadly female. Mason's young doctor, whom he had known in the army, is also in love with her even though he ominously dubs her 'Diana' – the second appearance of Artemis in James's work. Mason thinks that she is inclining towards him, but she accepts the doctor instead. After escorting Caroline to a party, Mason has a relapse. Following a short, unreported interview with her, he dies.

The doctor does not understand the case, but the experienced reader of James can make a diagnosis on the basis of the later novel, *The Sacred Fount*. Caroline gains in vitality and radiance as the story proceeds, and at the same time Mason's strength ebbs – a situation that is also suggested in *A Landscape-Painter*. Although there appears to be nothing organically wrong with him, he dies from lack of energy, an energy diminished in the first place by 'taking things too hard' in his doctor's words, during the war. The tribute that Mason then paid to his Venus, Caroline, was too much of a drain on what remained of his strength. The last interview in the bedroom is once more like the visit paid by the bronze Venus to her reluctant lover in Mérimée's story.

A Most Extraordinary Case has the highly-coloured quality of a Mérimée anecdote, although James tries to modify the melodrama of the theme by treating his story in a quiet-toned, realistic way. Its verisimilitude is deepened by the narration of the story largely from the point of view of, although not in the person of, Mason. When, at one place, James was tempted to shift to another character, he resisted with an aside to the reader that he felt 'compelled to let it stand in this simple shape' (CT, I, 332) – as if he were becoming more and more conscious of the gain in unity achieved by a single point of view.

The Hudson Valley, which James called in the story 'this long-settled, almost legendary region,' also supplied a congenial landscape for his pen. The commodious house itself, with its large verandahs strewn with basket chairs and light novels, is 'marked by a certain fastidious freshness which betrayed the uncontested dominion of women' (CT, I, 327). The surrounding scenery offered a tempting subject for James's pen, and he took the opportunity of describing a drive that Mason takes with Miss Hofmann to the river. 'The sun had sunk low, and the cloudless western sky glowed with an exquisite tone. The trees which concealed the view flung over the grass a great screen of shadow, which reached out into the road. Between their scattered stems gleamed the broad white current of the Hudson.' Leaving their carriage, they walk to the edge of the high bank, where 'the trees make a little amphitheatre on its summit.' 'To the right and to the left, a hundred feet below them, stretched the broad channel of the noble river. In the distance rose the gentle masses of the Catskills, with all the intervening region vague and neutral in the gathering twilight' (CT, I, 347–9).

James described a similar scene in a book he wrote forty years later. The description of a Hudson Valley house in *The American Scene* also supplies several clues to the nature of his original perception. The house is similar to the one in *A Most Extraordinary Case*, and James stressed its value in a country where so many of the relics of the short historic past had been destroyed. He looked out at the landscape from the high, deep gallery, and reflected: 'I know not what dignity of old afternoons suffused with what languor seems to me always, under the murmur of American trees and by the lap of American streams, to abide in these mild shades; there are combinations with depths of congruity beyond the plummet, it would seem, even of the most restless of analysts, and rather than try to say why my whole impression here melted into the general iridescence of a past of Indian summers hanging about mild ghosts half asleep, in hammocks, over still milder novels, I would renounce altogether the art of refining. For the iridescence consists, in this connection, of a shimmer of association that still more refuses to be reduced to terms; some sense of legend, of aboriginal mystery, with a still earlier past for its dim background and the insistent idea of the River as above all romantic for its warrant. Helplessly analyzed, perhaps, this amounts to no more than the very childish experience of a galleried house or two round about which the views and the trees and the peaches and the pony seemed prodigious, and to the remembrance of which the wonder of Rip Van Winkle and that of the "Hudson River School" of landscape art were, a little later on, to contribute their glamour.'[13]

In this nostalgic memory the elements that went to make up the setting and atmosphere of *A Most Extraordinary Case* are quite evident, and help to explain why this story was more concretely realized than most of the other early ones. Superimposed on James's childhood memories of the place – which heavily stress the Edenic charm – are the 'shimmers of association' derived from the legendary vision of Washington Irving. Behind Irving, of course, stretch the romantic tones of his chosen tradition. But Irving had successfully domesticated his European influences and had carved out, as very few early nineteenth-century American writers had managed to do, a territory that bore his stamp as unmistakably as that of Wordsworth's Lake district. The Hudson River School had shared the same kind of romantic perception of landscape as Irving. It was indeed a highly literary group, a point underlined by the most famous painting the group produced, Asher Brown Durand's *Kindred Spirits*, a picture of the poet, William Cullen Bryant, and the painter, Thomas Cole, standing on a platform of rock overlooking a wild, rocky valley.

Cole, along with Irving, William Cullen Bryant, and others of the school, frequented James's father's house in New York when Henry was a child. He attended the exhibitions of paintings they mounted and read the work that they produced, as he attests in *A Small Boy and Others*.[14] The massing and colouring of the scene observed by Mason as he looks over the Hudson might even be a representation in verbal terms of one of the canvasses of the school. The schema gave James a greater authority in *A Most Extraordinary Case* than he was able to demonstrate in his other early fiction. Significantly, in this story James did not feel that he had to refer to European comparisons to give his setting validity.

In both of these Civil War stories, James's protagonists seem to be invested with their creator's sense of his own inadequacy. Mason's invalidism, in particular, seems to have reflected James's own ailing, frustrated sense during and immediately after the war. Mason's aunt thinks him to be 'the most gifted, the most promising young man of his generation.' Mason himself remembers thinking during the war that 'the sense of lost time was ... his perpetual bugbear – the feeling that precious hours were now fleeting uncounted, which in more congenial labours would suffice for making a lasting mark' (CT,I,331). The personal note in all three Civil War stories may account for their intensity, which is much greater than that of most of the other early stories. James's mood as a beginning writer was closely attuned with those in battle, 'the particular taxed condition,' as he later called it, in which he was 'no less exaltedly than wastefully engaged in the common fact of endurance.'[15] Although the facts of war are absent from these stories, the sense of it appears in terms of the artistic representation of pain, guilt, and frustration. It was a grim and stirring time for a writer as sensitive as James to begin his work and he responded to it with all his imagination and the more limited resources of his artistic skill.

❊ 3 ❊

The Hawthorne Aspect

When James spoke of letting all the breezes of the west blow through him, he was presumably thinking of the influence of English and European writers. Fortunately, however, he did not shut out the airs from still further west; the voice of Hawthorne is heard increasingly in the stories that James wrote from the late 1860s on. Cornelia Kelley has surmised that Howells in particular was influential in turning James away from the realistic mode of his earlier work towards a more romantic strain. This may very well have been the case, not only because Howells himself was still very much in the romance camp, but also because he was taking over more and more responsibility on the *Atlantic*, of which he became editor in 1871. He was therefore in a particularly strong position to affect the type of fiction that James wrote for his magazine. It is possible, too, that James felt his stories after the manner of Mérimée, Balzac, Sand, and George Eliot had not been overwhelmingly successful and that he should look closer into the American tradition represented by Hawthorne's romances. It is clear that James increasingly felt the strain of representing a diversity of social types like those of the European writers and the difficulty in establishing a sense of community, which he so much admired in George Eliot's work. The romance tradition, with its possibilities of emphasis on individual psychology and its relative freedom from the kind of specific social detail that the realistic mode requires, obviously offered an attractive alternative.

The first direct response to the Hawthorne example is *The Story of a Masterpiece* (1868). A possible source for this tale is Hawthorne's *The Prophetic Pictures*, in which a great painter comes to the American colonies in the eighteenth century and does two portraits which are acknowledged to be his masterpieces. His sitters are a young engaged couple on the eve of marriage. The name of Hawthorne's hero, Ludlow, was, incidentally, that used by James for his earlier story, *A Day of Days*. The girl sees something terrible in the face of her future husband as painted by the artist, while he sees grief and terror in her portrait. She marries her fiancé anyway, but the prophecy of the picture is realized when, later, the husband goes mad and tries to stab his wife. Hawthorne, with his usual sense of ambiguities, suggests at one point that the artist was 'a chief agent of the coming evil which he had foreshadowed,'[1] but his major emphasis is on the painter's ability to discover and portray characteristics invisible to unskilled eyes and on the almost magical aspects of this kind of gift.

James's treatment of this theme centres on the psychological rather than the magical. His painter, Stephen Baxter, has known the girl, Marian Everett, before her fiancé, John Lennox, asks him to paint her picture. The painter had, in fact, been engaged to Marian some years earlier, but had ended the engagement when he discovered that she was continuing to see another man with far brighter financial prospects than himself. Baxter had concluded that Marian was a shallow and heartless girl. Lennox, another of James's rich bachelor heroes, does not know of this former intimacy. When he sees the completed picture, he realizes that his infatuation with Marian has blinded him to the essential heartlessness that it reveals. Yet he believes that, as a man of honour, he cannot back out of his engagement. 'He lacked the brutal consistency,' James wrote, 'necessary for taking away Marian's future. If he had mistaken her and overrated her, the fault was his own, and it was a hard thing that she should pay the penalty' (CT, I, 294–5). Even though he admits that the painting is a masterpiece, he destroys it with a poniard on the night before the marriage.

The conclusion is melodramatic and unconvincing, belonging far more to the Gothic literary convention than to the relatively realistic manner in which the story is written. *The Story of a Masterpiece* is, however, an interesting essay in the psychology of art in addition to being an unlikely romance. '[Baxter] had painted with something more than knowledge – with imagination, with feeling. He had almost *composed*; and his composition had embraced the truth' (CT, I, 285). Marian is perfectly happy with the portrait, but the more Lennox looks at it, the more he sees how heartless the image appears. But he cannot be sure how much is objectively represented by the portrait and how much has sprung from inklings about his *fiancée*'s nature that he has had all along. He also discovers that Baxter had been in love with Marian and so evolves the theory that the painting is the revenge of a rejected lover. But he is forced in the end to admit that the portrait has hit on the truth and that Baxter had been right when he told him 'I go in for reality; you must have seen that' (CT, I, 282).

The Story of a Masterpiece is undoubtedly one of the most significant of the early tales, as it looks forward to many of James's major themes. It is vitiated, however, because of its confusion of genres. Realism and romance fight an unresolved battle, as a Balzacian insistence on fact and the contemporaneity of the narrative disperse the mystery essential to such a story. The technique is also uncertain. The story is told largely from the point of view of Lennox, but there is a flashback to the period of Baxter's engagement to Marian and other excursions to different characters' minds as well as to that of the omniscient narrator. As a result, the narrative is too diffuse. It also lacks suspense, for the reader is told of Marian's heartlessness early in the story. If James had used the painting as a source of ambiguity, as Hawthorne had done, he could have explored the mind of the painter as well as that of the subject.

In the story that followed, *The Romance of Certain Old Clothes*, James tried to correct some of these defects by following much more closely in Hawthorne's footsteps. It is set in one of Hawthorne's favourite milieux, colonial Massachusetts, 'toward the middle of the eighteenth century.' But James soon reveals how uneasy he is in the twilight world, 'somewhere between fact and fancy,' as Hawthorne called it in the preface to *The Blithedale Romance*, which should have been the imaginative setting for the tale. James's passion for detail conflicts with a story that should have been touched with

romance and mystery, but he obviously felt constrained to preface
narrative sections with accounts of how thing were, as he nervously
comments, 'in those days.' Bernard Willoughby, of a rich colonial
family, is sent by his fond, widowed mother to England for his education. After Oxford and the Grand Tour, he returns to Massachusetts,
accompanied by an English friend, Arthur Lloyd, a rich and handsome young bachelor who is seeking to increase his fortune by invest-
ing in trade in the colonies. Bernard's two pretty sisters, Viola and
Perdita, both fall in love with Lloyd, whose appearance and manner
far eclipse the 'home-bred arts' of the young colonists. They commence
a silent but deadly struggle for his favour. After a decent interval he
proposes to the younger of the two girls, Perdita, to the unspeakable
mortification and bitterness of Viola. Sensing her sister's hostility,
Perdita begs her for a year of happiness at least. Plans for the wedding
go forward, but Viola, an expert needlewoman, makes no effort to
help Perdita with her trousseau until a splendid length of white silk,
brocaded in blue and silver, is sent to his bride by Lloyd. Perdita tells
her sister that it is a pity that the silk is not for Viola's use, since blue
is her colour. After this, Viola starts to sew the wedding dress. Her
jealousy is unabated, however. Directly after the ceremony, and
before Perdita leaves the house with Lloyd, Viola tries on the cast-off
wedding veil and wreath. Perdita, to her horror, catches her in the act.

The couple moves into a handsome house in Boston, which is
twenty-five miles away from the Willoughby's house in the country.
A year later, while Lloyd is visiting his mother and sister-in-law and
is out riding with Viola, Perdita gives birth to a girl. She is greatly
upset by Lloyd's apparent callousness in being away and out with her
sister during her confinement and she falls ill. A little over a week
later, she dies, but not before she has asked Lloyd to promise to keep
all her clothes locked away until her daughter can wear them. She
makes an exception of the blue and silver bridal gown, which she
bequeaths to Viola. Later on, Lloyd succumbs to the arts of Viola and
marries her. Three years afterward Viola asks for the key to the chest
in the attic in which the clothes are stored. Eventually Lloyd gives way
to her entreaties and passions and she goes off triumphantly to the
attic. When she does not come to the evening meal, he goes in search
of her and finds her in the attic in front of the chest. 'The lid of the

chest stood open, exposing, amid their perfumed napkins, its treasure of stuffs and jewels. Viola had fallen backward from a kneeling posture, with one hand supporting her on the floor and the other pressed to her heart. On her limbs was the stiffness of death, and on her face, in the fading light of the sun, the terror of something more than death. Her lips were parted in entreaty, in dismay, in agony; and on her bloodless brow and cheeks there glowed the marks of ten hideous wounds from two vengeful ghostly hands' (CT, 1, 318–19).

This is good writing of its kind and compares not unfavourably with Hawthorne's description of the corpse of Colonel Pyncheon in *The House of the Seven Gables.* The trouble is that such a conclusion is completely out of keeping with the rest of the tale, in spite of James's conscientious attempts at period atmosphere. He had apparently not realized that it required something more than historical detail to create the proper mood for supernatural events. Hawthorne's method was to create a warm haze of ambiguity so that there are always at least two possible explanations of mysterious events, one of them natural. James, on the other hand, in *A Romance of Certain Old Clothes,* simply transferred his evolving notions of psychological realism to the eighteenth century. He did not yet have much idea of what could be done with image and symbol to enrich and mystify a romantic tale. Imbued with ideas about the necessity of realism in fiction, he was not able, even when writing in the romance form, to profit at this time by Hawthorne's example. *The Romance of Certain Old Clothes,* as the title suggests, is, for all its high colour, a costume drama, unredeemed by historical insight or credibility.

In *De Grey: A Romance,* published six months later in the *Atlantic,* James attempted something more ambitious in this line, a long tale that has its origins in the characteristically Hawthornesque idea of the hereditary curse. The first love of every male heir of the De Grey family must die soon after betrothal. The time of the story is 1820; the place, somewhere on the edge of New York City. A widow, Mrs. De Grey, is living in her large house, with a priest, Father Herbert, who had been the companion of her late husband. She is, of course, Catholic. She feels lonely because her only son, Paul, is in Europe travelling to complete his education. She invites a young girl, called Margaret, whose mother has just died, to come to live with her as a companion. When

Paul returns in the springtime, the predictable happens. He falls in love with Margaret. Margaret is told by Father Herbert of the curse on the family, but she refuses to be bound by it. By an immense act of volition, she curses the curse in order to revoke it. She and Paul determine to marry in the fall of the year. However, the curse, instead of being revoked, is simply transferred. 'As she bloomed and prospered, he drooped and languished. While she was living for him, he was dying for her' (CT, I, 425). Here, as in *A Most Extraordinary Case*, James uses the situation that he was to exploit fully in *The Sacred Fount*. In *De Grey: A Romance*, the theme is enhanced by a variation that James probably derived from the Hawthorne tale, *Rappaccini's Daughter*. Margaret has a suspicion that Paul has begun to dislike her, as if 'a dim perception of her noxious influence had already taken possession of his senses.' It is the poisoned garden of her will that has begun to destroy his organism, and she is now powerless to prevent the outcome, as Beatrice was powerless to prevent the poisoning of the system of her lover. Paul De Grey falls from his horse while riding feverishly through the countryside. Margaret gets to the spot in time to see him die and in turn she herself goes mad. The curse ends with the line.

De Grey: A Romance is more successful than *The Romance of Certain Old Clothes*, for James at least attempted to create a certain ambiguity of causation. Paul's mother, for example, to Father Herbert's surprise, 'refused to accept the idea of a supernatural pressure upon her son's life,' cherishing the belief that he had died as a result of his fall. The action of the story, too, springs quite naturally from the characters' personalities, which are fancifully but solidly specified. James discarded many of the more obvious trappings of the Gothic convention to create romance and interest from character instead. Paul, dashing and handsome, is also moody and introspective, whereas Margaret develops from an innocent girl into a woman capable of deep passion and an almost terrible strength of will. In this story, then, James was, probably unconsciously, following a path that Edgar Allan Poe had taken when he used the Gothic romance as a means of exploring certain obsessive psychological traits. The mystery and the horror is found not so much in the plot as it is in the development and interaction of character.

But at this point in his career it seemed that for James the excursion into historical romance could be little more than a divergence from his main course. He was far too deeply committed to the European tradition of realism to take seriously what had up to this time been the more fruitful American tradition of the romance. He appeared to feel the need for more social and historical data for his romances than America could easily supply, as his invariable habit of introducing a hero who had lived or travelled in Europe would indicate. He realized that he had been exposed far too early and intensively to Europe ever to feel satisfied with what the United States could offer for this kind of fiction.

By the end of 1868, after an absence from Europe of more than eight years, James was growing decidedly restless. His state of mind may have been indicated by Paul De Grey who, given the opportunity of travelling in Europe after coming of age, had stayed and travelled in America instead. After this, 'he came back an ardent American, and felt that he might go abroad without danger' (CT, I, 390). By this time, James could feel secure about his opportunities for publication and he knew that he had a good, if small, reputation in American literary circles. Moreover, according to the fashion of the time, he believed his health merited some European treatment. He sailed for Liverpool in February 1869.

❧ 4 ❧

Transatlantic
Trials

The England that James encountered on this trip was precisely the one that he had expected. Or rather, the literary schemata that he had built up in his omnivorous readings in English literature and his scanning of English painting dominated his perception of the actual scene. Fifteen years later, in *The Author of 'Beltraffio,'* he was to reveal precisely this process of perception in the words of the Jamesian author-narrator: 'That was the way many things struck me at that time, in England: as if they were reproductions of something that existed primarily in art or literature. It was not the picture, the poem, the fictive page, that seemed to me a copy; these things were the originals, and the life of happy and distinguished people was fashioned in their image' (CT, V, 307). This observation is confirmed in his autobiography, when he talks of things 'hanging together with a romantic rightness that had the force of a revelation' with the vision of England that he had built up in his mind through his childhood exposure to the cartoons in *Punch* and those of Hogarth, and his reading of the novels of Smollett, Thackeray, and Dickens.[1] His journeys through London, the Cotswolds, and to Oxford, far from challenging these literary schemata, might have been calculated to reinforce them. Unconsciously, he was hardly observing closely at all, but merely seeing what he wanted to see through the spectacles of already-formed perceptions. James himself was aware of the dangers inherent in his romantic attitude towards Europe. He wrote to Charles Eliot Norton from Malvern before he left England to return to the United States from this trip: 'It behoves me as a luckless American diabolically tempted of the shallow and the superficial really to catch the flavour of an old civilization (it hardly matters which) and to strive to place myself for one brief moment at least in the attitude of observation.'[2] But the striving appears to have been of little use. On the continent as well as in England he travelled in an aura made up of child-hood memories and images formed by his reading – that of Balzac, Mérimée, Sand, and Taine. In Rome, just like Goëthe, he almost swooned from joy in the streets.

This is why James felt that in the deepest sense he was coming home in returning to Europe (as Hawthorne had, although in a far less personal sense), and why he felt his imaginative vision quicken to new life. Some of the consequences for the fiction he wrote at the time or soon afterwards were unfortunate. *Travelling Companions* and *At Isella* are merely extensive travelogues, with thin, sentimental plots added to round out the tale.

Happy as he was to be travelling and writing in Europe, James felt obscurely that by so doing he was avoiding his prime responsibility as an American writer. Determined to get to grips again with American subjects, he returned to Boston in April 1870, after fifteen months abroad. 'America is American,' he wrote to Grace Norton, soon after landing; 'that is incontestable, and consistency is a jewel. I wish I could tell you how characteristic every thing strikes me as being – everything from the vast white sky – to the stiff sparse individual blades of grass.'[3]

In the summer, armed with a commission from the *Nation*, he went on a tour of central New York, upper New England, and Canada. He obviously hoped that the tour would be as useful as his European one in filling his notebook with materials for fiction. He began with the most famous American resort, Saratoga, which he rather expected would be 'a sort of elegant wilderness.' To an ima-gination fed with Baden and the Mediterranean resorts, however, it proved to be a sad disappointment. It was neither elegant nor a wilderness, only 'dense, democratic, vulgar,' with its huge wooden hotels sprawling over the town, and its surrounding countryside not so much rural as untidy. James perambulated and gazed at the

visitors. The men suggested to him 'all the swarming vastness –
the multifarious possibilities and activities – of our young civilization.'
Their experience seemed to him to have been hard and narrow, yet
he had to concede that 'they had lived, in every fibre of the will.' He
compared these men, as they sat idly tilting up their chairs on the
wooden piazzas, with their European counterparts. 'They are not,' he
wrote patronizingly, 'the mellow fruit of a society which has walked
hand-in-hand with tradition and culture; they are hard nuts, which
have grown and ripened as they could. When they talk among themselves, I seem to hear the cracking of the shells.' His first impression
of the ladies was different. They wore the latest Parisian gowns and
looked lovely, but then he discovered that they had neither the conversation nor the occupations to match their appearance. They were
merely, James observed, 'rustling beauties whose rustle is their sole
occupation.' Leaving the town in search of the consolations of nature,
he was again disappointed. Nostalgically, he wrote: 'There are no
white villages gleaming in the distance, no spires of churches,
no salient details.' Only after finding a boat and floating out on a
lake, could James escape 'the vulgar and trivial associations' of the
town and listen to 'the eloquent silence of undedicated nature.' Fortunately, he reflected, Ruskin's assertion that human associations were
necessary to make natural scenery fully impressive did not hold true
in America.[4] It is clear from this essay that James did not really make
much effort to appreciate Saratoga. Behind every observation and
judgment is a European criterion. He made little attempt to see the
place on its own terms and could not keep a patronizing and disdain-
ful tone out of the essay.

The same is true of all the other sketches in this group. He complained of all the resorts and towns that the natural beauties of
America had nowhere been enhanced by man-made additions. Ticon-
deroga, for example, was 'more drearily, dirtily, glaringly void of any
poor pitiful incident of village prettiness' than any place with such a
name deserved to be. Niagara Falls, he found, was 'the most beautiful
object in the world' surrounded by 'horribly vulgar shops and booths,'
'catchpenny artifices,' and 'bedizened with placards and advertisements.' The only mitigation to this dreariness was his reflection that
this was 'one of those sordid foregrounds which Turner liked to use,

and which may be effective as a foil.'⁵ It seems that when James went in search of America on this tour, what he unconsciously looked for were echoes of Europe. Understandably, he was disappointed when he found very few.

Only when he came to write of Newport could he really feel at ease. By the time he wrote his sketch of the place it was an old story to him. The James family had visited and lived there for so long that Henry could bring to the place little freshness of perception, only considerable and rather unaccountable affection. With a trace of irony, he confessed to feeling rather shamefaced that he had turned to such a place for inspiration rather than to Saratoga, which was 'more characteristically democratic and American.' Newport at that time, as he later noted in *The American Scene*, was unprecedented in American conditions; it harboured 'a handful of mild, oh delightfully mild, cosmopolites, united by three common circumstances, that of their having for the most part more or less lived in Europe, that of their sacrificing openly to the ivory idol whose name is leisure, and that, not least, of a formed critical habit.'⁶ The town had an aristocratic air, he noted in his early essay. Business seemed remote and pleasure was organized there as in no other American resort. Newport had such an atmospheric ripeness that there 'the sweet, superior beauty of natural things' had triumphed over the destroyer or the reformer as it had done nowhere else in the land. Even the 'little warped and shingled boxes' of the colonial town had been magically transformed by the scintillating atmosphere. A few of the more recent cottages, James thought, gave 'some hope of a revival of the architectural art.' He was probably alluding to the eclectically romantic cottages that Richard Morris Hunt, brother of his old painting master William, had recently designed.⁷ Newport, James concluded, had suffered less from the encroachments of pleasure-seekers than any other watering-place. Here the views, the weather, and the leisure combined to make the 'sweet fruit of the lotus grow more than ever succulent and magical.' How it should purify the temper and refine the taste of the residents. 'How it should purge them of vulgarity!' he whimsically wound up. 'Happy *villeggianti* of Newport!'⁸

In the course of his sketch, James speculated about Newport as a possible setting for literature. The social element would be 'too light and thin' for tragedy, he thought. It would do, however, for drama of a comic nature. Anticipating *The Ivory Tower*, which he was to begin more than forty years later, he observed that it was even possible for a transient observer to dream of 'a great American novel, in which the heroine might be infinitely realistic and yet neither a schoolmistress nor an outcast.' A closer observer of the place, he went on, would conclude, however, that his possible heroines have 'too perfect a time' to make their lives interesting enough for fictional treatment. Perhaps James took his own warning too seriously, for he abandoned Newport, which he had used definitely as a setting for *The Story of a Masterpiece* and *Osborne's Revenge* and by suggestion in other stories, for more 'characteristically American' places when he began to write about his renewed experience in America. The place in the continent he knew best did not re-appear again in his fiction until almost ten years later.

The troubling problem of setting for his fiction was solved for James when he turned back to his recent European experience to write *A Passionate Pilgrim* which appeared in the *Atlantic* in March and April 1871. Evidently he had been comparing his experience with that of Nathaniel Hawthorne, for the story is based on two incidents which appear in 'Consular Experiences,' one of the essays in *Our Old Home*. There had come into the consular office in Liverpool one day a nearly penniless American, a shopkeeper from Connecticut. 'Like a great many other Americans,' Hawthorne had observed, '[he] had long cherished a fantastic notion that he was one of the rightful heirs of a rich English estate ...' He was now stranded in England without the evidence to prove his claim and without funds to return to America. Hawthorne later encountered another American who had discovered in the picture gallery of a country house to which he laid claim 'a portrait bearing a striking resemblance to himself.'[9]

Combining these two incidents and taking as his theme what Hawthorne called 'the blind pathetic tendency' of his countrymen to lay claim to their ancestral home, James created in *A Passionate Pilgrim* the story which he later chose officially to inaugurate his career when he collected his fiction for the New York Edition. Like Hawthorne, he revelled in England's rich resources for settings in his descriptions of London, Hampton Court, the country near Malvern, and Oxford. At the same time, he endeavoured to make these settings not merely decorative but functional to the narrative. The pilgrim, in perceiving these scenes, is initiated into a country which he feels to be his by heritage, even if he has lost the ancestral estate to which he had laid claim. The nostalgic perceptions which James had had of England matched exactly the technique that he chose for representing the story. By the happy choice of an observer-narrator, an obviously cultured young American coming for the first time to England, James was able to tell the story with a deep sympathy for the older passionate pilgrim. At the same time he used his narrator as a detached perceiver of the pathetic absurdity of the pilgrim's cumulative delusions. The narrator, at the beginning of the story, talks of 'the latent preparedness of the American mind' for English life, and of his seeing the coffee-room in which he is sitting 'years ago, at home, – at Saragossa, Illinois, – in books, in visions, in dreams, in Dickens, in Smollett, and Boswell' (CT, II, 227–8). And later on, in the village by Hampton Court, he recognizes that 'it was in this dark composite light that I had read all English prose; it was this mild moist air that had blown from the verses of English poets ...' He had felt a similar emotion in Italy, 'in which the mind, with a great passionate throb, achieves a magical synthesis of its impressions.' This is a perfect description of the 'matching and making' process that E. H. Gombrich speaks of, in which schemata and experience mingle precisely to present the image to be transferred to canvas or the page.[10] The result is the best prose that James had written to date, measured and leisurely yet glowing with the images of his felt experience.

Through Searle, the pilgrim, James was able to luxuriate in the dream which tempted him whenever he went to Europe in his early years – the dream of living in a picturesque past. In Oxford, after leaving the ancestral home to which he had thought to lay claim, Searle imagines that he had been to the university as an undergraduate. 'Thank heaven,' he says, 'that they had the wit to send me here in the other time. I'm not much with it, perhaps; but what should I have been without it? The misty spires and towers of Oxford seen far off on the level have been all these years one of the constant things of memory.' In an abrupt shift of tone, he compares Oxford to the United States: 'My soul reverts to the naked background of our own

education, the dead white wall before which we played our parts ...
We are nursed at the opposite pole. Naked come we into a naked
world. There is a certain grandeur in the absence of a *mise en scène*,
a certain heroic strain in those young imaginations of the West, which
find nothing made to their hands, which have to concoct their own
mysteries, and raise high into our morning air, with a ringing hammer
and nails, the castles in which they dwell' (CT, II, 293–4). The imagery
here is redolent of James's recent American travel essays; the bareness of the scenery is explicitly contrasted to the rich variety and
colouring of Europe. It was bare largely because James had no
schemata upon which to base his observations, because his mind,
filled with the images and forms of the European tradition, could not
come to grips with his skimpy American experience.

A Passionate Pilgrim has been cited by Van Wyck Brooks and
others as the story in which James first prostrated himself before
English standards. To say this is of course to ignore the qualifications
that James makes through his narrator. There is another aspect to the
theme of inheritance that Brooks conveniently ignored. The down-
and-out former Wadham man, Rawson, who wheels the stricken
Searle around Oxford in a bath-chair, is eager for another chance in
the new world. Rawson is in an analogous position to Searle in that
he has been deprived of his birth-right by the miserliness of an elder
brother who, through the outdated law of primogeniture, has inherited and kept all the family property. As Krishna Baldev Vaid has
pointed out, Rawson is Searle's *Doppelgänger*.[11] But whereas Searle,
dying, can feast visually and imaginatively on England and can thus
come aesthetically into his own, Rawson has a family to support. 'O,
for a cooling, cleansing plunge into the unknowing and the unknown!' he cries (CT, II, 301). He gets his chance. The dying Searle
gives Rawson his watch and chain and other trinkets which will be
sufficient to pay for his steamship ticket to America where he can
make a new start.

James was in this way careful to balance the hopeless pathos that
Hawthorne found in the situation of the deluded American claimant
to an English inheritance with the eagerness that the intending immigrant feels for the opportunities offered by a land unencumbered by
class, privilege, and tradition. In a sense, Rawson is to be a passionate

pilgrim too, and the illusion which caused the decline and death of Searle is at the same time to provide means by which the Englishman can renew his grasp on reality.

The American stories which immediately succeeded *A Passionate Pilgrim* do not by any means maintain this high quality of form and expression. *Master Eustace*, which is set very vaguely somewhere in the United States, is an absurdly melodramatic tale of a spoiled lad who refuses to accept the man whom, he finds, his mother has married during his absence on the Grand Tour of Europe, even after he discovers that the man is his father. The abandoned, passionate tone of the story, as Cornelia Kelley has observed, is ill-adapted to the manners of American life, and shows once more how little success James had in trying to adapt George Sand's vision to the more sober hues of the United States.

In the next, seeking greater concreteness, James called the town in which his narrative takes place 'L——.' There is little doubt, however, that he was drawing heavily on his impressions of Saratoga. For the first time in his American stories, James made a real attempt to make the scene a function of the plot and not merely a backdrop to it. The crude resort is a fit setting for *Guest's Confession*, the first of a long series of stories that James was to write about fraud. As a novelist, he was fascinated by the psychological problem posed by the idea of possessions. Fraud was somehow the most personal of crimes. As the swindled man cries to his defrauder in *Guest's Confession*: 'A man's property, sir, is a man's person. It's as if you had given me a blow in the chest!' (CT, II, 394). Also, from the beginning, James showed a mistrust for businessmen, an attitude which his father's ideas probably helped him to develop. Balzac's work provided him with plenty of examples of fraud. Miss Kelley has also suggested the influence of George Eliot on this theme. At any rate, James made a great effort to domesticate the idea through incorporating his observations of the tough nuts on Saratoga's piazzas with his ignorance and distrust of what they did to make their money.

The narrator is a rich, indolent, good-natured fellow, David Musgrave, who has gone to 'L——' to book a room in one of the 'various wooden barracks' for his step-brother Edgar. Edgar Musgrave is a shrivelled, evil-tempered, tight-fisted hypochondriac who arrives in a towering rage from the city, announcing that he has been swindled of twenty thousand dollars. He unexpectedly encounters his defrauder, Mr. Guest, at the resort. He tells him that he is about to prosecute but, at the intercession of the narrator, exacts a humiliating signed confession, and a promise of immediate restitution instead.

Before meeting his step-brother at the train, the narrator had entered the little wooden Episcopalian chapel of the resort to listen to someone playing an organ. He had added his voice to the music and then discovered that the player was an attractive girl. She had come into the church because to do so reminded her of visiting churches in Europe. The narrator goes on: 'I cast a glance over the naked tabernacle, with the counterfeit graining scarcely dry on its beams and planks, and a strong aroma of turpentine and putty representing the odor of sanctity. She followed my glance; our eyes met, and we laughed' (CT, II, 381). A friendship develops from their 'mutual urbanity,' but she leaves the chapel before he discovers that she is the daughter of the swindler, Mr. Guest.

The father leaves for New York to raise money to pay off his fraud and in the interim the narrator courts his daughter, not telling her that he has already met her father. An additional complication of plot is that Guest, a widower, had been in his turn paying marked attention to a widow, Mrs. Beck. In describing her, James invents a brilliant fantasy portrait, although it owes something to his observation of the rustling beauties of Saratoga: 'Mrs. Beck's great point was her "preservation" ... Her age really mattered little, for with as many years as you pleased one way or the other, she was still a triumph of juvenility. Plump, rosy, dimpled, frizzled, with rings on her fingers and rosettes on her toes, she used to seem to me a sort of fantastic vagary or humorous experiment of time. Or, she might have been fancied a strayed shepherdess from some rococo Arcadia ... All this was true, at least of her pretty face and figure; but there was another Mrs. Beck, visible chiefly to the moral eye, who seemed to me to be excessively wrinkled and faded and world-wise, and whom I used to fancy I could hear shaking about in this enamelled envelope, like a dried nut in its shell. Mrs. Beck's morality was not Arcadian; or if it was, it was that of a shepherdess with a keen eye to the state of the wool and the mutton market, and a lively perception of the possible advantages of judicious partnership' (CT, II, 405–6).

Was it that James, lacking real knowledge and insight into a character like Mrs. Beck, applied the schema of the Arcadian romance to represent, ironically, her make-up? The comparison is slightly absurd and out of place and it shows how he was tempted to fall back on convention instead of relying on observation. The wit and humour, however, justify the portrait and skilfully sum up Mrs. Beck's essential artifice. She gains another admirer, 'a certain Mr. Crawford out of the West,' the owner of a diamond mine in Arizona. This romantic creation again takes his start from James's observations on the Saratoga piazzas: 'He was a tall, lean gentleman, on the right side of forty, yellow-haired, with a somewhat arid complexion, an irrepressible tendency to cock back his hat and chew his toothpick, and a spasmodic liability, spasmodically repressed when in a sedentary posture, to a centrifugal movement of the heels' (CT, II, 407). The polysyllabic humour of this portrait denotes an emergent tendency in James's treatment of his American material. With his European notions of dress and decorum, the westerners begin to appear in the guise of caricature.

The courtship between the westerner and the artificial Arcadian shepherdess is couched very much in the comic mode and it supplies an amusing parallel to the more serious one that goes on between the narrator and Miss Guest. Mr. Guest finally returns to 'L——,' having sold all his property. When Mrs. Beck discovers this, she rejects him in favour of Mr. Crawford. Guest also soon discovers the identity of his daughter's suitor and, unable to forgive him for being the witness of his degradation, forbids her to have anything more to do with Musgrave. The sickly step-brother dies and the narrator retrieves the confession from among his effects. David Musgrave holds it over Guest's head with the threat that he will show it to his daughter if he does not consent to her marriage. Finally, in an Arcadian revulsion of feeling that comes after sitting alone by a rural stream in the countryside and seeing 'something in this vision ineffably pastoral, peaceful, and innocent ...' (CT, II, 442), he repents of his purpose. In a gesture that anticipates Christopher Newman's action at the end of *The American*, he burns the paper in the presence of Guest, and is accepted as a suitor and a future son-in-law.

Guest's Confession is technically the most sophisticated story that James had yet written. For the first time, he uses his narrator as an ironic instrument to his purpose. In this story of corruption – the first of many that James was to write about American life – the narrator himself is as tainted as the rest. His indolence and passivity he admits; what he does not realize is his own lack of compassion and sensitivity. That he could stand by and watch his step-brother extorting a confession from a fellow human being on his knees is bad enough. That he could then threaten his future father-in-law with exposure from this same confession reveals him to be a man as unscrupulous as he is unsympathetic. Only his last-minute repentance saves him from abasement. His indolence and ignorance detach him from those who are engaged in the savage competition of the business world. But his indifference implicates him in Guest's guilt, just as Edgar Musgrave, by his ruthlessness in exacting a confession, intensifies that guilt. The last-minute burning of the confession symbolically expiates the narrator's guilt, as well as releasing Guest from an intolerable shame.

James manages the self-revelation of the narrator without for one moment intruding on his point of view. At times, he ironically underlines the narrator's self-deception by giving him observations that reflect on himself. Early in the story, Musgrave ponders the delusive appearance of Mr. Guest. 'Indeed,' he thinks, 'from my cursory observation of my friend, I had rarely seen innocence so handsomely featured. Where, then, was the line which severed rectitude from error? Was manhood a baser thing than I had fancied, or was sin a thing less base?' (CT, II, 390). Under the excuse of his passion for Miss Guest, the narrator readily stoops to baseness without, apparently, ever asking himself the same question. The theme of the complicity of guilt and the irresponsibility of innocence is one that James was to return to with ever-increasing subtlety in his later fiction set in the United States.

Guest's Confession contains a good deal of the passionate melodrama, reminiscent of George Sand, that is characteristic of much of James's early American fiction. There is no doubt that melodramatic literature had a great appeal to James from the beginning. The pages of *A Small Boy and Others* are full of references to melodramatic forms, those of Poe, those of the contemporary American theatre, and those of Victorian writers. He was able, in time, to adapt the form to his own uses, so that in *The Bostonians* and even in the last great novels the melodramatic scenes are integrated with and seem natural to the story. In these early works, however, the melodrama does not seem organic, but merely pasted on to his plots. In lieu of sufficient American schemata, it seems, melodramatic devices of contemporary European literature had to serve James's turn.

A survey of the short stories that James wrote between 1865 and 1872 reveals again and again the sources of the problems that most troubled him in writing American fiction. In an article in the *Nation*, written in 1868, he observed that the American was born into a far simpler world than the European, and inherited far fewer 'obligations, conventions, responsibilities.'[12] This, he noted, made for a less complicated life, but there can be little doubt that James believed that simplicity complicated his work as an American novelist. Obligations, conventions, and responsibilities were precisely the things that he wished to deal with, just as Balzac and George Eliot had dealt with them in Europe. It must be assumed that America had its own kind of conventions and obligations, but James seems to have been unable to discover them. In trying to represent the American scene, James found a similar difficulty. 'I couldn't do without the *scene*,' he wrote of himself as a beginning novelist in his autobiography, 'whether actually or but possibly peopled (the people always calling for the background and the background insisting on the people) ...'[13] But, as we have seen, he practically did without scene for many of these early stories. When he tried to paint the background, he usually used a schema based so firmly on European models that the actual American picture was almost entirely obscured. Both these related problems of character and setting were most acutely felt when he came to write his first novel.

5

A Certain Form
Watch and Ward

Watch and Ward was serialized in the *Atlantic* in the latter part of 1871. Professor Leon Edel has rightly claimed for it an 'undeniable quaintness and rather old-time charm ...' (ww, 9). Surely these qualities were not, however, what the young realist had in mind for his book. James apparently believed he was writing an 'American' novel but, as Miss Cornelia Kelley has remarked, 'everything about it was not observed but imagined.' He brought little of his recent experience and travel in the United States to bear in the book, so that Miss Kelley is, on the whole, right in concluding that 'it is not a picture of a group of Americans whom James knew and respected. It is not a record of contemporary manners. It is something made up, invented, a figment of the imagination.'[1]

The main critical question about the novel has been, and still remains, that of the influences playing upon it. Ford Madox Ford, who began the search, certainly oversimplified the case by calling it 'a Balzac-Dickensian trifle,'[2] but the elements of both novelists are at least vestigially present. A certain meticulous observation of interiors and an assured and authoritative treatment of his characters in an omniscient way remind a reader strongly of Balzac at times, while melodramatic confrontations and incidents and, later in the novel, some treatment of the sordid realities of city life bring Dickens to mind. Oscar Cargill in his quite exhaustive treatment of sources in *The Novels of Henry James*, has emphasized the influence of Dr.

Oliver Wendell Holmes. He was still a great presence in *Atlantic* affairs and the author of the novels *Elsie Venner* and *The Guardian Angel*, which James probably read. But, as Mr. Cargill's own analysis shows, the influence was more a question of similar incidents and the anti-sentimental tone than of essential form and subject. James attempts none of Holmes's local colour and dialect, even though such trimming might have given his novel a greater authenticity. He was in fact, like George Eliot, much more concerned with the analysis of personal relationships and, above all, with the treatment of passion, where the obvious source is once again George Sand.

There is, as Mr. Cargill points out, a direct source in Madame Sand's fiction for the central situation of *Watch and Ward*. In *La Mare au Diable*, Germain, who is twenty-eight, is attracted to the fatherless Mary, aged sixteen. She eventually becomes his mistress. When *Watch and Ward* opens, the hero, Roger Lawrence, is twenty-nine, and Nora Lambert is twelve. He offers her his protection when her father commits suicide. Leon Edel has seen in this situation an analogy between James's novel and Nabokov's *Lolita,* but this seems to me to be misleading. There is very little overt sexuality in Roger's relationship with Nora in her early years. A closer analogy is to be found with the Pygmalion myth, for Roger deliberately sets out to make of his little protegée an ideal bride. 'I have begun at the beginning,' he writes to a confidante; 'it will be my own fault if I have not a perfect wife' (ww, 53).

It is George Sand's influence which would seem to have led James most astray from his natural road in this novel. He had seen from the first that most English novelists appeared to have 'omitted the erotic sentiment altogether,' and that Madame Sand, by contrast, treated it continually. She 'enlarged the novel-reader's conception,' he wrote, 'of the ardent forces of the heart.'[3] Neither Howells nor the *Atlantic* readership would, however, permit him to treat passions, particularly illicit ones, in the same free way as George Sand had done. In order to widen his readers' conceptions at all, James felt bound to enclose his passions within the conventional framework of the sentimental English novel, which chronicles the adventures of the chaste heroine until she finally winds up in the safe haven of her true lover's arms. James tried to bring to this old form, however, a degree of passionate expression that was presumably meant to liberate the novel. But the discrepancy between the passions and the characters who are supposed to feel them is so great that he succeeds simply in embarrassing the reader. One of Nora's suitors is a clergyman, Hubert Lawrence, who is perhaps ironically modelled on one of Trollope's low-church clerical bounders. Hubert is a high Episcopalian, full of unction, though little of it is sacred. It is he who makes the strongest plea for love in the novel.

'Nora, Nora!' he says, ' I stand up for passion! If a thing can take the shape of passion, that's a fact in its favour. The greater passion is the better cause. If my love wrestles with my faith, as the angel with Jacob, and if my love stands uppermost, I will admit it's a fair game ...' With passion outstripping reason, he tells her that he dreams of breaking some law for her sake. Nora, however, has a stiffer moral fibre. She replies that she dreams 'of the beauty of keeping laws' (ww, 163-6).

Most of the other characters in the novel, at different times, talk in the same passionate vein as Hubert, which hardly seems a realistic portrayal of American life in the 1870s. The irony of this situation is that James had already expressed his intention of breaking the mould of romantic fiction in America. In one of his long talks with Howells, he had asked how they could 'eliminate the everlasting young man and young woman' from their work.[4] One of the products of his concern for realism is presumably the anti-romantic hero, Roger, who is a short-sighted, balding, fastidiously neat little man – a prototype, in fact, of the fussy, rich bachelors who are a perennial element in James's fiction. The trouble is that James, having eliminated from his work the most obtrusive element of romantic fiction, replaced it by George Sand's extravagant passion, an even less appropriate element.

Presumably unaware of this discrepancy, James uses his characters to attack the conventions of sentimental fiction. Nora, although she is reading Charlotte Yonge's enormously popular *The Heir of Redclyffe* for the twentieth time, tells Roger that he is 'quite as good a hero as this stick of a Philip,' even though Roger has fallen asleep while she has been reading the romance to him (ww, 70). Roger toys with the idea of treating Nora as Rochester treated Jane Eyre, but rejects the idea as absurd. Later on, Hubert finds Nora reading a novel and asks her to tell him the plot. Afterwards, he cries: 'Heaven preserve us, what a hotch-potch! ... Is that what they are writing nowadays? I very seldom read a novel, but when I glance into one, I am sure to find some such stuff as that! Nothing irritates me so as the flatness of people's imagination. Common life, – I don't say it's a vision of bliss, but it's better than that. Their stories are like the underside of a carpet, – nothing but the stringy grain of the tissue, – a muddle of figures without shape and flowers without colour' (ww, 163).

One of the main defects of *Watch and Ward*, however, is that James was not as yet capable of using the stuff of common American life to impart some substance and vitality to his novel. Its social context is painfully thin. Apart from the characters already mentioned, and one or two Dickensian minor figures like Roger's housekeeper, Lucinda, the only other characters in the novel are Mrs. Keith, a widow to whom Roger had once been a suitor, and a young businessman, George Fenton. The widow is that stock figure of European light fiction, the chaperone. Fenton is probably the most original figure in the novel, since he is derived in part from James's observations at Saratoga. For the rest he is a caricature of the stock Western figure of fable. He is, James writes, 'a vulgar Missourian,' who 'knew the American continent as he knew the palm of his hand; he was redolent of enterprise, of "operations," of a certain fierce friction with mankind.' In contrast to Roger, he is tall, lean, dark-eyed and has straight black hair. He also wears a diamond in his shirt-front. Nora feels that he has 'an irresistible air of action, alertness, and purpose' (ww, 78–83). This is what attracts her to him at first in preference to the inactive and largely purposeless Roger, who feels like a boy or an old woman in Fenton's presence. Fenton, James tells us repeatedly, is not a gentleman; it turns out, in fact, that he is a swindler. His partner in a scrap-iron business in New York tells Nora that Fenton had made off with the 'thirty thousand dollars that I put into the d—d humbug of a business' (ww, 199). Near the end of the novel the caricature takes over from the character and Fenton degenerates into a conventional Victorian villain. He proposes to hold Nora to ransom after she has run away from Roger, threatens her with violence, and finally, in an absurd gesture of contrition after she has called him a coward, flings himself down moaning, 'O Lord! ... I am an ass!' (ww, 227).

Characteristically, in this novel, the West appears as a dire and violent region. As early as 1868 James had written a story, *Osborne's Revenge*, in which one of the characters commits suicide in Minneapolis. Nora's father, who has come east from St. Louis a few days before, begins *Watch and Ward* by shooting himself after an ineffectual attempt to shoot Nora. On the other hand, the West represents energy as well as violence and vulgarity. Nora's father is full of energy, even if it is the energy of despair. He moves rapidly, flings himself about, seizes Roger's arm in the hotel lobby and tries to hustle him into lending him a hundred dollars. Fenton, for his part, appeals to Nora by reminding her of her western origins and calling her, when grown, 'a regular Western girl.' The West, he says, 'is the only place for a man of ideas! In the West you can do something! Round here you're all stuck fast in ten feet of varnish' (ww, 86-7). To Roger, the West seems to represent all the features in Nora that he must overcome. Nurture must overcome what nature has given her, or at least direct and civilize the natural energy which seems her endowment.

By contrast, the East produces the effete characters in the novel, the indolent Roger and the corrupt Hubert, who is much more interested in bodily comfort than spiritual salvation. Midway through the novel, Hubert tells Nora that he wishes she had been left poor instead of having been taken up by Roger, so that he could have rescued her penniless from the street. At the end of the novel she goes to see Hubert after she has fled from Roger. She then learns that he had been engaged to a wealthy girl of Jewish descent all the time, and that he had gone back to her after Mrs. Keith had accused him of playing a double game. Denied what she believes to be her last refuge, Nora leaves his house and, in an ending worthy of Hollywood, sees Roger walking down 'the bright vista of the street.' Roger has been tried and chastened by his love, like any chivalric hero, and now deserves the heroine. Nora goes to him and takes his arm, saying that she is now a wiser girl.

It is curious that Henry James, who was later to be so scrupulous about the settings of his novels, was so careless about scene in this. The novel opens in a hotel that appears to be in Limbo. It is not until many chapters later that the reader discovers that it must have been Boston. Similarly, Roger's country house is the setting for Nora's upbringing, but it does not emerge until much later that it is situated about twelve miles from Boston in a place unsatisfactorily called 'C——.' The only graphically rendered scene is a poor section of New York where Nora goes in search of Fenton after leaving Roger. She is looking for Fenton's scrap-iron yard and passes a picturesque and dirty Dutch grocer's (that later did duty for *The Bostonians*) and walks through streets of 'mean and sinister' houses. Going into a fly-blown 'Ladies' Café,' she stays briefly to drink a bad cup of tea served her by a 'half-dressed woman with frowzy hair and tumid eyes' who charges her a dollar for it. She later sits for a while in a sordid square which has 'a frozen fountain, thawing fast' in the centre. Around her the benches are 'occupied by shabby men, sullen with fasting.' James renders here with some skill an image of poverty and exploitation that was not to appear again in his fiction until he wrote *The Princess Casamassima*. New York, even if he could not see in it a society complex enough for a significant novel of manners, could at least supply him with a fitting background for expressing his sense of the meanness and rapacity in urban American life. Its function in the novel is to make a significant contrast to the luxury and security of Nora's upbringing, a motif extended by the scrap-iron yard itself where Nora has to wait some hours for Fenton to appear. In the office, 'the desk, the stove, the iron safe, the chairs, the sordid ink-spotted walls, were as blank and impersonal as so many columns of figures' (ww, 197). The office makes her realize how little her cousin, for all his energy, had done to make his way in the world.

A little further on in the novel, it is true, James makes use of a February thaw to presage the happy ending. As Roger searches for Nora in the New York streets, James writes, 'The weather was perfect; one of those happy days of February which seems to snatch a mood from May, – a day when any sorrow is twice a sorrow. The winter was melting and trickling; you heard on all sides, in the still sunshine, the raising of windows; on the edges of opposing house-tops rested a vault of vernal blue. Where was she hidden, in the vast, bright city? The streets and crowds and houses that concealed her seemed hideous' (ww, 214–5). Roger turns into Central Park, which appears here for the first of many times in James's fiction. There he sets a brief scene in which Roger meets a girl whom he had earlier admired and in whom he can confide about his situation. On a 'little bed of raw verdure' he finds the first violet of the year, which he presents to the girl before he goes off once more renewed in his determination to find Nora.

But the reader has the distinct sense in this novel that James found the American resources for functional and dramatic scenery to be sparse to the point of poverty. In fact, in the middle, he pads his work by including letters that Nora writes home from Europe, where she is touring with Mrs. Keith. A good many pages are filled with descriptions of Rome, which are quite irrelevant to the action. James's notebooks obviously yielded up some colourful Roman material that he put into *Watch and Ward* as a contrast to its drab American background. 'Nothing can ever be the same after a winter in Rome,' writes Nora to Roger, revealing, no doubt, her creator's mind. 'Sometimes I am half frightened at having had it in my youth. It leaves such a chance to be dull afterwards' (ww, 133).

As so often in James's later fiction, the European journey is used to bring out the latent beauty and intelligence of the heroine. Before she sails, she rides for a long time in the rain in a closed carriage with the clergyman, Hubert. The scene is ironically reminiscent of the coach ride in *Madame Bovary*. 'You will not be able to do this kind of thing abroad,' says Hubert. 'Do you know we are monstrously improper? For a young girl it's by no means pure gain, going to Europe. She comes into a very pretty heritage of prohibitions ... Promise me not to lose this precious bandage of American innocence' (ww, 116). Nora comes back with her bandage intact, but she has been awakened to life. Hubert, on seeing her, calls her 'a Western version of the myth' of Pallas Athene springing fully-armed from the brain of Jove. This is a colourful but misleading analogy. The point is that all her potentialities were dormant. The myth that James was really using here, for the first of many times, was that of the sleeping beauty. Europe plays the part of the prince.

As *Watch and Ward* was being serialized, James wrote to C. E.

Norton: 'I have begun to print in the *Atlantic* a short serial story which you will see. The subject is something slight; but I have tried to make a work of art, and if you are good enough to read it I trust you will detect my intention. A certain form will be its chief merit.'[5] At least James had no illusions about the thinness of his subject, and he seems to be confessing a desire to conceal this slightness by his art. His intention was presumably to expand the simple subject by a dramatically arranged progression of encounters between the major characters. He does at least succeed in tracing the development and growth of Nora's perception of the value of her original discoverer, Roger, but the sequence of scenes with Hubert and Fenton and Roger is often too artificial and coincidental in nature. James was not yet able to write an organically sustained narrative.

However, the climax of the novel is skilfully prepared for and convincing. When Nora returns from Europe, she finds that Roger is ill. Then she realizes that he is 'her world, her strength, her life.' Later, when he appears to be dying, she saves him with an embrace, thus reversing her role as a sleeping beauty. During his long convalescence, Roger sees her as Scheherazade or Badoura from the *Arabian Nights*. In the story in which the Princess Badoura appears, she is awakened and restored from her illness by the Prince Camaralzaman. By literary analogy, then, James also reverses Nora's role. The important thing, however, is that the principle of vitality is transmitted and Roger regains his will to live. When he is recovered from his sickness, he proposes to Nora. But she is as yet unprepared for a new role in relation to Roger, having assumed that she was still in the situation of being a ward to him. The shock of his proposal causes her to refuse him and then run off to New York. As she tells George Fenton, her pride will not allow her 'to pay my debt and be his wife.' It is only after she has made trial of her other two suitors, Fenton and Hubert, in a pair of highly melodramatic scenes, that she can appreciate Roger as a man, rather than as a guardian, and accept him as a husband.

In spite of James's art in concealing the slight subject, there are times when he tries the reader's patience with the sentimental events that were the stock-in-trade of the magazine novelists of the period. The chief strength of the novel lies in its character-drawing and the indications of thematic ideas that are given, if not worked out, in mythical analogues. These myths, usually fairy tales, were the form of romance that James was best able to adapt to his realistic method. They embody his most deeply felt ideas and emotions, as their frequent recurrence in his fiction makes clear. The myths supply an analogical framework within which he could work out his characters' developments — as in the recurrent concern with the growth of a young girl into adulthood — and at the same time give a basis to what was to become his major theme, the relation of the United States to Europe. Even in this early 'American' novel, these twin concerns occur (perhaps even embryonically in the contrast of West and East in the United States) and serve to show that James could not imaginatively do without Europe as an essential part of his fictional world. For many years he regarded Europe as an essential element in the education and development of his major characters. There is a mystery in this process that perhaps James himself did not fully comprehend, a mystery echoed by Hubert when he first sees Nora after her return from Europe to the United States: 'What sudden magic had made her so handsome? She was the same tender slip of girlhood who had come trembling to hear him preach a year before; the same yet how different! And how sufficient she had grown, withal, to her beauty! How with an added burden had come an added strength ...' (ww, 147).

Much of the novel's interest to a student of James's work is in what it foreshadows, rather than in what it does. Many of the characters are drafts of later more richly detailed personalities — particularly Roger, who looks forward both to Acton in *The Europeans* and Ralph in *The Portrait of a Lady*. Nora too is the prototype of innumerable Jamesian heroines, although she lacks the complexity, or even the potential complexity, of an Isabel Archer. Some of the situations in *Watch and Ward*, too, are to crop up again, refined and complicated, in James's later work. Roger's proposal to Mrs. Keith, for example, is echoed in the late story, *Crapy Cornelia*, and the swindling businessman, George Fenton, appears frequently in other guises in James's late stories.

But on the whole, *Watch and Ward* is unsatisfactory. The social context is too thin to give the book any strong feeling of reality. The main trouble is that too many influences are fighting for mastery in the novel, some of them, like George Sand and George Eliot, being mutually exclusive. Without a ruling aesthetic idea or viable perceptual schema to apply to American life and scenes, James was groping uncertainly. It is not surprising that he tried to suppress the novel in later years and that he did not attempt another full-length American novel for a long time to come.

⚜6⚜

Experiment and Decision
The Attempt
to Be an American Artist

After nearly two years in America since his last visit to Europe, Henry James had neither properly settled down nor come to grips with his situation. On 4 February 1872, he summed up his discontent to Charles Eliot Norton, then in Europe, in a letter, which has often been quoted in part and thus somewhat distorted. 'It is not that I have anything very new and strange to relate. In fact when one sits down to sum up Cambridge life, *plume en main*, the strange thing seems its aridity.' After complaining about the lack of 'society' in Cambridge, he continued: 'I confess that my best company nowadays is that of various vague, nourishing dreams of getting to your side of the world with what speed I may. I carry the desire ... to a marked pitch, and I exaggerate the merits of Europe. It's the same world there after all and Italy isn't the absolute any more than Massachusetts. It's a complex fate, being an American, and one of the responsibilities it entails is fighting against a superstitious valuation of Europe.'

Percy Lubbock, in his introduction to the first section of *The Letters of Henry James,* quotes only the sentence containing the remark about the complex fate. The context makes plainer than Lubbock does how desperately bored James was with Cambridge, how sterile a climate he felt it to be for his art, and how much he was yearning for Europe at this time. He was obviously trying to caution himself against overvaluing it in the light of his earlier experience there. His intellectual doubts did not shake his emotional conviction, however, that for him at least Italy *was* better than Massachusetts. Steeling himself against disappointment, he made preparations to return to Europe once more. As he told Norton, 'It will be rather a sell, getting over there and finding the problems of the universe rather multiplied than diminished. Still, I incline to risk the discomfiture.'[1]

This discomfiture, partly a sense of guilt and inadequacy, partly a real confusion about his complex relationship to both Europe and America, kept James from feeling content on his next European tour, which began in May 1872. From Berne, he wrote to Howells: 'Your letter made me homesick, and when you told of the orchards by Fresh Pond I hung my head for melancholy. What is the meaning of this destiny of desolate exile – this dreary necessity of having month after month to do without our friends for the sake of this arrogant old Europe which so little befriends us?'[2] Even after he had taken up residence in Florence, his mind returned anxiously to the question of his relationship to America. Norton was by this time back in Cambridge and lamenting its inadequacies in letters to James. Commenting to Norton's sister, Grace, in one such letter, James wrote: 'It's not for me to blame him, for I take [America] hard enough even here in Florence, and though I have a vague theory that there is a way of being contented there, I am afraid that when I go back I shall need all my ingenuity to put it into practice. What Charles says about our civilization seems to me perfectly true, but practically I don't feel as if the facts were so melancholy. The great fact for us all there is that, relish Europe as we may, we belong much more to that than to this, and stand in a much less factitious and artificial relation to it. I feel forever how Europe keeps holding one at arm's length, and condemning one to a meagre scraping of the surface.' James went on to complain of how little reciprocity he had found in Europe, but admitted, ironically, that those Americans who had stayed on there and been happy found 'even Cambridge the Brilliant' not an easy place to live in. By this time, however, he had evolved a theory about the bareness and thinness of America. Might it be a source of original art? 'It would seem,' he wrote in the same letter to Grace Norton, 'that in our great unendowed, unfurnished, unentertained and un-entertaining continent, where we all sit sniffing, as it were, the very earth of our foundations, we ought to have leisure to turn out something handsome from the very heart of simple human nature. But after I have been at home a couple of months I will tell you what I think.'[3]

The proposition was only half-facetious. Certainly if Europe condemned him to a mere scraping of the surface, he would be better off trying to plumb the depths of American life. But James was irresolute. He could be neither happy in America nor content out of it; his loyalty conflicted with his desires, his intellect with his emotions. On the one hand, if he went home he would be less of a drain on the family purse and nearer the sources of publication. On the other, the expense of living in America might gobble up all the extra income he might receive there. It was obvious at least that he had to return home for a period to test his own theory about American conditions. In a letter to his mother he announced his intention of coming back in the autumn. If at the end of a decent period in America he did not feel an overwhelming desire to return to Europe, then he would have gained something. What he felt he most needed was 'a *régal* of intelligent and suggestive society, especially male.'[4] But he did not know where to find it in Paris or London, since he knew no one. He must have felt that to look for such a society in Cambridge, Massachusetts, would be a waste of time, but for the moment there seemed to be no alternative. In September 1874, he sailed once more for the United States.

The conflict of these two years abroad is dramatized in one of James's most effective early stories, *The Madonna of the Future*, published in 1873. The narrator meets in the streets of Florence the shabby little painter, Theobald, who, like Searle in *A Passionate Pilgrim*, is a sort of aesthetic invalid in Europe. It is he who gives the passionate speech about Americans as 'the disinherited of art' that has so often been quoted as proof of James's alienation from America. 'We are condemned to be superficial!' he says. 'We are excluded from the magic circle. The soil of American perception is a poor little barren, artificial deposit. Yes! we are wedded to imperfection. An American, to excel, has just ten times as much to learn as a European. We lack the deeper sense. We have neither taste, nor tact, nor force. How should we have them? Our crude and garish climate, our silent past, our deafening present, the constant pressure about us of unlovely circumstance, are as void of all that nourishes and prompts and inspires the artist, as my sad heart is void of bitterness in saying so! We poor aspirants must live in perpetual exile.'

The narrator, however, in a passage seldom quoted by critics, puts the other side of the argument equally forcibly. 'Nothing is so idle as to talk about our want of a nutritive soil, of opportunity, of inspiration, and all the rest of it. The worthy part is to do something fine! There's no law in our glorious Constitution against that. Invent, create, achieve! No matter if you've to study fifty times as much as one of these! What else are you an artist for?' (CT, III, 15).

The last question is one that James must have had strongly in his mind as he returned to America, and *The Madonna of the Future* reveals that he had a better grasp now of his problem. But what if 'the soil of American perception' did turn out to be barren? Theobald's phrase is ambiguous. It could mean, on the one hand, that there was not enough in the American environment worth perceiving or, on the other, that former American artists had not been able to create enough schemata to form a viable tradition for those that followed. The narrator ignores Theobald's problem. James, however, could not, and his return to America this time was a pilgrimage to see whether or not he could see, could work, could till the soil of American perception.

A notebook entry of 1881 records the result. 'I had returned from Europe ... [at] the beginning of September, '74, sailing for Boston with Wendell Holmes and his wife as my fellow passengers. I had come back then to "try New York," thinking it my duty to attempt to live at home before I should grow older, and not take for granted too much that Europe alone was possible; especially as Europe for me then meant simply Italy, where I had had some very discouraged hours, and which, lovely and desirable though it was, didn't seem as a permanent residence, to lead to anything. I wanted something more active, and I came back and sought it in New York. I came back with a certain amount of scepticism, but with very loyal intentions, and extremely eager to be "interested." As I say, I was interested but imperfectly, and I very soon decided what was the real issue of my experiment.'[5]

He spent the winter in New York, writing reviews of books and plays for the *Nation* as well as fiction. In spite of his discovery that New York was a bustling, growing, metropolitan, even cosmopolitan, city, he found it uncongenial. He was, as he recalled in a later preface, isolated uptown, on Twenty-fifth Street, along with the 'music-masters and French pastry-cooks, the ladies and children.' The 'serious male interest' was all at work downtown.[6] It was the old problem that had plagued him from the beginning. He felt outside the main current of American life. No amount of imaginative effort could enable him to grasp the complexities of the business world, which, he came more and more to see, was at the centre of American experience.

In this winter of decision, James must have realized that the cosmopolitan and artistic life that his father's peculiar theory of education had led him towards had disqualified him from chronicling the battles of the market, just as his injury had prevented him from fighting in the Civil War. Yet he could see the latent drama in the ferocity, intensity, and unscrupulousness of business competition in the post-Civil War decades. It was the period of the rise of many of the great American fortunes, of rapid physical and moral change that was accompanied by a startling increase of sharp and corrupt practice in public and commercial life.

Whenever James treated businessmen in his early fiction he tended to associate them with fraud or grasping shrewdness. The American writer's distrust of the commercial type did not originate with James, of course. Cooper, Poe, Hawthorne, and Melville all represented commercial characters in their fiction equivocally, at the least. After the Civil War, however, the distrust appears to have risen sharply. *The Gilded Age* by Mark Twain and C. Dudley Warner, a study of corruption in politics and business, gave the name to the period. Even the genial and optimistic Howells portrayed characters in business and the professions who are not particularly scrupulous about the conduct of their affairs.

Subsequent to the writing of *Guest's Confession*, however, James did not attempt to write about business as such. He did, though, on one occasion, follow the example of Hawthorne to make a study of corruption on the tattered fringes of American life, rather than at its

71

business centre. As he matured, James seemed more and more to feel that Hawthorne's subjects and methods could help him better than any other author to unlock the secrets of American existence. Professor Fargo in the story of that name, published in *Galaxy* in 1874, is modelled on the magician Westervelt in *The Blithedale Romance*.* Like Westervelt, Professor Fargo claims hypnotic power and travels around the rural areas of New England putting on his show in town and village halls.

The story opens with the narrator, a commercial traveller, waiting to see an absent client in a remote little country town called, with James's usual indefiniteness in these early tales, 'P——.' There is nothing for him to do but loiter around the tavern, walk up and down the dusty plank sidewalk of the main street, or visit the cemetery and bewail the lack of European accessories. 'Although we were at the end of September,' the narrator writes, 'the day was hot, and this youthful institution boasted but a scanty growth of funereal umbrage. No weeping willow, no dusky cypress offered a friendly shelter to the meditative visitor. The yellow grass and the white tombstones glared in the hot light ...' (CT, III, 259–60). The story goes on to sketch a few more details of this ragged and ugly place until the narrator comes across Professor Fargo in a large bare room in the Town Hall. He is getting ready for his show, which the narrator realizes with relief will help fill the slow hours in the town. On the same bill are a mathematician, Colonel Gifford, and his deaf and dumb daughter, who gives a demonstration of rapid calculation.

The narrator attends the show that evening and discovers that the Professor is a mountebank – as the circus imagery that James had used to describe him had already prefigured. Like his successor, Selah Tarrant in *The Bostonians*, he discourses 'upon the earth life and the summer land, and related surprising anecdotes of his intimacy with the inhabitants of the latter region' (CT, III, 269). On the other

---

*Daniel Lerner, in 'The Influence of Turgenev on Henry James' (*Slavonic Review*, XX, 1941, 40), maintains that James derived this story from Turgenev's 'A Strange Story' (1869). In Turgenev, however, the spiritualist medium is a religious fanatic, unlike the cynical and corrupt figures of Westervelt and Fargo. However, James probably did, as Lerner claims, borrow another detail from Turgenev in making the girl in *Professor Fargo* a deaf-mute, like the deaf-mute in 'Mumu.'

hand, the Colonel and his daughter, while they have no popular appeal, put on a performance which the narrator finds simple, charming, and genuine. The portrait of the young girl derives a good deal from Priscilla in *The Blithedale Romance* and may be taken also as a preliminary sketch for Verena, Selah Tarrant's daughter: 'It was no brilliant beauty, but a sort of meagre, attenuated, angular grace, the delicacy and fragility of the characteristic American type. Her chest was flat, her neck extremely thin, her visage narrow, and her forehead high and prominent. But her fair hair encircled her head in such fleecy tresses, her cheeks had such a pale pink flush, her eyes such an appealing innocence, her attitude such a quaint unconscious felicity, that one watched her with a kind of upstart belief that to such a stainless little spirit the working of miracles might be really possible' (CT, III, 272).

The Colonel loathes his collaborator, with whom he has been forced to associate because of his descent to abject poverty after many expensive and useless experiments. In the hotel bar after the performance he challenges the Professor, who has been drunkenly boasting of his powers, to make any man, woman, or child do anything against his will by 'supernatural operation.' The Professor takes up the challenge. What the Colonel does not know, however, is a fact that has already been conveyed to the reader by the narrator – that the Professor is seducing the deaf and dumb daughter.

The last section of the story takes place in New York, where the narrator happens to run across the trio once more. The Professor has engaged a hall there, but he has sadly misjudged the appeal of the act in the metropolis, for it is playing to almost empty houses. The Colonel explains to the narrator that they had had a run of bad luck since he last saw them, as they had been travelling in the wake of a circus. ' "What are my daughter and I," said the Colonel, "after the educated elephant and the female trapezist? What even is the Professor, after the great American clown?" ' (CT, III, 291). The Colonel has decided to dissolve the partnership after the end of the engagement. Turning up at that night's performance the narrator finds that, apart from the proprietor of the hall, who has come vainly for his rent, he is the entire audience.

The Professor, accepting the failure, announces his intention of exhibiting the Colonel's daughter for a month in his own way, and predicts a great sensation. The Colonel refuses to consent to this arrangement. The Professor then reminds him that his daughter is of age. He asks her to choose between them. The girl chooses the Professor, who goes off with her, exclaiming to the dumbfounded Colonel, 'What do you say now? ... Is spiritual magnetism a humbug?' (CT, III, 298). The Professor has won his bet and the narrator finishes the story by noting that he sometimes goes to see the Colonel in the asylum where he spends his days covering little squares of paper with algebraic signs.

In *Professor Fargo,* Hawthorne's example led James, through his realistic treatment of a theme from *The Blithedale Romance,* to considerable artistic success. Like the Colonel, the narrator is sceptical and ironic about the posturing Professor. Their attitude is reinforced by the circus imagery with which the travelling act is surrounded. At the same time, James manages to suggest that the unscrupulous and corrupt Professor is able to exploit his sexual attraction for the innocent deaf and dumb girl and thus undermine the influence of her good but totally impractical father. Under the spell of her fascination for him, the girl's will is completely overcome and she rejects her father without hesitation. She goes off with the Professor into an unimaginably tawdry life, while her father declines into insanity.

In this story, once more, James made the resources of the American scene functional to his theme. The squalid little town of 'P——,' with its ignorant and gullible townspeople, supplies a suitable setting for the original performance of the Professor's travelling show. The blasé, indifferent metropolis of New York and the bare, gas-lit hall functions in a similar fashion at the end. It appears that, given themes of squalor, deceit, and failure, James was able to make fairly good use of the American environment. Perhaps, too, the schemata provided him by the city scenes in *The Blithedale Romance* helped him here. However, it seems that his native land could not at this time function dramatically as a backdrop for less depressing narratives. To write about love and romance, James turned back to Europe for his setting, as he did for the stories that followed *Professor Fargo*: *Eugene Pickering* and *Benvolio.*

The Flat-iron Building

The vast money-making structure
quite horribly, quite romantically justified itself,
looming through the weather
with an insolent cliff-like sublimity.

The American Scene

Henry James's Portrait
1906

His eyes were singularly penetrating,
dark and a little prominent ...
My servants used to say: 'It always gives me a turn
to open the front door for Mr. James.
His eyes seems to look you through
to the very backbone.'

FORD MADOX FORD

It was not until that first dinner
was half over, and he suddenly turned and
looked at me very closely, that
I realized the strange power of Henry James's eyes.
They made me feel in those instants
as if he had read me to the soul –
and I rather think he had.

ELIZABETH JORDAN

The Legend of the Master
compiled by Simon Nowell-Smith
8, 6

The State House, Boston

... to crown the eminence and complete the picture,
high in the air, poised in the right place,
over everything that clustered below,
the most felicitous object in Boston, –
the gilded dome of the State House.

A New England Winter
ANS, 356

A Boston Street

The large clear windows of their curved fronts
faced each other, across the street,
like candid, inevitable eyes.
There was something almost terrible
in the windows ...

A New England Winter
ANS, 355–6

A New England Village Street

When the great elm-gallery happens to be garnished with old houses,
and the old houses happen to show style and form and proportion,
and the hand of time, further, has been so good
as to rest on them with all the pressure of protection
and none of that of interference,
then it is that the New England village may placidly await any comer.

The American Scene

California Landscape

California –
... a sort of prepared but
unconscious and inexperienced Italy,
the primitive *plate*, in perfect condition,
but with the impression of History
all yet to be made.

The American Scene
462

New York Waterfront

... it is the power of the most extravagant of cities, rejoicing,
as with the voice of the morning, in its might, its fortune,
its unsurpassable conditions, and
imparting to every object and element,
to the motion and expression of every floating, hurrying, panting thing,
to the throb of ferries and tugs, to the plash of waves
and the play of winds and the glint of lights and the shrill of whistles
and the quality and authority of breeze-born cries
... something of its sharp free accent ...

The American Scene

James's main concern in fiction during the winter of 1874–5 was not, however, in short stories but in writing *Roderick Hudson,* which had been begun in Florence during the previous spring. For this, his first major novel, he took greater pains with the theme and method than he had taken for *Watch and Ward. A Passionate Pilgrim* had indicated that his most fruitful subject was the international theme. He had an interesting guide to a contemporary treatment of the topic in a novel that his friend W. D. Howells had recently published. This was *A Foregone Conclusion,* which was set largely in Venice. James reviewed it in both the *Nation* and *The North American Review* in January 1875, the month in which *Roderick Hudson* began to appear in the *Atlantic.* The former review, in particular, reveals his sense of his contemporary's limitations and obliquely indicates how he was trying to surpass him.

Howells had served in Venice as Consul and knew the city intimately, but James rather perversely expressed the wish that his friend had kept his novel at home. 'A novelist,' he wrote, 'is always safer for laying his scene in his own country, and the best that can be said of his errors of tone and proportion, when he deals with foreign manners, is that the home reader is rarely wise enough to measure them.' But Howells, he went on to remark, was 'almost at home' in Venice, and had achieved some very fine effects with his story of the love of an Italian priest for an American girl.

Consideration of the novel led James on to a more general discussion of the achievements and shortcomings of American writing of this time, and, veiled though it had to be in a review of his friend and editor's work, there is little doubt that James believed Howells was as limited in his range as his other American contemporaries. 'He reminds us,' James wrote, 'how much our native-grown imaginative effort is a matter of details, of fine shades, of pale colors, a making of small things do great service. Civilization with us is monotonous, and in the way of contrasts, of salient points, of chiaroscuro, we have to take what we can get. We have to look for these things in fields where a less devoted glance would see little more than an arid blank, and, at the last, we manage to find them. All this refines and sharpens our perceptions, makes us in a literary way, on our own scale, very delicate, and stimulates greatly our sense of proportion and form. Mr.

Lowell and Mr. Longfellow among the poets, and Mr. Howells, Bret Harte, and Mr. Aldrich among the story-tellers ... have all pre-eminently the instinct of style and shape. It is true, in general, that the conditions here indicated give American writing a limited authority, but they often give it a great charm – how great a charm, may be measured in the volume before us.'[7]

James clearly saw a great deal of merit in these methods, particularly in distinction to the English novel, which, in the same review, he characterized as a 'ponderous, shapeless, diffuse piece of machinery.' But, equally clearly, he was not himself satisfied with the 'fireside' virtues of delicacy, proportion, and form, necessary as they were. He wanted to bring to the American novel a greater force and rigour, the kind of effect, in fact, that Balzac achieved with his studies of provincial life.

He alluded to this intention in the preface that he wrote for the New York Edition of *Roderick Hudson* many years later. He had set the opening part of the novel in Northampton, Massachusetts, and its environs, seeking to show thereby not only the kind of background from which a native genius like his sculptor could conceivably spring but also 'some more or less vivid antithesis to a state of civilisation providing for "art." ' In using this provincial town, James admitted in his preface that he believed he was following in the path of Balzac, in whose 'great shadow' he was nestling at the time. He remembered yearning over 'the preliminary representation of my small square patch of the American scene,' and yet he saw in retrospect that he was not aware that Balzac's high practice was delusive for his case. 'Balzac talked of Nemours and Provins: therefore why shouldn't one, with fond fatuity, talk of almost the only small American *ville de province* of which one had happened to lay up, long before, a pleased vision? The reason was plain: one was not in the least, in one's prudence, emulating his systematic closeness.' The question was not confused, James thought, by the fact that Balzac would have little enough to tackle in Northampton. 'He tackled no group of appearances,' James observed, 'no presented face of the social organism ..., *but* to make something of it.' Under his contagion, James had named his town. It would have been better, he reflected, if he had invented a fanciful place – presumably he was thinking of his unidentifiable

'L——' and 'P——' of his earlier American short stories. Having named Northampton, however, he had failed to represent it, so the early chapters of the novel, he thought, had quite failed of intensity. 'It was a peaceful, rural New England community *quelconque* – it was not, it was under no necessity of being, Northampton Mass.'[8]

It is clear that James wanted to render his fictional picture with a greater intensity and colour than he found in the work of Howells and his contemporaries, but he had neither enough experience nor sufficient schemata to go on. The rich chiaroscuro and detail of Balzacian *ville de province* had no place in an American setting, and yet James did not know how else to see and represent his native scene. Consequently, the Northampton settings are thin and unconvincing. They consist of the interiors of a couple of houses – Roderick's mother's and Cecilia's – rather quickly sketched in, a picnic in the woods, and the occasional glimpse of an elm-arched street. The only memorable scene is a piece of landscape painting of the place where Roderick Hudson and Rowland Mallet converse about the problem of the American artist. It is on an elevation overlooking 'the great shining curve' of the Connecticut River. Perhaps it is more than coincidence that one of Thomas Cole's most popular paintings, *The Oxbow, Connecticut River near Northampton,* shows a very similar scene.

Although the European settings of the book lack the precision and relevance that James achieved in his later work, they are certainly much more effective than those of Northampton. But in the second half of the novel there are other faults that Balzac would have avoided, according to James. The whole time-scheme of Roderick's ruin is wrong. As he noted in the preface, James realized that he had not known enough, as a beginning writer, to profit by the French novelist's example. He had dodged all the difficulties that he could, but he had still left more than enough unsolved. The failure brought him up against what he thought to be the most interesting problem that an artist had to consider: 'To give the image and the sense of certain things,' he wrote, 'while still keeping them subordinate to his plan, keeping them in relation to matters more immediate and apparent, to give all the sense, in a word, without all the substance or all the surface, and so to summarise and foreshorten, so to make values both rich and sharp, that the mere procession of items and profiles is not only, for the occasion, superseded, but is, for essential quality, almost "compromised" – such a case of delicacy proposes itself at every turn to the painter of life who wishes both to treat his chosen subject and to confine his necessary picture.'[9]

The extended painterly metaphor in this quotation is another reminder of how James always tended to think of composition in terms of pictorial form and also indicates his awareness of his lack of skills and schemata for his earlier American scenes. The old leisurely English novel would not serve for his model, nor were the pale shades and delicacies of his contemporary American writers good enough, but he could not yet achieve the Balzacian solution of rendering all the sense without all the substance and all the rich and sharp values without a mere procession of items.

The preface to *Roderick Hudson* is notable not only for what it contains, but also for what it leaves out. Although there can be little doubt that one of the main sources for the novel was *The Marble Faun* of Hawthorne, James does not mention his predecessor's name. Like Hawthorne, James set the novel largely in Rome; like him he used a quartet of figures to organize the structure of the novel, three of them similar in occupation or function. The sculptor, Kenyon, of *The Marble Faun*, is transformed into Roderick. The *femme fatale*, Miriam, becomes Christina Light. The New England maiden, Hilda, the dove, becomes Mary Garland. The typically Hawthornesque fantasy figure, the Faun, however, is transformed into the solidly realistic American, Rowland Mallet. James's sculptor is of course a far less phlegmatic figure than Kenyon. Viola Dunbar has suggested that a Dumas novel *L'Affaire Clemenceau* supplied some hints to James for that romantic personality, as well as for the Christina Light affair.[10] Christina is certainly a far more definite figure than the ambiguous Miriam, who never quite emerges from the mysterious unknown of her past into the present of Hawthorne's novel.

But it is with the figure of Rowland Mallet that James most departed from the example of *The Marble Faun*. Hawthorne's last novel had been written discursively, indeed at times garrulously, from the omniscient point of view. In *Roderick Hudson*, James drew on his own experience with Roger Lawrence in *Watch and Ward* and created in Rowland Mallet another meticulous bachelor of independent means who uses his money to give a protégé a European 'education.' Where Roger had done so in order to produce a suitable wife, Rowland does it in order to produce an artist. Both intend to get the best for their money; the one 'a perfect wife,' the other 'one of our great artists.' In *Watch and Ward*, however, Roger had only intermittently been the centre of the narrative. In *Roderick Hudson*, Mallet became almost exclusively the informing consciousness of the novel. In the preface written thirty years later, James claimed that this device had 'saved' the novel from its other, many faults. It had given it 'a principle of composition'; 'the drama,' he claimed, 'is the very drama of that consciousness ...'

James could not remember whether he had hit upon this device by 'instinct or calculation.' The question has been lengthily discussed by the critics and most opinion inclines towards crediting the influence of Turgenev. There can be no question of the deep impression made by the Russian on James, who had read his work as a very young man. He first wrote about him in 1874, in an essay that was ostensibly a review of a German translation of *The Torrents of Spring* and *A King Lear of the Steppe*. The essay reveals that James identified himself quite strongly with Turgenev, with what he called his 'sense of being out of harmony with his native land,' and 'his union of an aristocratic temperament with a democratic intellect.' If there were an American novelist 'of a large pattern,' James concluded, Turgenev's state of mind 'would probably be, in a degree, his own.'[11]

Paradoxically, Turgenev's conception of Russian girlhood appears to have helped James form his idea of the American girl. Turgenev's women had, James claimed, 'the faintly acrid perfume of the New England temperament – a hint of Puritan angularity. It is the women and young girls in our author's tales who mainly represent strength of will – the power to resist, to wait, to attain.'[12] Both Daniel Lerner and Gilbert Phelps have pointed out that the character of Mary Garland, as well as many later Jamesian heroines, fits remarkably well into this description. Both critics have also noted the resemblances between the sculptor, Shubin, in Turgenev's *On the Eve* and Roderick Hudson. They go on from this point, however, to make large claims for Turgenev's influence on James's technique at this time.[13] Oscar Cargill goes even further, writing: '[James] doubtless derived his idea of incorporating an observer within his cast from Turgenev's treatment of Lezhniov in *Rudin.*' He qualifies this claim by adding, 'but the creation of the "fine central intelligence" to unify the novel, to report intimately on the action, and to reveal unconsciously and completely itself, was his own.'[14] Lezhniov is used only intermittently as the observer in *Rudin*, and James himself had commented in his essay on Turgenev's 'passion for shifting his point of view.'[15]

In *Roderick Hudson*, the point of view is remarkably constant. The closest analogy to this is to be found not in Turgenev's fiction but, once again, in that of Hawthorne. In *The Blithedale Romance*, there is another quartet of figures. The narrative centre is one of them, Miles Coverdale, whom James described in his later study of Hawthorne as 'a portrait of a man ... whose passions are slender, whose imagination is active, and whose happiness lies, not in doing, but in perceiving – half a poet, half a critic, and all a spectator.'[16] This description fits Rowland remarkably well. Hawthorne's treatment of Coverdale also corresponds closely to what James thought to be his own task with Mallet: 'Discernible from the first the joy of such a "job" as this making of his relation to everything involved a sufficiently limited, a sufficiently pathetic, tragic, comic, ironic, personal state to be thoroughly natural, and yet at the same time a sufficiently clear medium to represent a whole.'[17] Both characters fall in love with the New England maiden who loves the other male member of the quartet; both are left alone in the end with the sense of having failed.

The most significant similarity between the two characters is in the moral ambiguity with which they are treated. James was temperamentally akin to Hawthorne in his interest in psychological investigation into motive and behaviour. Both were concerned about the fine line to be drawn between curiosity on the one hand, and 'the unpardonable sin' of the violation of another's personality on the other. In *Roderick Hudson*, certainly, this violation is not on the scale of Chillingworth's treatment of Dimmesdale in *The Scarlet Letter*; it is more like Holgrave's tentative experiments with Phoebe in *The House of the Seven Gables* or Coverdale's prying into the other characters' lives in *The Blithedale Romance*. Cecilia is angry when she finds out that Mallet has not consulted her before asking Roderick to go with him to Rome. If she had been consulted, she tells Rowland, her reply would have been: 'Let well alone,' and: 'For an habitually unofficious person, you were rather thrusting your oar in.'[18] Mallet is to a degree responsible for Roderick's ultimate tragedy, just as Coverdale is guilty, to a degree, of the suicide of Zenobia. But the beauty of the situation in both novels is that although both point-of-view figures are spectators to the action, they are also too deeply involved in it to be sufficiently aware of their own moral culpability.* Despite all the European influences that were, then, working so fruitfully on James's imagination in the writing of *Roderick Hudson*, Hawthorne's schemata were the most powerful determinants of the novel's location, subject, and technique.

When all is said, however, of influences and schemata, it must be added that James began in *Roderick Hudson* to apply on a large scale the powers of observation that he had been carefully training in recent years. He had in an earlier review of Hawthorne's *Passages from the French and Italian Notebooks* discussed his predecessor's provincial response to Europe: 'Exposed late in life to European influences,' he wrote, 'Mr. Hawthorne was but superficially affected by them – far less so than would be the case with a mind of the same temper growing up among us today. We seem to see him strolling through churches and galleries as the last pure American – attesting by his shy responses to dark canvas and cold marble his loyalty to a simpler and less encumbered civilization.'[19] As he did with Turgenev, James identified himself with Hawthorne and at the same time implied that, as a member of a more cosmopolitan generation, he was taking Europe in a far more appreciative and yet critical way. In writing *Roderick Hudson* he began, in a real sense, where Hawthorne left off in his last completed novel, *The Marble Faun*.

One striking example of the difference between Hawthorne's and James's response to Europe was in their estimation of the American expatriate sculptor, William Wetmore Story. Hawthorne had become friendly with Story when staying in Rome in 1858 and 1859. Although he did not base his portrait of Kenyon on Story, he did make use of

*Coverdale's revelation of his love for Priscilla at the very end of *Blithedale* is surely his confession to the reader of his guilt in encouraging the fatal fascination of Zenobia for Hollingsworth in order to clear the way for himself. Similarly, Mallet's love for Mary Garland complicates his attitude towards Roderick's fascination by Christina Light.

one of Story's pieces, *Cleopatra*, in his novel, for which he makes a humorous apology in the preface to *The Marble Faun*. His estimation of his countryman's talent was just this side of idolatry, as his fulsome description of *Cleopatra* in the novel shows. In the preface, he called Story 'an artist whom his country and the world will not long fail to appreciate.'[20] James met Story in Rome in 1873, and his appraising eye soon took the measure of the sculptor's abilities. 'I have rarely seen such a case of *prosperous* pretention as Story,' he wrote from Rome to Charles Eliot Norton. 'His cleverness is great, the world's good nature to him is greater.'[21] In the biography of the sculptor that James was to write many years later he was to elaborate on this remark and to find in the lesson of Story's failure the symbol of the yearning, amateur ambition of the American artist of the earlier generation when confronted by the European scene.

In writing *Roderick Hudson* and making the record of his sculptor's failure he was to draw on his recent experience of Story's work and, as Robert Gale has shown, on that of another American sculptor, Thomas Crawford, who had gone to Rome and died young after producing a great deal of work.[22] He was also recording his own sense, often expressed in his letters, of how difficult it was for an American to work consistently in the golden air of Rome. He was to write later of Story that it would have been better if he had stayed at home in Boston and worked his imagination and his material in that cold northern air. Similarly, several times in *Roderick Hudson*, it is pointed out that Hudson would be better off in Northampton. It is not, of course, that Rome is *per se* to blame for Roderick's decline and fall; it is simply that the place encourages some latent tendencies in him, overstimulates his provincial imagination, and makes him prey to a sophisticated flirt like Christina Light.

Roderick Hudson was begun in Florence and so it is almost certain that James wrote there Rowland's lament to Roderick about his attitude to America: ' " It's a wretched business," he said, "this practical quarrel of ours with our own country, this everlasting impatience to get out of it. Is one's only safety then in flight? This is an American day, an American landscape, an American atmosphere. It certainly has its merits, and some day when I am shivering with ague in classic Italy, I shall accuse myself of having slighted them." '

Roderick's answer to this complaint is not of much help to Rowland's problem. 'We had only to be true to ourselves, to pitch in and not be afraid, to fling Imitation overboard and fix our eyes upon our National Originality. "I declare," he cried, "there's a career for a man, and I've twenty minds to decide, on the spot, to embrace it – to be the consummate, typical, original, national American artist. It's inspiring." '[23] As Edwin T. Bowden has pointed out, this 'sounds like a parody of the genuine ideal of an Emerson,' and the parody is complete when at the first chance he gets Roderick immediately forgets his 'National Originality' and decides to go to Italy.[24]

By the time he finished the novel, James had probably already decided what his own solution to the problem of his residence was to be. It seemed that all his attempts at portraying the American landscape and character had in one way or another failed. Rowland's bafflement was in one sense James's own and the bombastic answer of Roderick had in another sense shown his inability to solve his problems. James in his younger years *had* wanted to be an 'original, national American artist,' if not a 'consummate, typical' one. He had not, however, been able to reconcile the schemata he had derived from English and European writers to his own perception of his native land. Howells and his *Atlantic* contemporaries were not rigorous and forceful enough to provide him with examples, and even Hawthorne seemed inadequate as a *maître*. James fought shy of his predecessor's fancifulness and his allegorical symbolism, still being convinced that realism was his right path.

As Richard Chase has shown, however, the romance form has traditionally been the most fruitful genre for American writers of fiction. 'They have found,' he wrote in the introduction to *The American Novel and Its Tradition*, 'that in the very freedom of romance from the conditions of actuality there are certain potential virtues of the mind, which may be suggested by such words as rapidity, irony, abstraction, profundity. These qualities have made romance a suitable, even, as it seems, an inevitable, vehicle for the intellectual and moral ideas of the American novelists.'* Had James been more receptive at this time to the tradition which Hawthorne best represented,

---

The American Novel and Its Tradition (New York, 1957). In chapter six, Chase treats *The Portrait of a Lady* as a 'romance,' but he qualifies his use of the term and ends by saying that 'James is not a romancer like Hawthorne or Melville; he is a novelist to his fingertips' (135).

he would have had a much easier time in his early years as a writer, for he was temperamentally as well as culturally attracted to what he himself called 'the rich passion for extremes' characteristic of romance forms. In the fiction of his later years, particularly of the major phase, he was able to find his *métier* and combine romance elements with realistic forms. But in 1875, convinced of the superiority of European realism, he was trying to apply these schemata to American life. His lack of success at least partly explains the constant note of perplexity that sounds in his letters of the 1870s.

Roderick Hudson in part showed him the way out of the labyrinth. He could take his Americans abroad and use what he knew of their yearning desires for experience against the backdrop of a 'furnished scene,' as he later called it in his autobiography. With patience and industry, he set out to master this scene and to convert it to the material for his fiction. The most fulfilled figure in *Roderick Hudson* is neither Rowland nor Roderick, but the little artist-man, Sam Singleton, whose 'turned back' is seen throughout the novel as he works away at his sketches and canvases. Perhaps the most remarkable scene in the novel is towards the end when a gigantic figure descends from a high eminence in the Swiss Alps towards the watching Roderick and Rowland. But it is only little Sam whose form had been magnified by some trick of the setting sun. When he reaches them he is still 'the same almost irritating image of happy diligence,' who has been working hard, as usual, sketching.

In the next few years, James, like Singleton, was to bend his back to the task, to take notes and sketches, to perfect his style. It was a tremendous relief to him to have settled where he was to live and work. The first letter that he wrote home after he landed in England in the autumn of 1875, began: 'I take possession of the old world – I inhale it – I appropriate it!'[25]

The choice did not, of course, release him from the tug of nostalgia which he was to feel for America, on and off, throughout most of his life in Europe. This was to be a continuing source of inspiration for his art. His best American fiction was, in fact, written while he was living out of the country. He published two stories with American settings in *Scribner's Monthly* in the latter half of 1876. The first, *Crawford's Consistency*, is insignificant; the second, however, *The*

Ghostly Rental, is his first ghost story and an unusual and imaginative tale.

It opens with some nostalgic glimpses of Cambridge by the narrator, a former student of divinity at Harvard, who afterwards renounces a career in the church with ardour. He gives a pleasant, quite detailed picture of the old Cambridge which has since, he notes, 'forfeited much of its mingled pastoral and scholastic quietude' to the 'multitudinous eruption of domiciliary pasteboard which now graces the landscape, in the direction of the low, blue Waltham Hills' (CT, IV, 49–50). The student likes to walk in the outlying countryside. On one occasion, on his way back from Medford, he sees by an apple orchard 'whose tangled boughs made a stretch of coarse black lace-work, hung across the coldly rosy west,' an abandoned, colonial house, its once painted sides laid bare to the grain. He finds out that this house is thought, locally, to be haunted. Later he discovers from an old gossip in Cambridge that the owner is an old sea-captain, called Diamond, who is now living by the River Charles. Twenty years before, Diamond had turned his daughter out of the house after she had taken as a lover a bewhiskered young man from Boston. Report has it that she had since died, had returned to haunt him, and finally driven him out of the house. The captain is destitute, but the ghost allows him a rent for the house, provided he returns in person every quarter to collect it from her.

The student seeks out Captain Diamond and gets a partial confirmation of the old woman's story and so, at the end of the next quarter, make his way to the house. He sees the captain enter it, light some candles within, and, a little later, emerge. The student confronts him and asks his permission to enter the house. The captain reluctantly gives his consent; the student goes in and prowls around the house looking for the ghost. Coming to the foot of the stairs, he scans the darkness above. 'Suddenly, with an inexpressible sensation, I became aware that this gloom was animated; it seemed to move and gather itself together. Slowly – I say slowly, for to my tense expectancy the instants appeared ages – it took the shape of a large, definite figure, and this figure advanced and stood at the top of the stairs' (CT, IV, 75). In fear, the student falls back before the apparition, but he manages to make an orderly retreat to the outside world.

At the end of the next quarter, the captain sends for the student. He tells him that his time is up but that he is too ill and weak to go for the ghostly rent. He asks the student to go for the money, which he needs for doctor's bills and for what he feels to be his own imminent funeral. The student reluctantly consents. He confronts the ghost again, realizes that it is human, and unveils it. She rushes away from him, only to be confronted in the hall with the ghost of her own father. In her agitation she returns to the student and reveals that she has all these years played the part of a ghost in order to revenge herself upon the old man. It appears now that, in counter-revenge, her father has returned to haunt *her*. She begs the student to go at once to find out how her father is and to leave a report on his condition by the well near the house. Back in Cambridge he discovers that while he had been at the old house, the captain had died.

That night, the student sees a red glow in the sky in the direction of the haunted house, and conjectures that the 'ghost' had dropped her candle on seeing the apparition of her father. Returning next morning to leave the note, he finds his supposition to be correct. The story concludes: 'The haunted house was a mass of charred beams and smoldering ashes; the well-cover had been pulled off, in quest of water, by the few neighbours who had had the audacity to contest what they must have regarded as a demon-kindled blaze, the loose stones were completely displaced, and the earth had been trampled into puddles.'

Houses are recurrent images in James's fiction. He used them as symbols of life-styles and reflectors of character. So dominant is the house imagery, in fact, that it seems to reflect patterns and associations in James's own experience. The old colonial house might be symbolic of that dimly-perceived American experience that had haunted James's artistic conscience for years. The Harvard Divinity School student who gives up his career in the church with such alacrity seems closely related to James and his own rapidly terminated experience as a law student. Like the student, James entered the American house to confront its mystery, failed to fathom its nature and retreated. The return visit gave him the courage to face the ghost, which he exposed as merely human. On the other hand, the house does not yield up all its secrets, because the father's ghost is still there, even though the place is burned to the ground. It was as if the ghost stayed in possession during all the years of James's expatriation, troubling his memory. Thirty years later, he was to write another ghost story, *The Jolly Corner*, which has affinities with *The Ghostly Rental*. Once again, he sent a fictional representative to exorcise the restless spirit of the house, the *alter ego* who had stayed on all those years while he was absent in Europe.

Whatever interpretation might be placed on *The Ghostly Rental*, it reveals that James by no means abandoned his native land imaginatively when he left it physically to live in Europe. In spite of the fantastic nature of *The Ghostly Rental*, setting and atmosphere are more effectively conveyed in it than in any of his previous American fiction. The details of clothing, houses, landscape, and weather are sharp and clear and therefore give an air of credibility to the fable. Captain Diamond is a Dickensian type of character, but he is also constructed out of a series of American details. His head, for example, reminds the narrator 'of portraits of Andrew Jackson.' At the same time his strangeness puts him in mind of 'a figure out of one of Hoffmann's tales' (CT, IV, 55–6).

The Gothic convention, here explicitly mentioned by James, gave him a schema for treating an American subject. It enabled him, as it had enabled Hawthorne (whose influence is once again prominent), to use the slender resources of American history for imaginative purposes. Since the tale took place in the very recent past, James did not have to invent costume figures and detail from a history only vaguely known, but he was able to use his knowledge of American colonial architecture and design to evoke a suitably archaic and ghostly atmosphere. He was also careful to emulate Hawthorne's example and maintain an ambiguity of meaning in the story. The first ghost turns out to be solidly human enough but the second, which is seen only by the daughter, is left to be judged either as a real spiritual emanation or the creature of her overwrought and guilty imagination.

James's development in the early years of his expatriation was very rapid, as a look at his bibliography shows. In addition to *The American, Daisy Miller,* and *The Europeans,* he wrote scores of travel and critical articles and reviews during his first three years in Europe. He was nurturing there the habit of close observation of things he could readily respond to, and he seems to have been able to apply that gift retrospectively to his American experience. As his perception grew more sophisticated, he began to realize more and more what he had missed at home. The old woman who reveals part of the story of the haunted house to the student points out, 'Observe closely enough, ... and it doesn't matter where you are ... All you want is something to start with; one thing leads to another, and all things are mixed up. Shut me up in a dark closet and I will observe after a while, that some places in it are darker than others. After that (give me time), and I will tell you what the President of the United States is going to have for dinner' (CT, IV, 63).

James could hardly have made a more exact image of the growth of his own imaginative and observational powers. Once he had found things to start with, both in terms of techniques and schemata, he could mix them with his remarkable powers of observation to create his fictional picture. Although parts of the American closet were to remain forever dark to his gaze, he was able in time to observe and record aspects of its experience more clearly than any previous writer.

⁂ 7 ⁂

Comic Pastoral
The Europeans

When Henry James wrote *The Europeans* in 1878, he avoided most of the mistakes in characterization and setting that he had made in *Roderick Hudson*. His main New England character, Gertrude Wentworth, is far more solidly presented than Mary Garland. The angularity and the 'faintly acrid perfume' that he had noted in Turgenev's heroines comes out vividly in Gertrude, even though, in the end, she seems to be ready to turn into a good European. The main scene of *The Europeans* is not named. The Wentworths' house is located a vague seven-and-a-half miles from Boston. James remained true to his subtitle, 'A Sketch,' throughout, making no attempt to paint a landscape in this tale. The first part of *Roderick Hudson* seems to have taught him that he could not yet trust himself to a full-scale American canvas.

Critical study of *The Europeans* has shown that James probably drew his inspiration for the story from many sources. Oscar Cargill notes that at this time James was reading enthusiastically in the nouvelles and well-made plays of French writers like Feuillet, Cherbuliez, Dumas *fils*, and Augier.[1] He was also still in the first flush of his enthusiasm for Turgenev, whose favourite form was the short novel. Edward Sackville-West has pointed out some of the similarities between James's story and Turgenev's play, *A Month in the Country*.[2] This cannot be ruled out as a source, even though a recent study has demonstrated the unlikelihood of James having seen it by 1878.* *The Europeans* is three months in the country (one of the few stories that James wrote with a rural background); it is dramatic in form and does exploit, as Turgenev does, the discrepancy between urbanity and rusticity. F. R. Leavis has commented on 'the extraordinary dramatic quality' of the book,[3] and he, H. S. Canby, and Richard Poirier have suggested the influence of Jane Austen on the nouvelle's dialogue, its commentary on manners and morals, and its wit.

Another possible source, as yet unmentioned by critics, is the Arcadian schema of Hawthorne's *The Blithedale Romance*; Matthiessen has suggested the influence of *The House of the Seven Gables*. The resemblances between James's nouvelle and *Blithedale* are striking enough. Hawthorne's novel begins with Coverdale and his companions setting off from Boston in a snow-storm towards the middle of the month of April bound for the farm. James's story begins in Boston in a snow-storm on the twelfth of May. Coverdale talks of setting out to begin 'the life of Paradise anew.'[4] Felix, when he gets to the Wentworths' home outside Boston says: 'This is a Paradise' (ANS, 83). Both novels frequently refer to man's pre-lapsarian state. Felix compares the Wentworths to people who lived 'in a mythological era, when they spread their tables upon the grass, replenished them from cornucopias, and had no particular need of kitchen stoves' (ANS, 73). Coverdale talks of an ideal Blithedale without kitchen and house work. 'It is odd enough,' he says, 'that the kind of labor which falls to the lot of women is just that which chiefly distinguishes artificial life – the kind of life of degenerate mortals – from the life of Paradise. Eve had no dinner-pot, and no clothes to mend, and no washing-day.'[5]

Oscar Cargill has maintained that *The Europeans* is surburban rather than rural, but the convention in which James wrote the nouvelle is not. He had used that convention earlier in *Guest's Confession* (1868), in which I suggest that he was employing the pastoral mode comically to represent the character of the ageless Mrs. Beck. He had described her as 'a strayed shepherdess from some rococo

*In an unpublished M.A. thesis, 'Turgenev and James: a Comparison' (University of Toronto, 1964), Miss Catherine Batten has shown that *A Month in the Country* was not translated into a language that James could understand until 1885. As she notes, however, this does not rule out the possibility that James had access to a manuscript translation of the play.

Arcadia ... with a keen eye to the state of the wool and the mutton market.' Now that James was settled in England and was remote from the uncertainties that the New England landscape and character seemed always to have produced in his mind, he could employ this comic technique on a larger scale and with a more confident hand. By consistent use of the Arcadian convention he could reduce the otherness of the region to manageable imaginative dimensions.

His use of the pastoral led to a quite different effect from the one achieved by Hawthorne in *Blithedale*. Hawthorne is continually employing Arcadian and Edenic imagery for ironic and pathetic purposes, and the irony increases as the colony is increasingly rent by the passions of its fallen inhabitants. In the end, in a weirdly effective scene, all the characters in the novel, who had been engaged in Arcadian and necromantic revelry, pursue the narrator, Coverdale, through the woods, 'so that,' he thinks, 'I was like a mad poet hunted by chimeras.'[6] James, although he uses Felix as Hawthorne uses Coverdale to create an imaginary new Arcadia out of the cold and unpromising materials of New England, develops the analogy not for pathetic but for purely comic purposes.

Extending and enriching the mythical schema of *The Europeans* is legendary material from the *Arabian Nights*. Just as Nora had appeared as the Princess Badoura to Roger in *Watch and Ward*, so Felix appears like a Prince to Gertrude when she is reading the story of Prince Camaralzaman and Princess Badoura. That story tells how the two lovers were brought together for one night of enchantment and then separated, and of the subsequent search of the Prince for the Princess which culminates in their reunion. James makes a precise parallel with this plot in his treatment of Felix's first visit to the Wentworths and his later return with his sister to stay with them. The reunion of Camaralzaman and Badoura symbolically unites China and Persia. In the persons of Felix and Gertrude, James unites Europe with America. He makes use of a further analogy with the *Arabian Nights* story by introducing the sleeping beauty theme once again, as he had in *Watch and Ward*. On his return, Prince Camaralzaman rouses the Princess from her sick-bed by an embrace. In *The Europeans*, Charlotte asks Felix what he has done to change her sister. 'I think she was asleep,' Felix replies. 'I have waked her up!'

(ANS, 148). James writes the sleeping beauty motif with the pastoral imagery of New England in Felix's exclamation: '[Gertrude]'s a folded flower. Let me pluck her from the parent tree and you will see her expand.'

By using in parallel the schemata of the myth of Arcadia and the exotic legend of the *Arabian Nights*, James was able to enrich his American material immeasurably. Each tradition supplied him with a treasure chest of imagery which he uses consistently and wittily throughout the story. One of the central metaphors, for example, is that of the various metallic ages traditionally associated with pastoral. Ending his description of the Wentworth house, James writes: 'And the front door of the big, unguarded home stood open, with the trustfulness of the golden age; or what is more to the purpose, with that of New England's silvery prime' (ANS, 51). The wooden house in its faded grey paint is designed in the Greek Revival style, with white wooden pilasters supporting a classic pediment. In exploiting this architectural style, James anticipates Eugene O'Neill's use of the same setting in *Mourning Becomes Electra* to graft a classical onto a New England tradition. O'Neill was seeking to make an analogue between the tragedy of the house of Atreus and the tragedy of the house of Mannon, whereas James is indicating the fading glory of the classical period of Puritan New England. Enough of the original virtue remains in James's descendants from the Puritans to make this the age of silver.

The nouvelle is set in the period before the Civil War. James's rather indefinite notation at the beginning of the story that it is 'upwards of thirty years since,' would put it some time in the 1840s. That 'earlier and simpler generation' of pre-Civil War Americans, as he put it in his study of Hawthorne, symbolized for him a lost age of romantic virtue. In the classical myth, the silver age had given way to an age of brass. Hesiod writes:

> The Sire of heaven and earth created then
> A race, the third of many-languaged men.
> Unlike the silver they: of brazen mould:
> With ashen war-spears terrible and bold:
> Their thoughts were bent on violence alone,
> The deeds of battle and the dying groan.[7]

Although James himself does not pursue the myth beyond the time scheme of *The Europeans,* he surely intends an analogy between the age of brass and the Civil War. The War and its iron-age aftermath had darkened the whole American picture for James, along with many of his generation. In *The Europeans,* he was seeking, nostalgically, to recapture its light, clear tones.

The transformation that takes place in the opening scene of the nouvelle is itself a kind of curtain-raiser to this comic pastoral version of the international theme. The Europeans see from the windows of their hotel in Boston a narrow graveyard filled with mouldy tombstones covered with 'dull, moist snow' (ANS, 37); beyond its iron railings, people, mostly ladies laden with shopping, wait in the slushy streets for horse-cars, into which they project themselves as if scrambling into lifeboats. No wonder that the Baroness Eugenia, confronted with such images of cold, desperation, and death, thinks the outlook the ugliest she has ever seen and wishes to return to Europe at once. Her brother, Felix, takes the opposite point of view. What is dreadful to her is comic to him, and he looks forward eagerly to their adventures in this strange country. His optimism is justified. It is the month of May; the sky clears, the sun comes out, and the pair go for a walk. The Baroness's distinguished, foreign air excites the admiration of the passers-by. Basking in their stares, she begins to feel that the fortune she has come for will not be far to seek: 'There was a promise of it in the gorgeous purity of the western sky; there was an intimation in the mild, unimpertinent gaze of the passers of a certain natural facility in things' (ANS, 45).

The symbolic overtones of the sky at sunset, even the somewhat sheeplike expression on the people's faces, are harbingers of the imagery of the rest of the story. In the following pages, James skilfully sketches in the Wentworth house, which stands surrounded by orchards, fields, and ponds. The way in which he begins at once to work these pastoral images into the emerging themes of the story demonstrates a rapidly increasing mastery of technique. The Baroness's appetite for gold-digging has already been whetted by the sight of the New England sunshine that gilds nature 'as with gold that was fresh from the mine' (ANS, 44). She is further excited by a report from Felix, sent to prospect, that her American cousins have about them 'the *ton* of the golden age' as well as more concrete evidence of wealth (ANS, 57). Her arrival at the Wentworths' does nothing to dispel her confidence. She is received like visiting royalty. The rich abundance of nature, 'like drinking new milk' (ANS, 71), as she calls it, the flowers and the fruit supply her with all the auguries of success.

Even so, she is dissatisfied with the simplicity of the Wentworths' style and, as Edwin T. Bowden has remarked, goes about redecorating the little house that her hosts lend her 'in the dark, cluttered, ornate fashion of her Europe of the day.'[8] Indian shawls are hung up in the parlour door and curious fabrics tumbled around on the chairs. The rooms are bedimmed with pink blinds, and 'along the chimney-piece was disposed a remarkable band of velvet, covered with coarse, dirty-looking lace.' Charlotte, the simplest of the three New England maidens in the book, had been on the point of proposing that she 'help her put her superfluous draperies away,' when the Baroness tells her that she had been making herself 'a little comfortable.' Only Gertrude sees that her own life in contrast to this had been a little garish, and she asks herself: 'What is life, indeed, without curtains?' (ANS, 72).

Robert Acton, the rich and travelled cousin of the Wentworths, has a house far more to the taste of the Baroness. A more skilfully drawn version of the rich bachelor, Lawrence, of *Watch and Ward*, he has filled his rooms with treasures from his travels in China. They make a strong appeal to the Baroness, who has, in common with Hawthorne's Zenobia, an 'Oriental or exotic aspect' (ANS, 39). When she is taken by Acton to see his invalid mother, however, she makes a bad blunder. They find her seated with a copy of Emerson's essays. Seeking to please, Eugenia remarks that her son had talked 'immensely' of his mother. Acton is vividly conscious that he has scarcely mentioned her to the Baroness. Although more worldly than the Wentworths, he would certainly subscribe to Charlotte's comment on Eugenia: 'There can surely be no good reason for telling an untruth ... I hope she does not think so' (ANS, 75). Acton's suspicions about her veracity gather force as the story progresses. The incident that determines him not to propose is apparently the one in which he comes across Eugenia 'educating' young Clifford Wentworth 'George Sand fashion,' as Miss Cornelia Kelley has observed.[9] The incident itself is innocent enough, he knows, but he cannot tolerate the fabrications she makes up in order to pass it off.

F. W. Dupee has remarked that Acton is 'something of a pretender to worldly experience, the sum of whose wisdom consists in an enlarged capacity for being suspicious.'[10] He keeps muttering to himself after this: 'She is not honest, she is not honest,' even though he feels more and more attracted to her. Like all the Americans in this nouvelle, he is always thinking. He is 'extremely fond of mathematics,' and tends to see all human relationships in terms of mathematical symbols. To him, the Baroness's 'words and motions ... were as interesting as the factors in an algebraic problem' (ANS, 118). The Baroness who, like her brother, looks at the world almost entirely in terms of emotions, distrusts this method of approaching human relations. 'One's reason is dismally flat,' she says to Felix. 'It's a bed with the mattress removed' (ANS, 157). In this Turgenev-like theme of passion versus reason, reason triumphs, aided by Acton's sexual coldness and perhaps that slightly sinister mother dying by inches upstairs in the expensively ornamented house. In this context, the last sentence of the story is suggestive: 'Robert Acton, after his mother's death, married a particularly nice young girl' (ANS, 161).

Thus, for the Baroness, the golden tone slowly fades and disappears. It is mostly her own fault, for she has interpreted what is largely a moral atmosphere in terms of material values. Towards the end of the story, she feels 'the annoyance of a rather wearied swimmer who, on nearing shore, to land, finds a smooth straight wall of rock when he had counted on a clean firm beach' (ANS, 129). Generalizing that 'the conditions of action on this provincial continent were not favorable to really superior women,' she quickly sets sail for Europe and returns to her meagre morganatic marriage with the Prince of Silberstadt-Schreckenstein's younger brother.

Some critics have been dissatisfied with James's presentation of the Baroness Eugenia. She has 'cynical motives'[11] and 'a corrupt attitude to society'; she shows 'an outrageous lack of breeding'; she is neither clever nor charming.[12] In an editorial aside, James admitted that he had, through reasons of length, 'to express things rather brutally' about her (ANS, 114). As a result, this characterization lacks the depth that her prominence in the story demands. At the same time, I think it wrong to say that his touch 'faltered' with her. He meant to show her as not only charming, when she wanted to be, but also as the vain, self-centred creature that she is – two aspects of character not by any means irreconcilable. Her intention is to make a good marriage (since she can have her present one annulled at any time), and her methods in going about this include a little calculation and deception. These tactics would be acceptable enough in her own European society; she fails to see that they are simply inappropriate for the American. She therefore fails not through any lack of cleverness or breeding, but because of the more typically Jamesian fault of lack of perception and sympathy. She is too much a creature of the old world to be able to adjust to the conditions of the new.

Her brother, Felix, is of a different mould. He also is a fortune-hunter, but one far less confident and calculating than his sister. He can properly appreciate, even if he does not much like, the moral tone of this silver age. Consequently he treads cautiously among the quicksands of American manners, although he often comically misunderstands how his actions will be interpreted. He continually fears, for example, that his courtship of Gertrude Wentworth will be interpreted as an abuse of hospitality, a deliberate attempt to line his pockets. As it turns out, his hosts have no such suspicion. His 'charming nature,' as his sister calls it, is their 'capital' (ANS, 40), and it pays a magnificent dividend in the form of his cousin's hand in marriage.

The characterization of Felix, as of his sister, is not extensive, but James gives them both an extra dimension by means of his functional imagery. Images defining them are mainly drawn from the arts. Felix has been in the course of his life a strolling actor and is now an itinerant portrait painter, although, by his own admission, a poor one. He wears the picturesque costume of the Bohemian artist, sets up a studio, and flourishes brushes. His profession as artist is his chief romantic appeal to Gertrude, although it is viewed with some suspicion by all the other Americans. Mr. Wentworth, in particular, has a Puritan mistrust of graven images, and he recoils in horror when Felix offers to paint his head in the likeness of 'an old cardinal or the prior of an order.' 'The Lord made it,' he says, 'I don't think it is for man to make it over again' (ANS, 80). Felix remains undaunted and paints him anyway. In fact he tenaciously views the whole American *milieu* in painterly terms: 'It was like a large sheet of clean, fine-grained drawing-paper, all ready to be washed over with effective splashes of water-color' (ANS, 73). He looks with pleasure at the clothes of the American girls, who are constantly in 'thin materials and clear colors,' and appear always 'in the right light.' By contrast, the European women he has known seem now to have been 'pictures under glass,' giving off interfering reflections (ANS, 74).

Images of the theatre are continually used to define the situation of both Europeans, more particularly the Baroness. The attitude of the Americans when first confronted by her implies that she is 'a kind of conversational mountebank, attired, intellectually, in gauze and spangles' (ANS, 64). Acton, summoned in the middle of the action to a sick friend in Newport, eagerly looks forward to his return to the Baroness: 'He felt as if he had been called away from the theatre during the progress of a remarkably interesting drama. The curtain was up all this time, and he was losing the fourth act; that fourth act which would have been so essential to a just appreciation of the fifth' (ANS, 119). But, as Mr. Dupee has said, the Baroness's grand manner 'is too big for the picture.'[13] Her 'well-fashioned roundness of contour' (ANS, 38), in James's euphemistic phrase, does not conform to the 'angular conditions of New England life' (ANS, 122). She can never get used to the limitations of this new stage. When she looks round the drawing-room of the little cottage given her for the duration of her stay before calling for her maid to pack up her gimcracks, curtains, and cushions, she, for the first time, sees herself in perspective: '*Bonté divine*, what rubbish! I feel like a strolling actress; these are my "properties!"' The play is over, and although, as Felix courteously says, she has played her part 'with great applause' (ANS, 159), she knows that her true art – that of coquetry – has been wasted.

The defining images of the Americans are drawn, antithetically, from nature. Indeed, James carries his antithesis so far as to say that Gertrude 'had never seen an artist before' (ANS, 79). The place is, as Felix remarks, 'a Paradise.' The garden overflows with the traditional images of fertility: water, flowers, and fruit, and has 'an odor of earth and blossom' (ANS, 43). The Wentworth household itself seems 'pervaded by a sort of dove-colored freshness' (ANS, 71) that is also reflected in the clothes and manners of the girls. In the ultimate marriage of Felix and Gertrude, James unites art and nature as is appropriate to a union of European and American.

Naturally, given the length of *The Europeans*, James could do little more than suggest the complexities of his international theme. The suggestions are nonetheless rich, and make this nouvelle one of the really significant early indices of James's increasing subtlety of vision. A strain of Middle and Far Eastern imagery runs through the text, for example, and, besides lending colour to the story, and support to its *Arabian Nights* overtones, gives a paradoxical piquancy to the American and European conflict. Felix observes the *bariolé* colouring of Boston and says: 'Instead of coming to the West we seem to have gone to the East. The way the sky touches the house-tops is just like Cairo; and the red and blue sign-boards patched over the face of everything remind one of Mahometan decorations' (ANS, 44). Relics of the eastern trade are scattered about the Wentworth house too, although the aesthetic senses of the dwellers seem to have been singularly untouched by them. It takes the Europeans to appreciate these objects for their real worth.

Analogously, it takes Felix to discover the real worth of Gertrude, whose 'beautiful nature' has been suppressed by her environment. In their marriage, James suggests more than the union of art and nature; it is also the union of innocence and experience, action and thought, concreteness and abstraction. It is Gertrude's desire for the concrete that first attracts Felix. Her family, in hoping for her marriage to Mr. Brand, the 'good as gold' Unitarian clergyman, have been building on what they think to be her desire for abstraction, her concern for what they often call 'the great questions of life' (ANS, 110). Felix makes Gertrude realize her true self; she rejects the pervasive New England concern with problems of conscience that the others have been forcing on her and makes them see, finally, that Mr. Brand is much better suited to her more conventional, perpetually worried sister, Charlotte.

Through variations on the themes of his imagery, James carefully avoids making the European and American pattern too schematic. New England may be a paradise but, as Eugenia discovers, its pastures are rocky. She realizes that 'the social soil on this big, vague continent was somehow not adapted for growing those plants whose fragrance she especially inclined to inhale ... a species of vegetation for which she carried a collection of seedlings, as we may say, in her pocket' (ANS, 129). The rock represents Puritanism, that irritable conscience and prickly moral sense that makes the Americans strangers in their own paradise. As Felix remarks, the Wentworths are very well placed for enjoying life and yet 'They take things hard' (ANS, 58), as he observes in one of James's favourite phrases. Puritanism in its most extreme form is represented by Mr. Wentworth who 'looks as if he were undergoing martyrdom, not by fire, but by freezing' (ANS, 58). While he listens to Felix proposing for his daughter, he sits bolt upright in his chair 'with a light in his face that might have been flashed back from an iceberg'(ANS, 150). Perhaps the ultimate defining image for Puritanism in this nouvelle relates back to the view of the Boston graveyard at the beginning of the story. Mr. Wentworth's face looks 'cadaverous' to Felix, who learns, however, that 'in these semi-mortuary manifestations there was no cause for alarm' (ANS, 59). Even in Gertrude, a Puritan strain evidences itself occasionally. After having harshly turned off her importunate suitor, Mr. Brand, she sheds a few tears with 'a kind of glee.' 'There was something a little hard about Gertrude,' James notes; 'and she never wept again' (ANS, 87). R. P. Blackmur goes rather far when he sees in her elements of 'both the fairy godmother and La Belle Dame sans Merci,'[14] but, certainly, Gertrude is a logical development from the archetype Vénus d'Ille and a member of the line of New England women that culminates in the hard ruthlessness of Olive Chancellor in *The Bostonians*.

As F. W. Dupee has observed, Felix, in carrying off Gertrude, 'actually rescues the family from possible disruption by this somewhat threatening daughter.'[15] She is the only one of them to accept Felix's proposition that in order to enjoy life it is not necessary to do something wrong. She chooses a life of art and travel, whereas the others are clearly to be content with an horizon bounded by orchards on one side and Boston on the other. Even the 'wild' son of the family, Clifford, who has been rusticated from Harvard for drinking, is really harmless enough, and looks forward complacently to marriage with his cousin, Lizzie Acton, a double-fronted house on the Common, and driving behind a pair of matched sorrel horses.

The three marriages which conclude *The Europeans* is a most unusual feature in James's work. A friend of James, Elizabeth Boott, must have expressed her surprise on this score in a letter to James, for he replied to her, in a letter dated 30 October 1878; 'The off-hand marrying in the end was *commandi* – likewise the length of the tale. I *do* incline to melancholy endings – but it had been a part of the bargain with Howells that *this* termination should be cheerful and that there should be distinct matrimony. So I hit it off mechanically in the closing paragraphs. I was not at all weary of the tale at the end, but I had agreed to write it in *100 Atlantic* pages, and its abrupt ending came from outward pressure – not from internal failing ... You are quite right to hate Gertrude, whom I personally dislike!'[16] This excerpt from a hitherto unpublished letter reveals how far James, at least in his early days, was willing to make compromises in order to please his editors, as well as showing his attitude towards typical New England womanhood.

The other characters in the nouvelle, Clifford, Lizzie, and Mr. Brand, are not much developed, for *The Europeans* is much fore-shortened. Characterization is deliberately limited, although it is adequate to the purpose. What counts in a story of this length and lightness is the immediate impression made on the reader. James makes this impression by playing on the varieties of comic confrontation of European with American, urbane with rustic, sophisticated with innocent. He makes it so well, in fact, and with such a deceptive air of ease that, until quite recently, this story has been consistently undervalued. Even such a discerning critic as Blackmur has written of *The Europeans*: 'He wrote easily ... almost spontaneously, and according to the easier models at hand in the modes of the time.'[17] There were very few writers about then who could have given James much help in the mode for this story. In particular, in his skillful use of imagery, James had outdistanced his contemporaries. Where he ran into trouble with *The Europeans* was in the handling of the point of view. A charming passage such as the following is marred by James's intrusion into the narrative: 'Felix had spent a good deal of his life in looking into courts, with a perhaps slightly tattered pair of elbows resting upon the ledge of a high-perched window, and the thin smoke of a cigarette rising into an atmosphere in which street-cries died away and the vibration of chimes from ancient belfries became sensible. He had never known anything so infinitely rural as these New England fields; and he took a great fancy to all their pastoral roughnesses. He had never had a greater sense of luxurious security; and at the risk of making him seem a rather sordid adventurer I must declare that he found an irresistible charm in the fact that he might dine every day at his uncle's. The charm was irresistible, however, because his fancy flung a rosy light over this homely privilege. He appreciated highly the fare that was set before him. There was a kind of fresh-looking abundance about it which made him think that people must have lived so in the mythological era, when they spread their tables upon the grass, replenished them from cornucopias, and had no particular need of kitchen stoves' (ANS, 73).

The intrusion of an arch Thackerayan narrative voice here disrupts the ironic tone of the story. It seems that James, at this stage in his development, could not represent the United States in fiction with the same detachment that he could represent its citizens in Europe; he has to patronize Felix, slightly, for liking the 'homely fare' of the Wentworths and 'risk,' in his own view, 'making him seem a sordid adventurer' simply because he likes to dine there every day. It is a real falling off from the controlled use of the narrative point of view of Rowland Mallet in *Roderick Hudson*. James appears to have had in mind not only the European schemata that he was to some extent using in *The Europeans* but also a European audience that might be reading the tale. He continually loads the dice against the American characters far more than the dialectic of art and nature in the story demands. One can feel a certain sympathy for the outrage of the Bostonian critic, Thomas Wentworth Higginson, who damned the story for its anachronistically provincial Boston society figures.[18] James's bias clearly shows in favour of the Europeans in his staged battle between prickly conscience and gay sophistication. In the context, it is plain that he would endorse the Baroness's parting remark to Felix: 'Europe seems to me much larger than America' (ANS, 161).

Underlying Higginson's condemnation, however, and the strictures of many later critics, is not only offended nationalism, but also the criterion of realism in fiction. James wrote *The Europeans* in an experimental vein in which he did not further proceed. In it, he abandoned the realistic mode in which he had been working since his experiments in Hawthornesque romance, in favour of comic pastoral. Had he written a preface for *The Europeans*, as he later did for *Daisy Miller*, he might have made the same plea for it as he did for *Daisy Miller*. He recalled that he had often been criticized for misrepresenting the American girl in his portrait of Daisy. His defence was that she was 'pure poetry, and had never been anything else ...'[19] *The Europeans*, with its combination of the comic mode, pastoral tradition, legendary analogues, and stylized characters, is poetry in James's sense of the word, rather than realistic fiction. The enrichment of his story by these cleverly interwoven strands enabled him for the first time to make use of the American scene in a longer fictional work. In applying these romantic schemata to a realistic situation, he had arrived at a viable artistic way of representing American life. Perhaps only the poor reception of *The Europeans*, reinforced by his brother William's withering condemnation of it, prevented him from exploiting the vein further.

The theme, if not the form, was to become a major creative pre-occupation with James in later years. He is showing in *The Europeans*, through antithetical patterns of imagery as well as behaviour, that codes of morals and manners are relative – as he does in *The Ambassadors*, among other novels. Graham Greene's assertion that James eventually decided to develop from *The American* rather than from *The Europeans* is true, then, only in the sense that he did not employ this particular mode again.[20] In terms of the handling of theme and image, Henry James learned as much from writing this nouvelle as he did from any of his early work.

❖ 8 ❖

American Episodes
and
The Portrait of a Lady

It is characteristic of James's development as a novelist that he should reach a certain peak of achievement with a given theme or technique and then turn back from there to exploit other situations germane to the new method. After *The Europeans*, he turned to more conventional versions of the international theme. One of these, *An International Episode*, is set largely in America and it enabled James to use some of his memories of Newport, which he had not resorted to since his sketch of the place for the *Nation* in 1870. Although the story has a fine sparkle, it is essentially superficial. The Anglo-American differences that James exploits are the obvious ones: the American girl and the English nobleman, New York and London, democratic manners and aristocratic bad manners. Fairly clearly, *An International Episode* was written in response to the demand created for his work by the success of *Daisy Miller* rather than as an opportunity to get to grips with a real artistic or social challenge.

The story is saved from banality by its lively descriptions and conversations. In a rare sally, James took his hero downtown, in the stifling heat of midsummer, to give him a baffling view of business on Wall Street. Lord Lambeth and his fellow-travelling Englishman, Percy Beaumont, are whirled up in an elevator to the seventh floor of 'a fresh, light, ornamental structure, ten stories high' (CT, IV, 249–50), where they meet a businessman, Mr. Westgate, to whom they have an introduction. As he looks out of the window, Lambeth

103

notices the weather-vane of a church steeple on a level with his eyes.
We can recognize from this description that the office building is
opposite Trinity Church, and that James is keenly aware of the
vertical development of the city and what it is doing to old architectural scales – a subject he will return to many years later in *The
American Scene*. The initiation of the Englishmen into business life
is minimal, however, for Mr. Westgate sends them off at once on
the boat to visit his summer house in Newport. There, much more at
his ease, James sets the balance of the American part of the story,
and gives a pleasant picture of resort life, based on close observation
of his favourite American town.

Mark Twain, with his customary trenchancy, called Newport a
'stud farm' for aristocracy, 'that auction mart where the English
nobilities come to trade hereditary titles for American girls and
cash.'[1] *An International Episode* turns the tables on that truism.
After a short stay in the Ocean Hotel, the two Englishmen go as
guests to the Westgate's 'magnified chalet' on the cliffs above the sea.
Their first view of the house shows James's sense of how the resort
style of architecture fitted the informal and accessible nature of
American society. 'The house had a verandah of extraordinary width
all around it, and a great many doors and windows standing open to
the verandah. These various apertures had, in common, such an
accessible, hospitable air, such a breezy flutter, within, of light curtains, such expansive thresholds and reassuring interiors, that our
friends hardly knew which was the regular entrance, and, after
hesitating a moment, presented themselves at one of the windows'
(CT, IV, 261). There they met Mrs. Westgate and her sister, Miss
Bessie Alden from Boston. Beaumont thinks at once that Bessie will
make a set at Lord Lambeth, especially after she asks him about the
young nobleman's position and expectations in England.

But Bessie, another slightly angular daughter of the Puritans,
well-read and thoughtful, is only trying to satisfy her curiosity. Lord
Lambeth, for his part, is nothing loth to pass all his time with her, in
days full of 'infinite lounging and talking and laughing and flirting
and lunching and dining.' They go shopping in 'the ancient town,' a
collection of 'fresh-looking little wooden houses painted white, scattered over a hill-side,' and walk together on the beaches and cliffs.

As Bessie's voluble sister says, 'I really believe that the most charming girl in the world is a Boston superstructure upon a New York *fonds*; or perhaps a New York superstructure upon a Boston *fonds*. At any rate, it's the mixture' (CT, IV, 276).

Much to the dismay of his family, Lord Lambeth proceeds to court Bessie when she goes to London in the second part of the story. But, ironically, she is too much the free-born American girl to take the English social system for granted. She expects Lord Lambeth to live up to his position, to speak in the House of Lords, to exert an influence and encourage the arts. She is upset to find that he never has 'ideas,' never goes to the House, and never meets artists, who seem to belong to another society altogether. In the end, she refuses his proposal of marriage (to the puzzlement of English critics of the story) and returns to the United States. It is the comic germ of the far more subtle treatment of a similar situation in *The Portrait of a Lady*.

James's next book, *Hawthorne* (1879), is, among other things, a defence of his own decision to give up the United States as a field for his fiction. Moreover, it was written at the request of John Morley, whom James had met at Lord Houghton's house. Morley wrote to James: 'As you may have seen, I am editing a series of short books on English Men of Letters, and it has occurred to us that there is no reason why we should not for the purposes of literature consider Americans as English. If so, I think that a short book on Washington Irving, or one on Hawthorne, would be proper and an attractive feature in our scheme.'[2]

James tailored his book to an English audience and possibly to the note of condescension that appears in Morley's letter. He goes to great pains to show how provincial Hawthorne was. Indeed all the American writers who appear in the book are peppered with this adjective, except Thoreau, who is called 'parochial.' His estimate of Hawthorne's achievement was also influenced by his own current notions about the superiority of the realistic novel over the romance. Although Morley considered the book 'certainly ... one of the most attractive of the whole series,' his praise was not echoed by the American reviewers, who treated it even more savagely than they had *The Europeans*.

One review by Elizabeth Stuart Phelps in a religious paper called

The Independent was entitled 'The Man without a Country.' It typifies the provincial moralism by which James's work was so often judged in the United States, and in itself offers a kind of justification for his expatriation. 'Our fastidious cosmopolitan,' she wrote, 'has been slowly smoothing away the still sturdy and respectable, if a little angular, qualities of love and reverence for home.' She was outraged at James's patronizing tone and built up to the ringing denunciation: 'It is not he who can represent our "literature." American literature will be a finer, broader, nobler thing than this.'[3] Howells too objected to the charge of provincialism that James had levelled against Hawthorne. Howells maintained that it was no more provincial for an American to be an American than it was for an Englishman to be English. James countered by saying that it was in the nature of some national types to be provincial; Russians and Portuguese, for example, were as provincial as Americans. He defended his claim that it takes 'an old civilization to set a novelist in motion.' What Howells called 'paraphernalia' represented the essential elements of life to James. He, for one, could not do without them.[4]

As if to prove this point, most of the fiction that he wrote in the next four years was set in Europe. The writer whom he seems to have been most consciously looking to for guidance was Turgenev, rather than Hawthorne. In particular, he was concerned with a theme that is central to Turgenev's work: the determining power of character, particularly of an eccentric kind. This was paramount in the odd and unsuccessful novel *Confidence* (1880) and *The Diary of a Man of Fifty*, of the same year, a story obviously inspired by Turgenev's *Diary of a Superfluous Man*. Only in one book of this period did James return to the United States for his setting. This was *Washington Square* (1881).

The notebook entry for this story reveals, however, that there was nothing particularly national about the theme of this novel. The anecdote on which it was based was told James by the English actress, Fanny Kemble, whose brother, a selfish but very handsome young ensign in a marching regiment, was transformed into Morris Townsend. The father in the anecdote was the Master of King's College, Cambridge, who had a private fortune. His daughter, who had 'a slow, sober, dutiful nature,' was the model for Catherine Sloper.

James added an empty-headed aunt, Mrs. Penniman as duenna, to his cast of characters, and his plot was in hand. As Richard Poirier has pointed out, *Washington Square* is 'a melodramatic fairy-tale, complete with characters who have archetypes in everyone's most rudimentary literary experience and imagination.'[5] Poirier claims that these archetypes, of cruel father, motherless daughter, handsome lover, and fairy godmother, are given a new vitality by being transferred to the New World, but in fact the conflict does not depend much on the national identity of the characters. Their archetypal function was stronger than James's particular concern with his characters' identities as Americans.

In looking for the specifically 'American' theme of the novel, Mr. William Wasserstrom has maintained, in *Heiress of All the Ages,* that James was dramatizing the peculiar American relationships between fathers and daughters. By training them to be excessively filial, Mr. Wasserstrom claims, American fathers raise girls who are ill-prepared for life and love. 'Sloper,' he writes, 'deprives his daughter of love and therefore reduces her charm as a woman.'[6] It is true that Sloper does not love his daughter, but this is *because* she is commonplace, not *vice versa.* He would have liked to have been proud of her, but none of his efforts to make her more attractive appear to have any effect, not even the European tour, the inevitable fairy-tale means that James used to awaken the American girl to wit and beauty.

As for the novel's setting, James did not gain much from locating it in New York. Poirier claims that it serves 'the important function of making us recognize the fantastic development of a great city in which everyone is both literally and metaphorically moving uptown.'[7] Actually this is very lightly emphasized in *Washington Square.* James himself seems strangely uncertain about how to introduce his scene. It is significant that, without any applicable schema, he seems forced to resort to sentimental memories of his own childhood as a way out of his problem. 'I know not whether it is owing to the tenderness of early associations,' he writes, 'but this portion of New York appears to many persons the most delectable.' He goes on to gossip about his aged grandmother's house on the Square and his own faltering, childhood steps there. The passage contributes little to the novel, but does serve to indicate James's own nostalgia for the area, which was later to supply the setting for *The Jolly Corner*. He concludes the childish ramble lamely enough: 'It was here, at any rate, that my heroine spent many years of her life; which is my excuse for this topographical parenthesis.' At least the handsome houses on the Square provided a good setting for the rich doctor's affairs and created in the novel what James called 'a kind of established repose which is not of frequent occurrence in other quarters of the long, shrill city' (ANS, 171).

As he told Howells, he did try hard to make the novel 'a tale truly American,' but he once again ran up against the problem that had plagued him during his earlier American years of apprenticeship. The writing of *Washington Square*, he complained to Howells, referring again to the latter's criticism of *Hawthorne*, 'made me feel acutely the want of the "paraphernalia." ' Lacking formed schemata for the scene of the novel, James was forced to resort to familiar conventions in writing it. Ivan Turgenev seems to have been of little help, but in this novel, if anywhere, it can be claimed that James was a kind of male Jane Austen. The style of *Washington Square* is remarkably Austenian in its use of parallelism and balance and in its pervasive precision, irony, and wit. As in Austen, the cast of characters is limited and the novel's conflicts are the result of deep psychological differences. The action is precipitated, as in Austen's plots, by the intrusion of a stranger on the central group of characters. Since the action is practically confined to drawing-rooms, it can be divorced almost completely from local physical conditions. The title, *Washington Square*, is consequently not particularly appropriate. Those who adapted the novel for the stage recognized this in changing the title to the nicely ironic, *The Heiress*. *Washington Square* is a remarkable achievement, but, like *The Europeans*, it was an experiment in a form that James was not subsequently to follow, a uniqueness recognized in its omission from the New York Edition.

The culmination of James's first period as a novelist came with the publication of *The Portrait of a Lady* in 1881. Extensive discussion of this novel is not germane to the theme of this book, but its central importance in James's development makes a limited treatment of it necessary here. As in *Roderick Hudson* and *The American*, the combination of American characters with European scenes worked together to create a remarkable richness of texture. The novel moves in its fine leisurely way from the first scene on the sunlit lawn of the ancient English house through Italian palazzi and gardens, museums, churches, and theatres to culminate on the same English lawn, now in darkness. These scenes not only had the tone of time that James so much desired, but also were sanctioned as schemata by the innumerable writers and painters who had used these or similar settings before. To give one important example: James uses houses throughout as complex symbols of life styles. It is likely, as R. W. Stallman has claimed, that he was influenced by Hawthorne in this respect. Support for this view comes from the fact that James used the house that Hawthorne occupied in Florence as the model for Gilbert Osmond's house, and took full advantage of its outward character to make it an analogue of his villain's nature. By the symbolic use of settings, objets d'art, and atmospheres, James was able to avoid the merely picturesque effects that he was sometimes guilty of in the earlier international novels, particularly *Roderick Hudson. The Portrait of a Lady* is consequently organic in form to a degree that far surpassed his earlier long fiction.

The most important element in this unity is of course Isabel Archer herself. This new manifestation of Artemis in James's fiction is not so much a hunter of men, however, as of experience. In the sketch of her background provided by James near the beginning of the novel, he stresses her intellectual pursuits. Isabel is found by Mrs. Touchett sitting in the 'office' of the house in provincial Albany, which symbolically has its door to the street permanently bolted and its side-lights filled in with green paper. She is engaged in 'trudging over the sandy plains of a history of German Thought.'[8] Both the isolation from life and the bookish transcendental strain here indicated are important for her character, even though 'she really preferred almost any source of information to the printed page ...'[9] In her capacity for abstraction she is reminiscent of the Wentworth girls in *The Europeans*, and she shares their Puritanism and sexual coldness.

Much of the novel is seen from her point of view. In the first part, we can see where her capacity for abstraction and her radical unwillingness to feel lead her. She winds up with her 'sterile dilettante,' Osmond. Osmond himself is an American and perhaps an example of one who began like Isabel with highly intellectual and abstract attitudes towards experience. His long expatriation seems only to have increased his isolation and to have severed him from meaningful contact with the human and social worlds.

It is, however, not too late for Isabel to learn, which she painfully proceeds to do. Dorothy Van Ghent has shown how James uses the settings and art objects of Europe to emphasize 'modulations of perception' in his heroine.[10] Whereas when she first arrives at Gardencourt she sees the paintings in the gallery as only 'vague squares of rich colour,' by the time she has realized how she has been used by Madame Merle and Osmond, she has learned to see and feel Rome 'as an immensity of human time, as a great human continuum of sadness and loneliness and passion and despair and aspiration and patience.' Returning to Gardencourt at the end of the novel, she identifies a Bonington landscape and sees through it all she has experienced and discovered. The range and complexity of her perceptions are a measure of her maturity.

By this time in his career, James had quite thoroughly developed the theory that the point of view from which the individual perceived reality conditioned both what he saw and how he judged experience. In a significant exchange with Mrs. Touchett early in *The Portrait of a Lady*, Isabel asks: 'Now what is your point of view? ... When you criticize everything here you should have a point of view. Yours doesn't seem to be American – you thought everything over there so disagreeable. When I criticize, I have mine; it's thoroughly American!'

' "My dear young lady," said Mrs. Touchett, "there are as many points of view in the world as people of sense ... My point of view, thank God, is personal!" '[11] She illustrates this remark by her eccentric behaviour throughout the novel. Each character illustrates it in his own way. Goodwood's point of view is that of the practical, forceful American man of business, who never can see any moral objection to doing whatever one has the power to do to secure one's own happiness. Lord Warburton for all his 'radicalism' is stuck fast in the varnish of his caste and class. Even Henrietta Stackpole, that liberated American career-woman and fifth wheel to James's novelistic coach, is thoroughly consistent in her good-natured, ruthless desire to 'see

Europe' and in doing so missing almost every shade of the experience. Perhaps only Ralph has both the commitment to life and the necessary detachment to transcend the limitations that perception usually places on character. He is the only one to see the pathos and, at the end, the promise of Isabel's situation.

Thus Henry James anticipated by some nine years the theory of perception that his brother William was to put forward in his *Principles of Psychology* (1890) : 'Whilst part of what we perceive comes through our senses from the object before us, another part (and it may be the larger part) always comes ... out of our own head.'[12] James dramatizes this theory in many ways in *The Portrait*. For example, the dialogue in chapter nineteen between Madame Merle and Isabel about the relation of things to the self is essential for the definition of each character and for their respective cosmopolitan and American outlooks. 'One's self,' Madame Merle says, ' – for other people – is one's expression of one's self; and one's house, one's clothes, the book one reads, the company one keeps – these things are all expressive.' Isabel replies: 'I think just the other way. I don't know whether I succeed in expressing myself, but I know that nothing else expresses me. Nothing that belongs to me is any measure of me; on the contrary, it's a limit, a barrier, and a perfectly arbitrary one.'[13]

This brief exchange has many ramifications for the novel, and James is wise enough not to add any comment to it. Isabel has to discover, painfully, that her innocent American belief in the integrity of the self and the unimportance of what Howells had called 'the paraphernalia' are to prove woefully inadequate to her perception of the European scene, the deviousness of Osmond, and the machinations of Madame Merle herself. Emersonian self-reliance has to give way to a recognition of limits, and Isabel realizes at the end of the novel that she has to return to the self that she has defined by all her previous actions and acquisitions.

In writing *The Portrait of a Lady*, however, James could not rest content with the dramatic representation of scenes and points of view. He was very much aware of his own role as author as a note to a friend while writing *The Portrait of a Lady* reveals: 'It is from that I myself shall pretend to date,' he wrote, 'on that I myself shall take my stand.'[14] His stand is often far too evident in the narrative as the benevolent, omniscient author familiar to us from Victorian fiction. Particularly in the earlier parts, he is often mediating between the reader and the point of view of his audacious heroine. After the long passage in chapter six in which he gives a sketch of her temperament, he adds: 'She would be an easy victim of scientific criticism, if she were not intended to awaken on the reader's part an impulse more tender and more purely expectant.'[15] In this manner, James attempted to interpose norms of judgment between his reader and his characters, and to control in advance his reader's reaction to the plot. Technically, he was not yet fully committed to the dramatic principle in the long work, even though he does, in *The Portrait*, perform wonders of dramatization. The tradition of the omniscient narrator, so powerful a part of the narrative technique of the novelist of the period, would not allow James to rest content with the representation of the conflict of opposed points of view. He had to learn more about how they could function artistically before he could move one more step towards the fully dramatized novel.

❄ 9 ❄

Points of View

Between the completion of *The Portrait of a Lady* and the commencement of *The Bostonians*, James made a series of experiments within the limits of the international theme. He was to write a number of mediocre and tentative stories before he could at length break the bonds of his old perceptions and write a novel as strikingly different from his previous work as *The Bostonians*. Some of the reasons for this marked change are to be found in the experience of two visits that James made to his native land in 1881 and 1882–3.

He himself did not think that there was any artistic necessity for the first journey. He confided to his notebook in a hotel room in Boston soon after his arrival in November 1881 that he had come only to see his family. His impressions of the new world were exactly what he had anticipated. It was not necessary for a European writer to deal with America, he thought, although it was the unavoidable fate for the American writer to deal with Europe, if only by implication, and it seemed unjust that he too should have to assume 'that terrible burden.' He conceded that in one hundred, or even fifty, years time, the painter of manners would have to take America into account, but in the present he felt that his own time was 'terribly wasted' there.[1]

His prognosis was wrong. This visit, and the second one of a year later, gave him a rich fund of ideas, impressions, and materials for fiction. He acknowledged this later in the preface to volume XIV of the New York Edition, which contained some of the stories of the period.

113

He stayed for a month in Boston and another in New York. After Christmas, he travelled down to Washington, his first visit to the capital. He had an easy *entrée* to society there through his friend Henry Adams, but took rooms in a 'slightly sordid tenement.' He remembered later how 'the whole place, a nest of rickety tables and chairs, lame and disqualified utensils of every sort, and of smiling, shuffling, procrastinating persons of colour, had exhaled for me, to pungency, the domestic spirit of the "old South." '[2] Washington stamped itself vividly on his imagination, as the story *Pandora* and a number of contemporary letters show. In one, written to a friend in England on 9 January 1882, he rejoiced at being in his native land, 'where one is someone and something.' This was quite unlike his situation in Europe, where he was ignored. With 'the right point of view and *diapason*,' he added, 'it is a wonderfully entertaining and amusing country.' Washington, with its 'enormous spaces, hundreds of miles of asphalte, a charming climate and the most entertaining society in America,' was like nothing else in the old or new worlds.[3]

Another letter, previously unpublished, reveals how he could express, a mere two weeks later, a far from flattering opinion of the place. He wrote to Mrs. Jack Gardner in Boston, 23 January 1882: 'I have been here nearly three weeks and I ought to have a good many impressions. I have indeed a certain number, but when I write to you these generalities somehow grow vague and pointless. Everything sifts itself down to *one* impression – which I leave to your delicate imagination ... Washington is on the whole as pleasant as you told me I should find it – or at least that you had found it ... – Washington is too much of a village materially, but socially and conversationally bigger and more varied, I think, than anything we have. I should [not] care to live here – it is too rustic and familiar; but I should certainly come here for a part of every winter if I lived in the u.s. ... The Adamses tell me I succeed – that I am better than I was in London.' James went on to discuss the happy specimens of 'finished' American girlhood he had met who had profited by the social education that Washington gave. He had also found that men were much more socially available there, since they were not tied up in business as they seemed to be everywhere else in America. Even Oscar Wilde, a visitor to America at the same time, he observed, was not being looked at while he was at this party. James had met the President, Chester A. Arthur, whom he thought 'a good fellow – even attractive' a gentleman who seemed to want to please. James confessed to Mrs. Jack that he had almost asked the President for a foreign mission. He thought it would be a good idea for the states of the Union to send one another ambassadors. He himself would like to be 'at the head of a New York legation in Boston.'⁴ In this remark he quite accurately, if indirectly, sums up his own American literary affiliations.

The letter reveals that James was neither above the vanity of lionization, nor above feeling satisfaction at the social discomfiture of another lion, especially one who roared as loudly as Oscar Wilde. In fact, Wilde's American tour was, with a few exceptions, a great social success. The man who declared nothing but his genius at the New York Customs was hailed as such from there to San Francisco. In America, James realized, an artist of any significance was given a degree of social recognition that he seldom received in England. But even this was not sufficient to sway him from his chosen course. He ended his letter to Mrs. Gardner by expressing his longing for Europe. His emotion must also have been plain to his friends. Henry Adams later wrote to a common acquaintance: 'Henry James has been in Washington for a month, very homesick for London and for all the soft embraces of the old world.'⁵

James planned to return to New York and then make a little tour of the South. Before he could embark on this plan, however, he received a telegram from Cambridge informing him that his mother was ill. He left by the first train for Boston, but arrived after she had died. Her death was a great shock to him. He later wrote: 'She was our life, she was the house, she was the keystone of the arch. She held us all together, and without her we are scattered reeds. She was patience, she was wisdom, she was exquisite maternity.'⁶ He remained for some months in Boston to be near his father and only sister, Alice. Washington drew him back in the spring and he returned to Boston only to see his father and Alice settled in a house on Mount Vernon Street. Almost his last act before returning to England in May 1882 was to attend the 'curious, sociable, cheerful public funeral' of Ralph Waldo Emerson in Concord.⁷

James's own ambivalent attitude to the Concord sage was expressed in two long essays and many other references to him in his work. Although he looked with an ironic eye on Emerson's 'ripe unconsciousness of evil,' his provincialism, and his unruffled serenity, James regarded him as one of the great moral landmarks of New England. His pervasively lofty spirit, his love of freedom and belief in democracy, his easy distinction and noble bearing were symbolic to James of the best in the latter-day Puritan tradition. His death must have been to him a symbol of the gradual passing of the old order. Back in England, the whole American episode seemed to fade gradually away, 'like a very painful dream.'

In December of the same year, 1882, he received word that his father was dangerously ill. He returned at once to Boston, but arrived after his father's death. Since William was in Europe, much of the business of the estate fell to Henry. He had to travel westward to Milwaukee to see his younger brother Wilky and his family in this connection. His first visit to the Midwest confirmed his vague fears about the region. He wrote to Fanny Kemble on his return to Boston, on 1 February 1883: 'I think I shall never again willingly cross the Atlantic – though indeed I don't know what a blasé old age may in the fulness of time make me desire to do ... I have just returned from a fortnight's journey to the West – a hundred miles beyond Chicago! A thermometer 20 degrees below zero, and the rest *à l'avenant*. Those parts make New England seem like Italy, and Chicago renders Boston – as seen from there – adorable! ... The worst of the West is that it is a great country, with an extraordinary material civilization, and doesn't care one straw what one thinks of it ...'[8]

The quickly successive deaths of his parents and the dreary journey to the frozen West seem to have thrown a pall over James's whole relationship with his native land. Responsibility for family affairs prevented his return to England until August 1883, and he settled down to work in his father's house on Beacon Hill. He worked hard during the period but, as Leon Edel has pointed out, he did not initiate much new work. A good deal of his time was spent on collecting previous fictions into new editions.[9] He did, however, write some short stories and make a draft proposal to the publisher, J. R. Osgood, for his new novel, *The Bostonians*.

The first of the short stories to be published was *The Point of View* and the title might have been used for the other two American tales he wrote at this time, *Pandora* and *The Impressions of a Cousin*. All exploit the problem of how particular points of view colour experience. In *The Point of View* James returned to the epistolary form which he had first employed in *A Bundle of Letters* in 1879. The tone and themes of the letters, however, owe very little to the innovator of the form, Samuel Richardson, as they have nothing to do with sentimental relations. James's intention is primarily satiric, though the satire is good-humoured and never biting. *The Point of View* commemorates, in James's own words, 'its author's perverse and incurable disposition to interest himself less in his own (always so quickly stale) experience, under certain sorts of pressure, than in that of conceivable fellow mortals, which might be mysteriously and refreshingly different.'[10] This was one way of justifying the form, but it might also be pointed out that the epistolary method provided him with an easy way out of the problem of presenting sharply conflicting or irreconcilable opinions in fictional form. By opening successive windows on identical or similar experiences, he achieved some good ironic and comic effects but at the same time he avoided the destructive consequences that these conflicting views would have produced within the framework of the conventional form. The letters are written by American, British, and French correspondents as they travel to and in the United States, and each shows how narrowly their angles of vision are confined by the blinkers of national and social prejudice. James's own experience in the United States, as the two letters from Washington demonstrate, showed him how easy it was to have radically varying attitudes towards life there, depending on the frame of mind. Fundamentally, it was his own ambivalence towards his native land and his lack of literary schemata to apply to his experience there that made him resort to the simplifying technique of representing different national points of view.

James went back to *A Bundle of Letters* for one of his characters, the aesthete Louis Leverett, and to an even earlier story, *The Pension Beaurepas*, for two others, the American-born '*jeune-fille,*' Aurora Church, and her sou-pinching mother, who are both former denizens of *pensions* the length and breadth of Europe. Letters from Aurora begin and end the series of eight which make up *The Point of View* and thus make a certain factitious unity of the bundle. There are four other writers, all but one of whom take a rather bleak view of the United States. The odd man out is Marcellus Cockerell, a self-confessed 'roaring Yankee,' whose picture of America is painted in broad and aggressive strokes.

The 'moral' of the other seven letters is that to those used to European conditions, either through birth or expatriation, life in the United States can be very trying. The 'norm' of the group, that is to say the observer who appears to be the most objective and impersonal, is Miss Sturdy, an American spinster who has lived much abroad but who has 'gone to and fro so often' that she has ceased either to like or dislike America – which is the attitude that James, in his notebook, mentioned as the one he took towards Boston. In fact many of the remarks that James puts in Miss Sturdy's letter are those that he used in his own letters to various correspondents. Many more are those which he might well have used.

Miss Sturdy reveals herself as a tough-minded, witty, and hyperbolical observer. Echoing, perhaps, James's experience with the magazine editors, she asserts that there is not enough coarseness in America – although there is plenty of vulgarity, which is quite different. Using sophisticated European society as her standard, Miss Sturdy berates American manners. About the domination of children in America, she writes: 'Longfellow wrote a charming little poem called "The Children's Hour," but he ought to have called it "The Children's Century." ' She inveighs against the harshness of American speech and the twaddle of the conversation, the bourgeois manners, and the lack of great people. On the other hand, she thinks that since her last visit the country has become much more agreeable. She is able to appreciate the advantages of a democratic system in regard to manners. It deprived people 'of weapons that everyone doesn't equally possess.' This meant that there was little arrogance or social cruelty and a greater *bonhomie* than in England. One's 'merely personal and unclassified value' was greater. The familiar Jamesian antithesis reappears in Miss Sturdy's observation that the American order and climate gave people a 'nature they *can* let loose,' whereas Europe 'has to protect itself with more art.' Miss Sturdy is amazed at the amount of freedom allowed young women, who 'knock about' all over the place and yet are unmolested. Flirtations are 'child's play' and the men seem to have no time for making love (ANS, 308–14).

These conditions make the lot of Miss Church extremely hard. She has come over with her mother, at great expense, to find a husband, a pursuit which has been fruitless in Europe. She is a pathetic case, since she is dowerless in Europe and doomed to be considered Europeanized in America. None of her relations with American men leads to anything. She writes to her friend at the end of three months to say that 'passions don't rage' and that 'society seems oddly to consist of a sort of innocent jilting' (ANS, 334). In desperation, her mother has announced that they must go West in search of further prospects. It is obvious that the search will be no more successful there. One of the ironies of this bundle of letters is that even Louis Leverett, the expatriate American who should be most sympathetic to Aurora, and is drawn to her, in the end backs away because 'she is not of this country.' In this vignette, James touches on the pathos of expatriation with a light but sympathetic hand.

The most amusing of the points of view is that of the French Academician, M. Gustave Lejaune, who has come to collect material for a book about America. He is, according to Aurora, 'the first French writer of distinction who has been to America since De Tocqueville ...' The irony of this claim is at once apparent, as the Frenchman takes the most jaundiced, cynical view of everything American. Since he speaks no English, he is unable to communicate with any native. This does not, however, prevent him from freely judging everything. A comprehensive symbol for the country is, for him, the 'false classic, white marble, iron and stucco' Capitol building. 'The goddess of Liberty on the top,' he writes, 'dressed in a bear's skin; their liberty over here is the liberty of bears.' Awful trains, bad inns, loud newspapers; 'as for the people, they're the English *minus* the conventions. You can fancy what remains.' M. Lejaune has even been reading Henry James, and his letter contains a capsule (and typical contemporary) criticism of his fiction: '*C'est proprement écrit*, but it's terribly pale' (ANS, 324–6). Above all, M. Lejaune misunderstands the nature of American women. He is in hot pursuit of a married woman whom he has met in Philadelphia. He thinks that she has encouraged him. The reader can see that she has merely been flirting with him in the innocent American way and that the Frenchman is bound to be frustrated. The letter caricatures French logic and cynicism. James would have obtained some quiet amusement from the knowledge that years later an American critic, John Curtis Underwood, was to quote part of M. Lejaune's letter and then go on to remark: 'The attitude towards America and life at large of our most misrepresentative and un-American novelist of contemporary cosmopolitan life is sufficiently indicated by [this] quotation.'[11]

The letter of the Right Hon. Edward Antrobus, M.P., is equally a caricature of the indefatigable, official English traveller. It is an amusing document of facts, statistics, and bewilderment. He is a radical M.P., but he finds most things in America far too radical for his taste. He is so wedded to a class system that he is disconcerted at every turn by democratic manners. He is taken in by 'American humour,' confused by the slang, and shocked at the commanding situation of women. Although he has come to 'look into' everything, he is so effectively blinkered by his prejudices that he sees nothing.

The opposite angle of vision is represented by Marcellus Cockerell, the returned American patriot. He pours scorn on many of the institutions of France and England: their 'big pompous armies drawn up in great silly rows, their gold lace, their salaams,' and their aristocracies, which Cockerell characterizes as 'bad manners organised.' 'I've got rid of a superstition,' Cockerell writes, 'that there's no salvation but through Europe.' He crows over the fact that 'a mighty tide is sweeping the world to democracy.' This makes the European topics seem 'petty and parochial' (ANS, 328–31).

Probably James's own ambivalent attitudes are revealed in Cockerell's claim, on the one hand, that the salvation of Europe lies in the spread of democracy from America, and, on the other, M. Lejaune's observation that American development should be 'the biggest warning' for France. With Sir Roger de Coverley, James would have said that there was much to be said on both sides. Even in Cockerell's letter, however, James found it hard to praise America except by negatives. Cockerell boasts of the 'pie-eating plainness,' the lack of squalor, wife-beating, social distinctions, and ceremonials. But there was sound prophecy in Cockerell's claim that 'we shall have all the Titians by and by, and we shall move over a few cathedrals' (ANS, 332).

In the view of the aesthete, Louis Leverett, culture is not an exportable commodity. In a state of aesthetic agony, Leverett writes to his friend, Harvard Tremont, who is still in Paris. Significantly, Leverett pens his letter on a marble-topped table in a Boston hotel-room, which was exactly the situation that James was in when he made his first notebook entry on his return to the United States. James no doubt gave to Leverett the same exaggerated emotions that he himself felt on that occasion, only in an even more intensified form. As in most of the other letters in *The Point of View*, hyperbole is the main source of humour. 'A terrible crude glare is over everything,' Leverett writes, 'the earth looks peeled and excoriated; the raw heavens seem to bleed with the quick hard light.' He complains of those durable American hotel hazards, the icewater, the overheating, and the transom windows which pour floods of light into the room from the corridors. He hates the food, the newspapers, and the children. Everyone looks the same to him. 'They're thin,' he complains, 'they're diluted in the great tepid bath of Democracy!' He cries out for his little corner of Paris, for the 'rich, the deep, the dark Old World' (ANS, 321–3). With Louis Leverett's reactions, James cleverly illuminates the feelings of the aesthetic pilgrims who left America by the hundreds in the late nineteenth century to live out their lives in nooks and crannies of old European cities.

James appears to have believed that he was making an objective appraisal of the United States through these seven 'refreshingly different' correspondents. It is true that he displays amazing virtuosity in capturing their different flavours through differing styles, but his overall critical bias is not much concealed. Only the roaring patriot responds wholeheartedly to American life and even he does so largely by negatives. The rest of them, expatriates and visitors alike, find life in the United States difficult and uncomfortable and look forward to returning to the old world. In this respect they were all echoing the attitude of their creator. All the same, *The Point of View* shows James's understanding of the ways in which perception is conditioned – and his consequent awareness that there is no ultimate and objective truth in judgment about any country or situation. It was on the basis of this understanding that he was to build up his thorough-going point-of-view and reflector techniques in his subsequent novels. Perhaps more important at this time was his discovery that stereotypes of perception can distort reality to the point of absurdity. Only a sturdy pragmatism could do any sort of justice to the complex appearance and fabric of life.

Another story in this American group is *Pandora*, a product of his experience in Washington. He chose the capital as the main setting for the *début* of the most interesting type that he found on his return to America, the 'new' American girl. He probably saw in the story a chance to repeat the success of *Daisy Miller*. With *Julia Bride*, published in 1908, he was to complete a trilogy in which he summarized the evolution of this most representative American type over a span of thirty years.[12]

The story is told from the point of view of a young Junker diplomatist, Count Otto Vogelstein. He is intelligent, but closely circumscribed in his perception by the prejudices of his caste and country. His 'flights' of imagination are weighed down by the 'stone' of his cultural limitations. But he does make a good vehicle for strong reactions to the remarkable national type whom he first encounters on his sea-voyage from Germany to America, where he is to take up his post as secretary of embassy. James had by this time become fully conscious of how perception of reality is conditioned by literary schemata. Vogelstein is reading *Daisy Miller* when he first encounters Pandora Day. He naturally identifies the girl with Daisy and sees himself in the position of the young Winterbourne. Although he comes to see, in time, that Pandora is quite different from Daisy, he obviously fails to comprehend that he continues to share most of Winterbourne's limitations. His nature has all the coldness and detachment of his predecessor, and a good deal of Winterbourne's experimental scepticism. Pandora, like Daisy, comes from a town in upstate New York. She has the same lightness, spontaneity, and ease as Daisy and, although she does not have her predecessor's beauty, she is much more developed intellectually. She reads French critics in the original and, for dissipation, Alfred de Musset.

Vogelstein observes that Pandora seems to have considerable power over people. She is treated with deference by the captain of the liner; she is quickly escorted through customs by an obliging officer; she organizes and controls her obviously inferior and helpless parents, her sister (a Daisy Miller *en herbe*), and her brother (a Randolph *en fleur*). Vogelstein is attracted to her but he is too cautious to pursue her. Like Winterbourne he is confirmed in his hesitancy by an elderly lady, a fellow passenger, Mrs. Dangerfield, who warns the young Count about Pandora's low social position.

He does not see Pandora again for two years. In the meantime he has been making the best of the meagre society of Washington. His two years have taught him that the only way to enjoy life in the great Republic was 'to burn one's standards and warm one's self at the blaze.' But he goes often for consolation to the civilized and hospitable house of Mr. and Mrs. Alfred Bonnycastle – who are a very thinly disguised version of Mr. and Mrs. Henry Adams. The Count understands what Mr. Bonnycastle, chafing at his wife's exclusiveness, had meant when he said, near the end of the season: 'Hang it, there's only a month left; let us be vulgar and have some fun – let us invite the President.' This is a remark that Adams actually made.

It is a year after this remark that the story resumes, and the Bonnycastles are preparing to be reckless again, though James hastens to add that there is a different President in the White House. His style admirably captures the tone of the Adams' life, just as, later on, T. S. Eliot was to capture the note of the aging Adams in 'Gerontion.' 'Toward the end of the social year, in those soft scented days of the Washington spring when the air began to show a southern glow and the Squares and Circles (to which the wide empty avenues converged according to a plan so ingenious, yet so bewildering) to flush with pink blossom and to make one wish to sit on benches – under this magic of expansion and condonation Mrs. Bonnycastle, who during the winter had been a good deal on the defensive, relaxed her vigilance a little, became whimsically wilful, vernally reckless, as it were, and ceased to calculate the consequences of an hospitality which a reference to the back files or even to the morning's issue of the newspapers might easily prove a mistake' (ANS, 401).

Vogelstein is invited to the resultant party along with the new President, whom the Count had seen inaugurated after he had had the rare advantage of witnessing an electoral campaign and a distribution of the spoils. Vogelstein goes in search of the President in order to pay his respects. He always does this with some apprehension, as he feels he is often mistaken for an office-seeker. The chief of state he finds at length, seated on a sofa in a secluded recess of a small tea-room. To his surprise, he sees that the beautifully-dressed girl seated at the President's side is none other than Pandora. As he approaches, he hears her say, 'Well now, remember; I consider it a promise.' She has an air of elation, and is obviously now a person of great conse-quence, for, as soon as the President leaves, after bidding good-bye 'to these bright folks,' his hosts, Pandora is taken up by a Supreme Court judge and two foreign ministers. Vogelstein resists his impulse to join the group around her but he can see that in the interim since he had last met this 'daughter of small burghers,' she had grown really bril-liant. At the end of the party, after all the other guests have left, the bewildered Count asks his hosts what Pandora is.

'My dear Vogelstein,' Alfred Bonnycastle replies, 'she's the latest freshest fruit of our great American evolution. She's the self-made girl!' He goes on to elaborate. 'She was possible doubtless only in America ... She was not fast, nor emancipated, nor crude, nor loud, and there wasn't in her, of necessity at least, a grain of the stuff of which the adventuress is made. She was simply very successful, and her success was entirely personal. She hadn't been born with the silver spoon of social opportunity; she had grasped it by honest exertion. You knew her by many different signs, but chiefly, infallibly, by the appearance of her parents; ... you always saw how little her parents could have made her ... Naturally she was possible only in America – only in a country where whole ranges of competition and comparison were absent' (ANS, 412–3).

Vogelstein goes with Pandora on a tour through the Capitol, wondering all the time what he is doing, for, having seen it all before, he thinks it 'a hideous place.' 'In the lower House were certain be-daubed walls, in the basest style of imitation, which made him feel faintly sick, not to speak of a lobby adorned with artless prints and photographs of eminent defunct Congressmen that was all too serious for a joke and too comic for a Valhalla' (ANS, 415). However, he finds Pandora fascinating, and, later on, goes with her and a party of young people on an excursion by boat to Mount Vernon.

He is on the verge of falling in love with her when, on the return voyage up the Potomac, he is told by Mrs. Bonnycastle that her hus-band had omitted one item of information about the self-made girl.

In her past was always that piece of 'peculiarly American enterprise a premature engagement ...' (ANS, 420). This disconcerting generalization turns out to be true in this particular case; a young man from Utica is waiting on the dockside to meet the boat. The President's promise has been fulfilled; he has in his hand an offer of the consulate in Holland.

'I may make the thing a "little gem" – if I try hard enough,' James wrote in his notebook.[13] It did not, obviously, turn out as well as he expected. Looking critically at the story in his later preface, he observed that not much of the latent drama in the case had survived the story. This was a just observation. James gives few clues about the source of Pandora's power and none to the growth of her mind, although this is partially because she is seen throughout by the uncomprehending Count. James wondered why this 'none so very precious particle' should have been fished up at the time as if it were one of the pearls of his American experience. The answer to this was that it was a case once again, he thought, of his 'insuperably restricted experience' and his 'various missing American clues.' He knew so little of the downtown world that had partly produced Pandora that he had had to make the uptown count for everything. The story implies that downtown's refusal to participate in the world uptown had opened Pandora's box and given her the opportunity to operate in a realm reserved in other societies for men – the world of power, politics, and patronage.

James noted, rightly, that a good deal of the element of poetry had sneaked into *Pandora*, as it had into *Daisy Miller*.[14] He meant by this, presumably, the element of romance. It is a fanciful story, but it is nonetheless a significant *exemplum* of American experience. It gave him an opportunity to analyze some aspects of social life and politics in a way which may seem ephemeral on the surface but which in fact cuts quite deeply into the facts of post-Civil War Washington reality.

He used the house of the Adams, which, socially, 'left out ... more people than it took in,' to show the peculiar divorce of democratic politics from enlightened society. Their rooms were 'garnished with an occasional Senator,' but 'members of the House were very rare.' The bareness of the social scene and its lack of sophistication are mirrored in the bareness of the Washington that James represents.

With its unkempt look, its pretentious architecture and its deserted spaces, the capital symbolizes an unfinished, provincial society. The Capitol itself was 'the great white edifice that unfolds its repeated colonnades and uplifts its isolated dome at the end of a long vista of saloons and tobacco-shops.' This was not, of course, James's last word on Washington. When Pandora and the Count stroll on the terrace after seeing the interior of the Capitol they gaze at the splendid view. 'Washington was beneath them, bristling and geometrical; the long lines of its avenues seemed to stretch into national futures' (ANS, 414–15).

In 1879 James's tutor in American politics, Henry Adams, had published his novel about the Washington scene, *Democracy*. James's reactions to it were recorded by the wife of the British historian, John Richard Green, in a letter to Mrs. Henry Adams: 'Mr. James looked very severe and grave over it, but I am not sure whether it was on patriotic or artistic grounds.'[15] Probably James disapproved on both grounds. There is little doubt, however, that he made use of Adams' Washington and his insights into the corruption and graft of American politics as schemata for his own fiction. Although, like business, politics was one of the many aspects of American life that were to remain essentially unknown to him, he could imply the nature of American politics in *Pandora* by showing how determinedly society excluded it. Moreover, in the little scene in which Pandora is seen extracting a promise from the President, there is a hint of the pervasive odour of Washington's affairs. In this case, instead of coarser methods, Pandora's qualities of charm and boldness are used to get results. Nonetheless, the note of the spoils system is sounded and the American girl, exercising her power in a new realm, is the victor.

Nineteen-twentieths of American town-life, 'or in other words the huge organised mystery of the consummately, the supremely applied money-passion, were inexorably closed to him,' James recorded in one of his prefaces.[16] This did not prevent him from speculating about financial affairs particularly as they affected the women in the uptown world. A story based on this theme is *The Impressions of a Cousin*, published in *Century Magazine* in 1883. It is the weakest of the stories in this American group. Even before writing it, at the request of Richard Watson Gilder, James observed in his notebook that he had lost his fancy for the theme, which he thought 'thin and conventional.' He added, 'actuality must be my line at present. I may work it with infinite profit. The thing is to do so!'[17]

Actuality is not the strong note of *The Impressions of a Cousin*. It is written in the form of a journal, but James was no more successful with this than with his previous imitation of Turgenev in *The Diary of a Man of Fifty*. The 'writer' of the story thinks her own narrative should be called 'The Diary of a Morbid Woman.' In spite of its weakness, however, the story has considerable interest, not the least for the self-projection of James into the diarist, Miss Condit, a spinster painter, long resident in Europe, who has returned to live in New York. Another centre of interest is Mr. Caliph, an exotic type of businessman.

Miss Condit is not merely the channel through which the story flows, but is also a typical Jamesian point-of-view character, like Rowland Mallet or Miss Sturdy, commonsensical, self-deprecating, trenchant in opinion, slightly withdrawn from life. Her occupation as a painter gives James the opportunity to chronicle his own impressions of the city. He observed in his notebook, 'The New York streets are fatal to the imagination.' Miss Condit tells us why. 'How can I sketch Fifty-third Street? ... How can I even inhabit Fifty-third Street?' she asks. 'When I turn into it from the Fifth Avenue, the vista seems too hideous: the narrow, impersonal houses, with the dry, hard tone of their brown-stone, a surface as uninteresting as that of sandpaper; their steep, stiff stoops, giving you such a climb to the door; their lumpish balustrades, porticoes, and cornices, turned out by the hundred and adorned with heavy excrescences – such an eruption of ornament and such a poverty of effect! ... The city of New York is like a tall sum in addition, and the streets are like columns of figures. What a place for me to live, who hate arithmetic!' No matter how hard she tries, she cannot get excited about the artistic possibilities of New York, even Central Park. Nothing 'composes' there; there is no mellowness to the air or to the colours of the town. There are no gradations of light, only a harsh glare. Once again, through Miss Condit, James is expressing his frustration at the absence of European schemata and his inability to come to grips with the physical characteristics of the United States scene. Miss Condit's lament is the familiar cry from James's earlier attempts to 'do' New York. 'I believe I should be a good patriot,' she writes, 'if I could sketch my native town' (CT, V, 112). She finally gives up her search for paintable scenes and turns to discuss the emotional lives of the other characters in the story instead.

She is living with her cousin, Eunice, who has asked her to come back from Europe to be her companion. Eunice is an orphan, without other relatives, whose considerable fortune has been placed in trust with Mr. Caliph. Miss Condit is suspicious of Caliph from the start, but she realizes that she cannot discuss her suspicions with Eunice when she finds out that her cousin is in love with him. Mr. Caliph has promised to visit Eunice and her new companion, but he puts off his appearance many times before finally calling on them. Miss Condit's impressions of him through second-hand report have not prepared her for the imposing Caliph, who turns out to be a great talker with a face of 'a fine, expressive, pictorial ugliness' (CT, V, 126). Miss Condit thinks that his oriental richness of aspect connotes a Jewish origin. 'He has a way of his own of doing things,' she writes, 'and carries imagination and humour, and a sense of the beautiful, into Wall Street and the Stock Exchange.' She regrets, however, that she cannot go downtown to see what they think of him there.

Without much surprise, the reader discovers that Mr. Caliph is defrauding Eunice. But he is also having financial troubles himself. He does not know that Eunice is in love with him, and, to save her from poverty, he persuades his rich half-brother, Adrian Frank, to court her. Adrian, an amiable, rather weak, character, complies. Eunice refuses his proposal of marriage. Later on he proposes to Miss Condit, much to her surprise. She also refuses him and tells him to apply again to Eunice, who is by now, she tells him, practically penniless. Acting on hints from Miss Condit, Adrian finds out why, and he makes over his own fortune to Caliph so that his half-brother can restore the money to Eunice. When Caliph does this, Eunice suddenly falls out of love with him. 'It was sweeter,' Miss Condit writes, 'for her to suffer at Mr. Caliph's hands than to receive her simple dues from them' (CT, V, 190). Eunice, finding out that Miss Condit has meddled in her affairs, also becomes estranged from her cousin. Miss Condit feels that her scheming has come to nothing and decides to return to Europe. Normally, James would have ended the story there, but, perhaps at the urging of Gilder, or at least knowing what the *Century* readers wanted, he tacked on a happy ending. He implies that Eunice will marry her Caliph after a time and, when this happens, that Miss Condit will marry Adrian, who is now a poor man. This seems odd, since she has expressed no great affection for him in the course of her diary entries.

The Impressions of a Cousin has been justly neglected by the critics, but there are two short complementary commentaries on the story. The first is by Raymond D. Havens, who thinks that the self-revelation of Miss Condit 'is one of the best things in the story.' He adds that she becomes more likable as her prejudices fade in the process of the story and her sterling qualities of character appear. He also thinks that her sudden turnabout with Adrian Frank at the end of the story is quite understandable.[18] Unfortunately, in his short article he offers no support for either view. It fell to Wayne C. Booth to take up the defence in that notable study of narrative technique, *The Rhetoric of Fiction*. He maintains that a new heroine emerges between James's notebook entry for the story and the finished work. Instead of merely observing and recording, as James intended her to do, apparently, in the notebook, in the story she acts. Mr. Booth concludes: 'The original idea is completely transformed by having one of the key characters fall in love with the narrator who was originally conceived as a mere reflector.'[19]

Precisely the problem of the end of the story, however, is that this sudden falling in love appears to be an afterthought rather than a deliberately planned development. There is little or no transformation of Miss Condit since, like Miss Sturdy in *The Point of View*, she is not organically involved in the action; she merely observes and records and towards the end of the story begins to meddle. Nor does there seem to me to be much development in her character, except that she becomes more officious as the story proceeds. In fact, taken all round, this story appears to be, at this stage in James's development, almost incomprehensibly inept.

James apparently made a half-hearted attempt to model his situation on Hawthorne's novel, *The Marble Faun*. Miss Condit writes of Adrian Frank: 'He is a charming creature – a kind of Yankee Donatello. If I could only be his Miriam, the situation would

129

be almost complete, for Eunice is an excellent Hilda.' Hawthorne's schema, however, is quite inappropriate for the New York situation. Adrian has none of the wild, rustic, Italianate grace of Donatello, and Miss Condit is a pretty pallid Miriam. Eunice will do well enough as Hilda, but where is the fourth member of Hawthorne's quartet, the sculptor, Kenyon, to come in? Caliph bears no resemblance to him. If anything, James transposed Miriam's exotic, passionate, and Semitic qualities to Caliph. He then watered down Hawthorne's theme of the 'unpardonable sin' into Miss Condit's interference with Eunice's affairs, and ended up with a complete botch.

In spite of the artistic failure of the story, Mr. Caliph's character is worth examining further, Miss Condit calls him Haroun-al-Raschid, and his other attributes certainly suggest the Middle Eastern merchant much more than they do any New York businessman. The appearance of such a character in James's fiction is almost unaccountable in the light of his own repeated references to the monotony of type among the Americans of the commercial class. The only imaginative link between New York and the Middle East in James's work is in his quite frequent references to the colourings of the city in Eastern terms. From this association he may have made an imaginative leap to one or other of the people whom he saw in the city in the winter of 1883, where, as he told George du Maurier, he had found many 'types and figures and curious social idiosyncrasies.' He wished for a fifteenth part of du Maurier's talent in order to hold up the mirror to its variety.[20] Perhaps *The Impressions of a Cousin* is an attempt to imitate du Maurier's method of drawing exotic and fascinating types as he did so brilliantly in the pages of *Punch* at the time.

Whatever the source for Mr. Caliph, there can be little doubt about James's intention in representing him. It relates to his long-standing mistrust of business, and his deep concern with fraud, as seen in *Watch and Ward* and numerous short stories. Mr. Caliph, according to Miss Condit, is 'no better than a common swindler.' Yet there is a style about his method of swindling Eunice that gives it an almost artistic authority. The more he is described in the story, the closer he appears to the first gentleman and wily seducer, Satan himself. James even stages a garden scene as an analogue to Michael's appearance in Eden after the Fall.

This takes place in the second part of the story when the scene shifts to Eunice's summer house on the Hudson, opposite West Point. For the first time, Miss Condit is happy to be sketching and painting in this country which she thinks to be 'as beautiful as the Rhine.' Once again as in *A Most Extraordinary Case*, the Hudson River School seems to have given James a schema which he could fall back on in representing the colours and light of the area. In Miss Condit's description of the setting, there is a hint that she has been influenced by, and is reacting against the large shiny canvasses that the members of the school turned out. 'The great condition, of course, is the splendid river, lying beneath our rounded headland in vast silvery stretches and growing almost vague on the opposite shore. It is a country of views; you are always peeping down an avenue, or ascending a mound, or going round a corner, to look at one. They are rather too shining, too high-pitched, for my little purposes; all nature seems glazed with light and varnished with freshness. But I manage to scrape something off' (CT, V, 159). Eunice gives a garden party and Mr. Caliph comes down from New York for the occasion. He approaches Eunice and Miss Condit, who describes the scene in unmistakable terms: 'When I found myself face to face with him, and it came over me that, blooming there in his diabolical assurance, it was he – he with his smiles, his bows, his gorgeous *boutonnière*, the wonderful air he has of being anointed and gilded – he that had ruined my poor Eunice, who grew whiter than ever as he approached: when I felt all this, my blood began to tingle, and if I were only a handsome woman I might believe that my eyes shone like those of an avenging angel. He was as fresh as a day in June, enormous, and more than ever like Haroun-al-Raschid' (CT, V, 173).

This extraordinary adaptation of the scene of Eve's temptation concludes the description of Caliph. Throughout the story he has been characterized by a surprising number of literary allusions. It seems that James, unable to see any strong male element in American life, created this fanciful businessman out of the archetypal figure of the wandering, mercantile Jew to compensate for the lack. This Satanic figure despoils the innocent orphan Eunice of her property.

131

He is detected by the Gabriel-like avenging angel of art. But the implications of this allegorical scheme are dissipated by the story's probable happy ending. Business will marry property, and art retreats to Europe to marry the now penniless Yankee who has sacrificed his inherited fortune for the love of art.

Such an allegorical interpretation of the story is not really satisfactory, and it is probable that James had no such clear scheme in mind. *The Impressions of a Cousin* shows once again how James could flounder and grope with images and conventions totally unsuited to American experience when he was deprived of the schemata on which he had come to rely in his work. Miss Condit's spinsterish point of view and her amateurish techniques are inadequate to deal with the problems that the story raised, so James solved them in the end according to the clichés of contemporary magazine fiction. Contributing to this failure may also be James's fears about his recent 'orphaned' condition and about the looming shape of the money-passion in the United States

⁑ 10 ⁑

Evasive Boston
and
Threadbare Internationalism

From the artistic nadir of *The Impressions of a Cousin*, Henry James found a way of climbing up, as he did often in his career, by means of his technique. *A New England Winter*, published almost a year after *The Impressions of a Cousin* in August and September 1884, cannot be numbered among the most successful of James's stories, but it is one of the most interesting, since it clearly indicates a major change in his technique.

The plot of the story is slight and is merely a peg on which James hangs what he calls his 'perhaps too descriptive tale' (ANS, 356). It centres on the comic improbability of a European-style adulterous affair in Boston. In order to make more endurable the return of her expatriate painter-son, Florimond, Mrs. Daintry arranges a visit of a beautiful cousin, Rachel Torrance, to coincide with her son's stay. Rachel becomes the guest of another distant relation of Mrs. Daintry, the young Mrs. Mesh. Florimond, apparently acting in accord with his mother's plan, spends a good deal of time visiting the Mesh household. He does not, however, go in order to see Rachel, who cannot stand his conceitedness, but to see Mrs. Mesh. Mrs. Daintry finally discovers this and, scandalized, announces her intention of spending the summer in Europe. She embarks almost at once, taking Florimond back with her. As a matter of fact, the relationship between Mrs. Mesh and Florimond is innocent. Both are bored, but both are satisfied with sociable talk around the parlour fire. After he has gone, Mrs.

Mesh says only 'I kind of miss him, afternoons.' Florimond, on his side, a painter 'of considerable, if not the highest, promise,' seems incapable of any passion.

The story gave Howells great pleasure in representing, he wrote his friend, 'a more artistically difficult and evasive Boston than I ever get at.'[1] James himself was less enthusiastic about it, but it is easy to see what Howells meant. The action is seen partly from the point of view of Mrs. Daintry. James brilliantly dramatizes, through her, the painful, prickly, excitable moral consciousness of a Boston society woman. She can take nothing easily or simply. For example, she spends some agonizing minutes after leaving her house in the Back Bay at the beginning of the story trying to decide whether or not to go back to tell her parlourmaid that she should not shut the door so precipitately after she has left. Her personal and moral scruples about the arrangements she should make for her son's visit to Boston amount to a comedy of nervous indecision. Florimond himself is also a fine comic figure, a kind of Louis Leverett with a paint brush. Obviously, he is not much of a painter. He claims to be an impressionist, although, James adds, 'you would never have guessed' this from his neat and sleek appearance. He has what they call in Paris 'a great deal of eye.' The phrase recalls Cézanne's description of Monet: 'Monet n'est qu'un œil – mais quel œil!' Florimond sees things 'with great intensity' even though he cannot apparently paint them.

The appearance of an impressionist painter in James's fiction owes a good deal to an earlier episode in his career. In 1876, while living in Paris, James reviewed the second group show of the painters who had recently been dubbed 'the Impressionists.' He discussed the whole group without mentioning names. According to John Rewald, Degas, Monet, Pissarro, and Renoir, among others, exhibited on that occasion.[2] The most popular art critic of the day, Albert Wolff, wrote of this exhibition: 'It is a frightening spectacle of human vanity gone astray to the point of madness ...' James did not go this far, but he joined the wolf-pack of attacking critics with considerable enthusiasm. With striking lack of prescience, he wrote of the group: 'None of its members show signs of possessing first-rate talent, and indeed the "Impressionist" doctrines strike me as incompatible, in an artist's mind, with the existence of first-rate talent. To embrace them you must be provided with a plentiful absence of imagination.' He did, on the other hand, find the show decidedly interesting as evidence of the painters' desire to present 'unadorned reality.' They were foes to the idea of the beautiful in which, according to James, all previous artists had found their best account. 'The beautiful, to them,' he went on, 'is what the supernatural is to the Positivists – a metaphysical notion, which can only get one into a muddle and is to be severely let alone. Let it alone, they say, and it will come at its own pleasure; the painter's proper field is simply the actual, and to give a vivid impression of how a thing happens to look, at a particular moment, is the essence of his mission.'[3] Much as he disliked their work, he, as a writer always concerned with the methods of representing reality, could not help being struck by the honesty of their programme. These painters' canvasses and his own remarks about them dropped seeds into his consciousness which were to flower in remarkable ways eight years later.

Impressionism, also known as naturalism, was the storm centre of debate in Paris in 1876. Both Zola and Daudet staunchly defended the Impressionists against their many enemies. James was acquainted with them both, and he must have been fully aware of the issues. At the time, their writings appealed to him not much more than the paintings of their friends. But, as G. V. Dobie remarks in her study of Daudet, 'In the autumn of 1876 [James] moved to England and it was only in the course of subsequent visits to France that his feelings towards his acquaintances gradually underwent a change.'[4]

He made such a visit early in 1884, six months after he had returned from the United States to England. To quote Dobie again, 'In the blank made by the death of Turgenev, he seems to have come a degree nearer to Daudet.'[5] In a letter to his brother, William, Henry remarked on Daudet's remarkable personal charm and added that the French novelist had been 'extremely nice' to him.[6] To W. D. Howells, he wrote: 'I have been seeing something of Daudet, Goncourt, and Zola; and there is nothing more interesting to me now than the effort and experiment of this little group, with its truly infernal intelligence of art, form, manner – its intense artistic life. They do the only kind of work, to-day, that I respect; and in spite of their ferocious pessimism and their handling of unclean things, they are at least serious and honest.' He went on to reprove Howells for not going far enough towards naturalism, observing that his work was 'haunted with romantic phantoms and a tendency to factitious glosses.' He then had the grace to admit that his own characters also had 'too damnably much' gloss.[7] It is clear from this remark that he intended to get rid of this in order to do the kind of work that he had learned to respect.*

Daudet was, to James, by far the most appealing of the French naturalists. He admired above all what he called his pictorial ability. The metaphor he used most frequently in discussing his work was, in fact, that of painting. In a reference to him in an essay on Trollope, for example, he unfavourably compares the comfortable and profuse style of the English novelist with the 'minute stippling' of Daudet.[8] And, commenting on the way in which Daudet represented the light, the sky, the streets, and the vistas of Paris, James wrote that it reminds the reader 'again and again that if he paints with a pen he writes with a brush.'[9] Like the Impressionists, Daudet worked directly from life. James was now ready to try to emulate the vivacity and intensity of what he called this 'newly-invented' perception.[10]

A New England Winter was written about the same time as the famous essay *The Art of Fiction*, in which James defined good fiction as 'a direct impression of life.' The story is in part an attempt to make

*Probably, James revised his original estimate of the Impressionist painters about this time too, but he appears to have made no written comments on their work then. What he thought about them in 1904 is revealed by a passage in *The American Scene* on a private collection of Impressionists in a house in Farmington, Connecticut, which is now open to the public. In this section he is discussing the lack of 'social and sensual margin, overflow and by-play' in New England village life. 'Never was such by-play,' he goes on, 'as in a great new house on a hilltop that overlooked the most composed of communities; a house apparently conceived – and with great felicity – on the lines of a magnified Mount Vernon, and in which an array of modern "impressionistic" pictures, mainly French, wondrous examples of Manet, of Degas, of Claude Monet, of Whistler, of other rare recent hands, treated us to the momentary effect of a large slippery sweet inserted, without a warning, between the compressed lips of half-conscious inanition. One hadn't quite known one was starved, but the morsel went down by the mere authority of the thing consummately *prepared* ... It happened to be that particular art – it might as well, no doubt, have been another; it made everything else shrivel and fade: it was like the trill of a nightingale, lord of the hushed evening' (45–6).

a series of impressionistic verbal paintings of Boston after the manner of Daudet. Florimond actually paints very little; he spends his time wandering around the city getting the 'visual impression' and attempting to discover 'with regard to such and such an object or a place, of what its "character" would consist.' There is obviously a good deal of self-reference in James's presentation of his painter, who sees with the fresh eyes of the American 'who returns to his native land after a few years spent in the foreign element' (ANS, 355). He makes effective verbal pictures of Boston interiors, of Cambridge and Harvard, of slushy streets and packed street-cars deriving his schemata from the French Impressionists in their paintings of Paris. The largest verbal canvas is reminiscent in style of Monet's cityscapes. It is of the upper part of Beacon Street, with its 'long, wide, sunny slope, the uneven line of the older houses, the contrasted, differing, bulging fronts, the painted bricks, the tidy facings, the immaculate doors, the burnished silver plates, the denuded twigs of the far extent of the Common, on the other side; and to crown the eminence and complete the picture, high in the air, poised in the right place, over everything that clustered below, the most felicitous object in Boston, – the gilded dome of the State House' (ANS, 356).

This is little more than decorative writing, though very good of its kind. The seeing eye of the returned expatriate was, in addition, used to represent the appearance of things as emblems for the social order that produced them. Here we see the beginnings of James's technique of finding the 'sense' of the place, as he later called it, which reached fruition in *The American Scene*. Climate, geography, land- and cityscape, interior decoration, furniture, and faces all speak to Florimond with a peculiar accent of *place*. In *A New England Winter*, however, scenes are used not so much for dramatic as for symbolic purposes. There is, for example, a correspondence between the somewhat oppressive moral purity of Boston and the cleanness of the place. The fronts of the houses on Beacon Street on a frosty morning 'seemed to have been scoured, with a kind of friction, by the hard, salutary light.' The large, clear windows along the street are indications of the absurdity of the idea of an intrigue between Mrs. Mesh and Florimond. 'This continuity of glass constituted a kind of exposure, within and without, and gave the street the appearance of an enormous corridor, in which the public and the private were familiar and intermingled.'

The insistent hideousness of the town in winter is conveyed graphically by James's description of the muddy, snow-bound streets, the packed horse-cars, the staring advertisements, the ragged lines of houses in the newer districts, the tangle of telegraph-wires, and the goods in the shops – all 'of the latest modern ugliness.' It is a frigid and sterile background for what to Florimond appears to be 'a city of women, in a country of women.' The social life is so dominated by them that he could have believed himself at times to be 'in a country stricken by a war, where the men had all gone to the army ...' Only a trip across the river to Harvard eases this impression. There, in the spring, Florimond remembers, 'there would be a smell of earth and vegetation, – a smell more primitive than the odor of Europe ...' (ANS, 374–5). But this hint of male presence is erased by the rest of the story, which is a comprehensive image of an emasculated society. The title of the story itself seems to be intended as a symbol of a state of society as well as of place.

Unfortunately, the story as a whole does not live up to the promise of its parts, even though it merits more than the complete neglect that it has so far suffered at the hands of critics. While it is lively and witty, its subject is not clearly enough defined, so that it moves uncertainly among international manners, satire, social comedy, and travel literature. Showing through the story is the antipathy that James felt towards Bostonians, whose queerness, he observes in an editorial aside 'was collective, not individual' (ANS, 354). In spite of this distaste and in spite of the indulgent contempt that he shows for his artist-hero, Florimond, there are several glimpses of processes taking place in his mind that seem analogous to those that had already taken place in James's. 'He perceived,' James wrote, 'that when one changes one's sky, one inevitably changes, more or less, one's standard' (ANS, 363). Florimond concludes, after a long look around, that 'even amid the simple civilization of New England there was material for the naturalist' (ANS, 373).

This recalls the remark that James made to C. E. Norton in 1871, after a return from a less protracted stay in Europe: 'The face of nature and civilization in this our country is to a certain point a very sufficient literary field. But it will yield its secrets only to a really *grasping* imagination.' As we have seen, the attempt to grasp the secrets had failed at that time. Armed with the techniques and attitudes of the Impressionists, he could see his way clear to making a new attempt. Through Florimond's consciousness, James revealed that he was turning away from normative European forms and Ruskinian ideals of beauty that he had been using as late as a year before in representing the consciousness of Miss Condit in *The Impressions of a Cousin* to a more scientific representation of experience. For Florimond, James wrote, 'It was not important ... that things should be beautiful; what he sought to discover was their identity, – the signs by which he should know them' (ANS, 355). As he also wrote in *The Art of Fiction*: 'One perceives ... that the province of art is all life, all feeling, all observation, all vision.'[11] Using impressionist techniques, James no longer felt that he had to select his material according to abstract ideals of aesthetics, but according to their value as symbols of meaning about society and as values in a composition.

Before he embarked on the novel that was to test this new theory, James wrote one more international story that gave dramatic form to the strictures of his French academician, Gustave Lejaune, in *The Point of View*. In 1884, he read a book recently published by an English Tory M.P., Sir Lepel Griffin, called *The Great Republic*. This was precisely the book that James's imaginary Frenchman would have writen on his return to France – one full of dire warnings to his countrymen about the possible spread of American democracy.

Sir Lepel wrote solemnly in his introduction: 'It is necessary that Englishmen should understand ... the demoralization which may fall upon a country which is so unwise as to surrender political power into the hands of the uneducated masses ...'[12] 'Democracy,' he later asserted, 'is everywhere tyranny.' As usual, life is copying art. Although Sir Lepel told James nothing that he had not already imagined, he did provide him with a factual precedent for a fiction. With this germ in mind, James wrote *The Modern Warning*, which is also the title of the book that the fictional 'resolute and consistent conservative,' Sir Rufus Chasemore, K.C.B., M.P., writes.

Agatha Grice marries Sir Rufus against the advice of her brother

Macarthy Grice, 'a passionate democrat, an unshrinking radical' (CT, VII, 35), like Marcellus Cockerell. Sir Rufus visits the United States with his wife, and does the usual tour. On his return to England he writes his book of impressions. When it is published the gulf between the Englishman and his American brother-in-law is fully revealed. The wife and sister is torn between her loyalties to her husband on the one hand and her brother and native country on the other. This is the sort of irreconcilable conflict that James had avoided in *The Point of View*. In *The Modern Warning*, it seems that the only way out for the girl is suicide – James's usual solution for a fictional deadlock, as in *Roderick Hudson* and *The Princess Casamassima*. Lady Chasemore's death, however, only delivers the *coup de grâce* to a story that held little promise from the beginning. *The Modern Warning* reveals as much as anything else the cessation of interest in a theme that had served him well for over ten years. As he wrote perceptively in his notebook after outlining the story, he was afraid that its internationalism might be found 'overdone, threadbare.'[13]

The time had come for James to concentrate on one country, to bring his various impressions and points of view about the United States into one sharp, dramatic focus. One thing seemed clear. Every point of view that James had invented, whether of returned expatriate, French Academician, German Count, or English Member of Parliament, had been made the vehicle for James's own amazement and concern at the domination of American society by women. It is the one consistent *leit-motiv* of this whole series of stories. An attempt to escape from it had led only to the creation of the absurd Mr. Caliph, a fantasy figure symbolizing the domination of the businessman. What was the explanation for this 'country of women'? Henry James's sole completed full-scale American novel was an attempt to answer this central question.

·Jc· 11 ·Jc·

A Very American Tale
The Bostonians

The recent spate of criticism on that long-neglected novel, *The Bostonians*, as good as some of it has been, has consistently missed the most important difference between it and James's previous novels: that it derives directly from French naturalism and signifies a radical, if temporary, shift in his fictional method and style.*

I do not mean to deny the importance of Hawthorne's influence on the novel, which has been rightly stressed. James was obviously recalling the reformers of *The Blithedale Romance* and some of the characters in Hawthorne's other novels and short stories, but the romance elements that dominate Hawthorne's fiction and that James himself had drawn on for some early tales and *The Europeans* were almost totally abandoned in *The Bostonians* in favour of a sharp realism. This is why Marius Bewley's claim of the almost complete indebtedness of *The Bostonians* to *Blithedale* is, in spite of the many parallels he draws, so misguided.[1] Some of the elements that Bewley claims that James drew directly from *Blithedale* for *The Bostonians* he used earlier in *Professor Fargo*. Verena is as much like the mathe-

---

*Two of the most perceptive discussions of *The Bostonians* are Lionel Trilling's introduction to the Chiltern edition (London, 1952) and Irving Howe's chapter in *Politics and the Novel*. Trilling's emphasis is on the sexual dislocation and the thinness of the social fabric, whereas Howe centres his discussion on James's irony and the novel's psychological penetration. He notes that while James was not politically oriented, his attitude in the novel is one of conservative scepticism.

matician's daughter as she is like Priscilla of *Blithedale*, and Selah Tarrant is more like Professor Fargo than he is like the magician Westervelt. Tarrant shares with Fargo a dubious past of communal societies, quack remedies, and delusions of fame. By the time that James wrote *The Bostonians*, he had assimilated and turned to different uses characters and events that had their origins in Hawthorne's fiction.

Most of the characters in *The Bostonians* had predecessors in James's own fiction. Basil Ransom is evolved from a long series of conservatives, generally European in origin. Some of these are M. Lejaune of *The Point of View*, Count Vogelstein in *Pandora*, and Sir Rufus Chasemore in *The Modern Warning*. Ransom's physical characteristics can be traced to a childhood acquaintance of Henry James when his family lived on Washington Place. Next door to them lived for a while a Southern family. A son, Eugene Norcom, was described in *A Small Boy and Others* as 'the slim, the sallow, the straight-haired and dark-eyed Eugene.'[2] These are also the physical characteristics of Basil Ransom. Mrs. Luna had her origins in the merry, rococo widow in *Guest's Confession*, and Olive Chancellor is prefigured by Lizzie Crow in *The Story of a Year* and Gertrude Wentworth of *The Europeans*.

The important thing, however, is not so much the origin of these types as how James put them all into the new form that grew out of his adaptation of impressionistic schemata, as first seen in *A New England Winter*. The primary source for *The Bostonians* is named by James himself, in a very rare confession of this sort. After outlining the novel in his notebook, he wrote: 'Daudet's *Evangéliste* has given me the idea for this thing.'[3] Critics have been reluctant to take James at his word. Mr. Bewley dismisses the remark by writing: 'Such a notice as this serves only as a distraction' – a distraction, of course, from the real source of the novel, *The Blithedale Romance*.[4] Oscar Cargill writes: '*L'Evangéliste* can be said to have supplied only one important element to ... *The Bostonians*'; that is, the situation of a strong, rich woman enslaving a less experienced member of her own sex.[5] Professors Matthiessen and Murdock also remark that James could have taken no more than the initial impulse from Daudet's novel.

All these critics have ignored a whole series of correspondences between the two novels and, what is more important, the fact that James borrowed from Daudet, as he had earlier from Turgenev, ways of observing and presenting reality in the United States. This is made clear, not only by comparison of the novels, but also by reference to an essay that James wrote on Daudet in 1883, a few months before he wrote his outline for *The Bostonians*. It is possible to project both his enthusiasm for and reservations about Daudet's *L'Evangéliste* forward to his own novel to see how he reshaped the schema he derived from Daudet in order to profit not only from his predecessor's success, but also from his mistakes.

The evangelist of Daudet's book is a Danish Protestant woman, a religious fanatic who has married a French banker of enormous wealth, M. Autheman. He is a mere cipher in the tale, which is largely devoted to an account of how she spends his money in propagating her repressive, cold, puritanical beliefs by training her converts in her own school, and sending them on foreign missions. James wrote of her: 'The figure is painted with Alphonse Daudet's inimitable art; no-one that handles the pen to-day is such a pictorial artist as he. But Madame Autheman strikes me as quite automatic; psychologically she is a blank. One does not see the operation of her character. She must have had a soul, and a very curious one. It was a great opportunity for a piece of spiritual portraiture; but we know nothing about Madame Autheman's inner springs, and I think we fail to believe in her.'[6]

Madame Autheman gets hold of a young and innocent country-woman of hers, living in Paris, called Eline Ebsen, in whom she sees a promising disciple. She is a sweet, intelligent girl who, shortly before coming under Madame's Autheman's influence, had promised to marry a widower with two young children. But Madame Autheman so works upon Eline's innocence and credulity that she renounces the world, gives up the widower and his family, leaves her adoring widowed mother, and devotes herself to religion. All this is achieved in about two-thirds of the novel. The remaining third is taken up with the pathetic attempts of Eline's mother to reclaim her daughter. But *L'Evangéliste* ends on a note of desolation as Eline is finally and irrevocably lost to her mother as she devotes herself to the cause.

James thought that Daudet had not presented Eline Ebsen any more convincingly than he had Madame Autheman. 'The logic of the matter,' he wrote, 'is absent in both cases.' The central flaw of the novel, James thought, was simply that Daudet did not know his subject. 'Proposing to himself to describe a particular phase of French Protestantism,' he wrote, 'he has "got up" certain of his facts with commendable zeal; but he has not felt nor understood the matter, has looked at it solely from the outside, sought to make it above all things grotesque and extravagant.'[7]

But when James came to outline *The Bostonians*, he proposed the subject to himself in a remarkably similar manner. 'I asked myself,' he wrote in his notebook, 'what was the most salient and peculiar point in our social life. The answer was: the situation of women, the decline of the sentiment of sex, the agitation on their behalf.' This means of selecting his subject was very different from James's more customary practice of enlarging upon anecdotes and incidents in his own experience. His consciousness of his debt to Daudet both in conception and plot is reflected in his concern for the title of the novel. Before selecting *The Bostonians*, he rejected 'The Reformers' and 'The Precursors' for fear that these titles would be clues to the origin of the novel in *L'Evangéliste*.

He had reason to be concerned, as even a comparison of the plots of the two novels reveals. Madame Autheman suggested the role of Olive Chancellor, who has been left a rich woman by her father. The innocent Eline Ebsen supplies the role of Verena Tarrant. Madame Autheman's large town house in Paris gives the idea for the snug house on Charles Street; the Autheman chateau finds its American equivalent in the cottage on Cape Cod. In addition, James adapted several of Daudet's incidents for his novel. For example, Madame Autheman tries to 'buy' Eline Ebsen from her mother in order to avoid a struggle for possession, but without success. James converts this incident into the successful 'purchase' of Verena from her parents by Olive. Even an apparently native touch like the 'immemorial waterproof' that Selah Tarrant perpetually wears, has its origins, seemingly, in the customary *'waterproofs plein de boue'* of Madame Autheman's followers.

In writing *The Bostonians*, however, James made vast improvements over *L'Evangéliste*, in part by following the pattern of his own criticism of Daudet's novel. He put the relationship between his two women at the centre of his work and explored it with great psychological insight. Moreover, he used this relationship, 'one of those friendships between women which are so common in New England,' as he put it in his notebook, as a means of commenting on a feminized society. Whereas in *L'Evangéliste*, Daudet had made Eline's mother the chief antagonist to Madame Autheman, James pushes Verena's ineffectual mother into the background. Eline's lover in *L'Evangéliste*, Lorie, is a weak and rather colourless civil servant who has been dismissed from his post in Algeria. Verena's lover, Ransom, is also from the South, but he brings with him a range of associations and a force of character that make him a worthy opponent to Olive. By this improvement on Daudet's schema, James not only makes the conflict more dramatic, he also underlines the sexual battle that lies at the heart of his novel.

It is in the style and tone of *The Bostonians*, however, that James owes most to Daudet. As he noted in the essay, Daudet achieved the feat of getting 'outside of his ingredients and judging them.' He was 'objective to his own vision.'[8] His detached, often scornful, attitude affected his style, which was sharp and epigrammatic. Following Daudet, James in *The Bostonians*, for the time being, abandoned the impartiality that he had derived from Turgenev and adopted the socially conscious role of the naturalist writer. The harsh, cold environment of New England is seen to have done much to shape the Bostonians into a sexless, rigid, radicalism, just as Ransom's Southern upbringing has given him the warmth and conservatism that sets him against everything the Bostonians stand for. In this novel, James abandoned the device of the point-of-view character that he had been experimenting with for so long. He found the model for his technique in the Gascon Daudet's fundamentally unsympathetic attitude towards his northern Protestant characters. Like Daudet he judged and commented on his characters freely. Sometimes the commentary is carried to the point of caricature, as it is with Mrs. Farrinder, the women's rights leader, and Miss Birdseye.

No wonder the novel caused an outcry in Boston. There was, after all, some justice, although also a good deal of offended local pride, in the charge that James had treated some of its representative types harshly. Since he did not get inside his characters to see their situations from their own points of view, he was able to treat them instead as figures not only formed by their environment but also easily manipulable for his comic and satiric purposes. It is true, as Irving Howe remarks, that James felt 'a free and happy release of aggressive feelings' in his novel,[9] and the satiric style that resulted sparkles brightly, but in some instances the characters are straw men and women set up only to be knocked down by his wit.

James did feel a certain sympathy for Olive Chancellor, more than he did, perhaps, for his 'hero,' Basil Ransom. Whatever her failings, she is a representative of 'good' Boston society, a transmitter of the Emersonian ideals of plain living and high thinking; she is 'distinguished and discriminating' (ANS, 562) and has 'a rich moral consciousness' (ANS, 545). The worst cross she has to bear (and it is her mission in life to bear crosses), is the necessity of associating with all the cranks and racketeers of the women's rights movement. Her attempted education of Verena's virginal and pliable nature is also a justification for her isolation from these cruderies and publicities in her cosy Charles Street drawing room. In the end, however, she has to come out and make her compromises with the newspaper world of Pardon, the lecture-platform mentality of Mrs. Farrinder, and the social world of Mrs. Burrage. Olive is not fundamentally interested in the women's rights movement, but is simply using it as a means of gaining power at the expense of the opposite sex. She would seem to be that familiar type of a woman in revolt against a dominant father figure who has become identified with the male sex in general. 'Any man that one would look at –' she says, 'with him, as a matter of course, it is war upon us to the knife' (ANS, 520). She wants, as Verena perceptively remarks, 'not only justice but vengeance' (ANS, 587).

The dammed currents of her passion are turned, therefore, in the direction of Verena, who, all innocence, seems unaware of any unnatural overtones in their relationship. The intensity of Olive's sexual involvement with Verena makes her battle with Ransom a fierce and bitter thing. With great skill, James combined the two elements of latent lesbianism and the women's rights movement into one character and theme and thus dramatized a central aspect of American experience after the Civil War. In many of his previous stories, he had ascribed the absence of the male from social life to his absorption in business. In *The Bostonians* he returns to the more fundamental theme that he had dramatized in the early Civil War tales *The Story of a Year* and *A Most Extraordinary Case*: the wounding and death of the hero. Ransom, of course, has survived the War, but he has seen many of his friends die and is himself a symbolic representative of defeat. He bears on his shoulders the whole burden of re-establishing (or ransoming) the male element in the life he sees around him. As such he fights against overwhelming odds.*

The central episode of the novel takes place in the Memorial Hall at Harvard. Verena, after saying to Ransom that it might be indelicate to take a Mississippian there, leads him to the monument dedicated to the fallen student-soldiers. Ransom says ironically, 'I must be brave enough to face them – it isn't the first time.' In the comment that follows, James is obviously recalling his own emotions on visiting the hall: 'The effect of the place is singularly noble and solemn, and it is impossible to feel it without a lifting of the heart. It stands there for duty and honour, it speaks of sacrifice and example, seems a kind of temple to youth, manhood, generosity. Most of them were young, all were in their prime, and all of them had fallen; this simple idea hovers before the visitor and makes him read with tenderness each name and place – names often without other history, and forgotten Southern battles' (ANS, 597). Ransom is deeply moved. Even Verena, who had first observed that it was a sin to put up a building to glorify bloodshed, finally admits it is very peaceful. After inspecting some of the tablets commemorating battles at which he had fought, Ransom's remarks to Verena take a personal turn. Their conversation becomes more intimate than it has ever been before. Significantly, too, he traces a pattern on the mosaic floor with his cane, a version of the 'figure in the carpet' that often indicates a

---

*Wasserstrom, noting that in popular fiction of the day, the Southerner was generally portrayed as one sunk in lust and carnality, maintains that James 'relied on the myth of Southern eroticism to underscore Ransom's effect' (34–5). Certainly the images of the north – ice, coldness, paleness – imply virginity, while Ransom's colouring, his language, and his gestures connote a tropical sexuality and warmth.

nodal point in James's work. 'They were discussing their affairs,' he adds, 'which had nothing to do with the heroic symbols that surrounded them; but their affairs had suddenly grown so serious that there was no want of decency in their lingering there for the purpose.' When they leave the Hall, they feel the first vague breath of spring.

In this significant passage, it seems that James is recalling the emotions he felt on his own return to the place of his substitute service in the War. The Memorial Hall of Harvard was a monument to the high hopes, the glory, the sacrifice 'of the best among them.' It also signifies the destruction of the irreplaceable flower of New England youth. The architecture of the Hall itself, however, seems to symbolize another of the results of the War – the sacrifice of proportion and taste in American life. It was, James writes, 'buttressed, cloistered, turreted, dedicated, superscribed.' Even Ransom sees that 'there was rather too much brick about it' (ANS, 596).

But the effect of the place on Verena's consciousness is sufficient to enable Ransom to break through the hard shell of her naïveté and knowingness, as well as the 'fine web of authority' that Olive has woven around her, to reach the essentially feminine nature beneath. Verena does not tell Olive of her meeting with Ransom, and it remains a constituted link between the couple, in spite of all Olive's subsequent attempts to destroy 'the sentiment of sex' in Verena's heart. On this link, Ransom constructs his chain of memory, of tenderness, and of love by which he finally draws Verena away from Olive's obsessed grip.

It is clear, however, that James did not intend to make Olive's defeat a noble victory for Ransom. Verena is a true American girl and she is not going to be subdued by a husband, as several remarks in the novel indicate. James obviously feels that American women have usurped men's roles so far as to make Ransom's mission practically hopeless. Ransom himself has a heroic concept of his task. 'My interest is in my own sex;' he tells Verena, 'yours evidently can look after itself.' He wants to save men 'from the most damnable feminisation.' 'The whole generation is womanised;' he goes on, 'the masculine tone is passing out of the world; it's a feminine, a nervous, hysterical, chattering, canting age, an age of hollow phrases and false delicacy and exaggerated solicitudes and coddled sensibilities ... The masculine character, the ability to dare and endure, to know and yet not fear reality, to look the world in the face and take it for what it is – a very queer and partly very base mixture – that is what I want to preserve, or rather, as I may say, to recover; and I must tell you that I don't in the least care what becomes of you ladies while I make the attempt!' (ANS, 663–4).

This is not so much heroic, however, as quixotic. Basil Ransom is a man born out of his time as well as one thrown out of his place. His rhetoric is part of the Walter Scott type of romanticism in the Southern temperament that Mark Twain was castigating about this same time. To underline this trait in Ransom, James uses several images of former aristocratic orders to describe his hero. 'Was he not like a French *gentilhomme de province* after the Revolution,' Mrs. Luna thinks, 'or an old monarchical *émigré* from the Languedoc?' (ANS, 571). Ransom is an aristocratic remnant in a bourgeois society. At a time when the nation's best male element had been destroyed by war, a war largely caused, Ransom maintains, by the motive power of female abolitionists, the misdirected energy of a soured Puritanism had driven women to establish a political as well as a numerical and moral superiority over men. Ransom's belief that he can correct this situation, noble as it is, is a part of what James called 'a thread of moral tinsel' in his make-up – the same thread that existed in 'the Southern idea of chivalry' itself (ANS, 653).

The hopelessness of Ransom's battle is dramatized by the extreme inequality of the sexes in this book. All the other males in the novel are on the women's side, and a poor collection they make. Verena's father, Selah, a 'moralist without moral sense,' is merely 'a charlatan of the poor, lean, shabby sort' (ANS, 505). From him stem the cheap theatrical elements in James's early definitions of Verena as a rope-dancer, circus-performer, and actress. His past consists of ventures in mesmerism, spiritualism, and Utopian communism; his present, of some vaguely defined faith-healing, which entails numerous visits to the ladies and a futile haunting of newspaper offices in the hope of 'columns' on himself or Verena. It is a needle-sharp portrait of New England reformism in its most decadent and shabby form. The news-paperman, Matthias Pardon, on the other hand, does not live for him-self at all but only for the press. For him the women's rights movement is merely the latest opportunity for brazen publicity. With his 'remarkably neat and pretty features,' he seems both impersonal and effeminate. His proposal of marriage to Verena appears to have no element of sexuality in it. His passion, James observes, 'included a remarkable disposition to share the object of his affection with the American people' (ANS, 511).

The last contender for Verena's affection is the rich young New Yorker, Henry Burrage, who seems at first sight to be the most masculine of the lot. It soon appears, however, that he is controlled by his mother, Mrs. Burrage, the typical society matron. Henry is the familiar Jamesian dilettante, 'weakly pretentious, softly original' (ANS, 544). Although he regards Verena as something to add to his collection of intaglio work and enamels, he has none of the viciousness of a character like Gilbert Osmond. At one point, Olive even considers marrying Henry to Verena, knowing that it would be easy enough for her to take over his mother's role and control him.

This completes the small cast of male characters. The rest of the novel, proportionate to its theme, is given over to the ladies. They are indeed an odd lot. The most likable is that wonderful example of the 'Yankee female,' Dr. Prance. She is, in fact, hardly a female at all, 'spare, dry, hard, without a curve.' Ransom sums her up as a product of 'the New England school-system, the Puritan code, the ungenial climate, the absence of chivalry' (ANS, 450). Her lack of sexuality has reached the point of annihilation: 'If she had been a boy she would have borne some relation to a girl, whereas Doctor Prance appeared to bear none whatever.' At least she is free of the cant of causes; caring only for medicine, she is as tough as she is technical. She is the other side of the coin to Mrs. Tarrant, whose sex appears to have been eroded by all the vagaries of her life with the unspeakable Selah. James has admirably caught the pathetic ineffectuality of the daughter of a great abolitionist, Abraham Greenstreet. Her sole occupation in the novel is nourishing delusive hopes of a social rise through her daughter's association with Olive. The images that James uses to characterize her are those of some piece of jetsam. She is 'bleached and tumid,' and her complexion has a 'kind of withered glaze' (ANS, 502).

The most notable portrait is Miss Eliza Birdseye, that relic of the heroic age of New England and of Emersonian self-reliance, who remembers 'Concord as it used to be' (ANS, 553). She had sheltered fugitive slaves from the South and refugees from defeated European revolutions. As a matter of course she had preached temperance and had been a member of every reforming league from the Short-Skirts on down. Although tired and vague now, she is a kind of monument in her own person. 'She was heroic,' James summed her up, 'she was sublime, the whole moral history of Boston was reflected in her displaced spectacles ...' (ANS, 446). She is not merely a comic figure, however. Ransom, who at first regards her with contempt, comes to like and even respect the old lady. When he discovers that she is dying, near the end of the novel, he offers to Dr. Prance to watch by the 'sacred flame,' to the outrage of Olive who thinks his presence is a mockery at the departure of this last link to the crusading spirit of New England.

William James and others protested that Miss Birdseye bore entirely too much resemblance to Hawthorne's reforming sister-in-law, Eliza Peabody. The charge greatly upset James, and he wrote his brother protesting that 'she was not in the smallest degree my starting-point or example.' He asserted that he had evolved Miss Birdseye entirely from his 'moral consciousness, like every other person I have ever drawn ...'[10] And yet, in his essay on Daudet in 1883, James, in defending Daudet's propensity to use acquaintances and figures of the day, remarked: 'The temptation to "put people into a book" is a temptation of which every writer of fiction knows something, and I hold that to succumb to it is not only legitimate but inevitable.' The real question, James went on, is the novelist's delicacy in conjuring away recognition or insisting on it.[11] It seems that in *The Bostonians*, James was, like Daudet, working much closer to life than had formerly been his custom, using his observations and memories of Boston scenes and characters. This method is essentially different from the one he had employed in writing *The Portrait of a Lady*, the characters of which, he recalled in his preface, 'simply, by an impulse of their own, floated into my ken ...'[12]

Irving Howe has wittily summed up the character of Olive's sister, Mrs. Luna. Her virginal name at first seems puzzling in association with the hair that is curled 'like bunches of grapes,' and her bodice which seems to 'crack with her vivacity.' Mr. Howe's observation that 'her sexuality has turned rancid,' and has been 'corrupted into a strategy for social acquisition' adequately explains the imagery.[18] James reinforces her essential falseness and sterility when he has Mrs. Luna refer to herself as 'a painted Jezebel' and Olive characterize her as 'a bundle of dress trimmings.' James sufficiently illustrates how low the fortunes of Ransom fall in the novel by having him for a short time consider marrying Mrs. Luna.

The two other women in the novel are not given as much space, but still come through with a startling clarity. There is Mrs. Burrage, who provokes Olive by having 'the air of a New Yorker who didn't particularly notice whether a Bostonian called or not' (ANS, 531). Mrs. Farrinder is the women's movement organizer who, 'at almost any time, had the air of being introduced by a few remarks' (ANS, 443). One of the remarks with which James introduces her precisely projects her force of character and her pomposity: 'She lectured on temperance and the rights of women; the ends she laboured for were to give the ballot to every woman in the country and to take the flowing bowl from every man.' The relative importance of Mrs. Farrinder's husband is indicated by this one of the three references he gets in the novel: 'She had a husband, and his name was Amariah.'

The range of characters in the novel sufficiently represents James's ruling ideas about the Bostonians. All of them except Ransom, an outsider, and Verena, an innocent, represent some distortion of personality that relates in some way to a dislocation of the sexual role. All James's sense of the misproportions, provincialisms and corruptions in American life were poured into his devastating observations about these creations. Yet he writes with an irony and urbanity reminiscent of Pope in his *Epistles*.* James, like Pope, satirizes manners and morals from a firm conviction of what they ought to be. Implicitly he is judging Boston by cosmopolitan standards of culture and traditional codes of morality.

In *The Bostonians*, James set out deliberately to reproduce the

---

*The Popean parallel is reinforced by James's description of Verena in terms reminiscent of Belinda in *The Rape of the Lock*, Canto II: 'Nature had given her a beautiful smile, which fell impartially on every one, man and woman, alike' (ANS, 508).

pictorial quality of Daudet's work, as he had in *A New England Winter*. In the earlier story he had had Florimond pick out 'bits' that would appeal to the eye of a painter. In the novel, however, he makes scenes functional to characters, none of whom has a painter's eye. Ransom, James remarks, is unobservant of his surroundings, but even he can see that the drawing room of Olive Chancellor's house on Charles Street, with its German books, its photographs and paintings, represents culture as well as comfort. Yet James intends many other things by the scene. It is a queer corridor-shaped room – as narrow as her personality. It overlooks at the back, as Irving Howe has remarked, 'the slowly accumulating seediness of the city itself as it stumbles into the factory age.'[14] The ugly images of industry and religion present Boston as a symbolic wasteland, a place where Olive's twisted ideas can flourish. Miss Birdseye's room is shaped like Olive's, but it is 'loose and empty.' When chairs are arranged along its sides it has 'the similitude of an enormous street-car' (ANS, 443), the democratic vehicle that Miss Birdseye is so fond of taking. Verena's parents' temporary lair in a back street in Cambridge has all the 'bald barrenness' of the Tarrants' life. There is nothing in it, to Olive's sense, 'but a smell of kerosene.' On the other hand, the temptations to which Verena is subject, as well as the character of Henry Burrage, are symbolized by his room at Harvard, in which the faint fragance of burning logs mingles with the perfumes of the melodies of Schubert and Mendelssohn. Ivory carvings and other precious objects gleam in the red fire-light. By contrast, Ransom, congruent with his own past and present circumstances, lives in New York, in 'two small, shabby rooms in a somewhat decayed mansion' next door to a Dutch grocer's. James mentions the store once again in *The Bostonians*, 'for old acquaintance sake and that of local colour' (ANS, 555).

The first part of the novel takes place almost entirely in these interiors in Boston at mid-winter, an appropriate time for such events. The recurrent imagery of ice and snow in the novel is also a metaphor for the city's Puritanism. When James compares the colour of Olive Chancellor's eyes to 'the glitter of green ice,' the reader is reminded of a similar use of imagery to characterize Mr. Wentworth in *The Europeans*. It is not until Verena and Ransom go out walking to look around Harvard at the first hint of spring that the novel comes out

into *le plein air*. It opens out again when in New York Ransom spirits
Verena away from Olive and takes her into James's old stand-by,
Central Park. In this 'cockneyfied landscape ... bright with the sense
of air and space,' Ransom begins to break through the wall of ideas
and attitudes that Olive has built around Verena (ANS, 668). When
they leave, they enter again the sterile setting of the city, with its
rattling street-cars, beer saloons, and groups of immigrants propping
themselves up against the wall of the park.

The New York episode is immediately followed by the events on
Cape Cod. Ransom has escaped the sweltering heat of the city to follow Verena to Olive's summer house. On an August evening, he
travels down from Boston in a train that rambles fitfully by straggling,
shabby woods and vague ponds and marshes. 'The ripeness of summer,' James writes, 'lay upon the land, and yet there was nothing of
the country Basil Ransom traversed that seemed capable of maturity;
nothing but the apples in the little tough, dense orchards, which gave
a suggestion of sour fruition here and there, and the tall, bright
golden-rod at the bottom of the bare stone dykes' (ANS, 670). The
imagery suggests the sterility of Olive's household, where Olive is
training Verena for her appearance at the Boston Music Hall, and
where Miss Birdseye, attended by Dr. Prance, is passing her last days.

When Ransom gets to Marmion (a fictional counterpart to Marion
that James mentions having visited in *The American Scene*), he stays
in a run-down hotel, and courts Verena like a 'follower' of a maid-
servant. In this tranquil backwater, amidst a comically rudimentary
society, the tone of the novel is low-keyed, in deliberate contrast to
the hysteria prevailing in the Boston scenes and the phrenetic quality
of those set in New York. All the while Olive, ice-cold yet feverish,
sits reading to the dying Miss Birdseye. In a last desperate exercise
of her power, Olive suddenly sends Verena into hiding, knowing that
she is now passionately in love with Ransom. When he comes to see
Verena, Olive tells him what she has done, with a shrill laugh of
triumph which 'might have passed almost as well for a wail of despair'
(ANS, 721).

In the last three chapters, the novel comes full circle. It is
November. Ransom arrives once more at Olive's house in search of
Verena, only to find, again, Mrs. Luna, whose desire for him has

been turned into rancour by his neglect. She would not tell him where
Verena was hidden, even if she knew. Neither would Matthias
Pardon, who comes round once more, notebook in hand, in search of
news. Ransom goes to the only place he can think of, the Music Hall,
where the lecture is to take place. Here the action of the novel builds
up to its splendid melodramatic climax. Inside, the hall looks to him
like a Roman arena. People are pouring in without seeming to begin
to fill it up. Soon the other actors in James's drama step on the stage
to see Verena's triumph: Mrs. Farrinder and Amariah, Mrs. Burrage
and Henry, and Verena's parents. Verena and Olive are out of sight.
An organ peals out and Ransom, knowing that his moment has
arrived, prepares to seek out Verena. He pauses for a moment with
his back to the stage and looks at the audience. What he sees is
reminiscent of Degas's paintings of the theatre: 'It had become
densely numerous, and, suffused with the evenly distributed gaslight,
which fell from a great elevation, and the thick atmosphere that
hangs for ever in such places, it appeared to pile itself high and to
look dimly expectant and formidable.' He then has a prevision of
'the ferocity that lurks in a disappointed mob' (ANS, 733), but this
only confirms him in his endeavour to save Verena from exposure to
the roaring crowd.

Ransom finally succeeds in penetrating to the room where Verena,
having sensed his approach, is delaying her entry onto the stage. In
spite of the uproar in the audience above, and all of the pleas of the
other characters, Ransom insists on taking Verena away at once. The
manager appears and shouts that this is 'the most magnificent
audience ever brought together! The city of Boston is under this
roof!' 'The city of Boston be damned,' says Ransom, echoing the
famous retort of William Henry Vanderbilt. As he leaves with
Verena, Olive rushes on stage to try to quieten the mob. It is her
final degradation, but at the same time, with acute psychological
penetration, James sees it as 'the fierce expiation' of her failure and
the fulfilment of her desire for martyrdom. She seems like 'some
feminine firebrand of Paris revolutions, erect on a barricade, or even
the sacrificial figure of Hypatia, whirled through the furious mob of
Alexandria' (ANS, 745).

Ransom throws Verena's long cloak around her head and body

and guides her, unresisting, through the groups of people, a little scared, who are already leaving. Verena says, 'Ah, now I am glad!' but Ransom sees that, beneath the hood, she is in tears. James cannot resist one last, omniscient turn of the screw: 'It is to be feared that with the union, so far from brilliant, into which she was about to enter, these were not the last she was destined to shed.'

In this way, James undercuts the victory of his hero and, at the same time, the significance of this rare 'happy ending.' Verena sacrifices a life of fame and comfort for poverty and adversity. As William McMurray points out, she only exchanges one set of absolutes for another in choosing Basil instead of Olive. And yet, James clearly does not intend this resolution to be entirely ironic. Verena's task, as McMurray observes, 'will be to learn how to live' in the actual and potential freedom of her own will and the challenge of her union with Basil.[15] Verena is redeemed by Basil's love from the idols of publicity and the sterile grip of Olive. The theme of the novel transcends its provincial ambience. James is concerned with dramatizing not merely a local political issue but also a universal moral problem. This is shown by the analogy that James draws between Olive's instruction of Verena and Michael's revelation to Adam of the future history of the world in Books XI and XII of *Paradise Lost*. 'Olive had taken her up,' James writes, 'in the literal sense of the phrase, like a bird of the air, had spread an extraordinary pair of wings, and carried her through the dizzying void of space. Verena liked it, for the most part; liked to shoot upward without an effort of her own and look down upon all creation, upon all history, from such a height' (ANS, 478). The implication is that for a time Verena is seduced from her proper role, both sexually and intellectually, and becomes a kind of false Adam. She says in her address to the social world of New York: 'Good gentlemen all, if I could make you believe how much brighter and fairer and sweeter the garden of life would be for you, if you would only let us help you to keep it in order! You would like so much better to walk there, and you would find grass and trees and flowers that would make you think you were in Eden.' This is 'the vision of the world' that Verena puts before her audience, one 'redeemed, transfigured, by a new moral tone' (ANS, 615).

Ransom takes a poor view of this 'tissue of generalities' and sees clearly the corruption that is taking place in Verena's pure nature. She has become the devil's advocate. He has to save her from these delusions by his love. Ransom's view is that of the fallen Adam, after the vision of Michael. Life he sees as hard and painful. He has no Utopian theories, has never seen any progress, and knows that man's only hopes for happiness in a fallen world depend on the private virtues of love and compassion, not on the illusions of power and publicity. He sees Olive as she can never see herself, as an exploiter of natural genius, as one intent on turning a beautiful, generous, and gentle young woman into a flaming Joan of Arc. Verena sees all the possibilities of her power in the glimpse of the huge crowd in the Boston Music Hall, but she also sees the face of Ransom, the one person who has come to mean more to her than all the citizens of Boston. She renounces her ambitions, puts Olive behind her, and goes off with him. It is the triumph of love, but also of the 'consummate innocence of the American girl' (ANS, 510), through which she has resisted the most subtle efforts to betray her sex and her own powers.

The happy ending of the novel, in all its ambiguity, does not obscure James's main contention. Verena is the exception that proves the rule that Boston women ruled its social, intellectual, and emotional life. James saw that the general dislocation of the Civil War, itself partly caused by New England's reforming womanhood, had left a power vacuum that American women, whom James had always seen as being full of energy and moral purpose, had rushed to fill. The consequence, as James saw it at least, had not been the achievement of the freedom and emancipation that they had happily anticipated. Instead there was a release of hysteria that revealed, as Lionel Trilling has remarked, a profound sexual disorientation. American men, for their part, had been eager not only to countenance this womanly zeal, but also to encourage it. The servile quackery of such men as Selah Tarrant had ministered to women's neuroses, while the brazen journalism of men like Matthias Pardon had made available the power that publicity exerted over a gullible populace. To make matters worse, the whole women's rights movement had been invested with such a rich cloak of altruism that its basic hypocrisy had been totally concealed. The sharp light of James's wit and the strong colours and symbols of his impressionist pictures of this society and its environment show up in detail the vast pretentions of post-Civil War Bostonian reformism.

James had high hopes for this novel, which he thought by far the best he had written up to that time. Its failure on publication was one of the bitterest set-backs he had to sustain in a lifetime of publishing reverses. Seeking to explain the novel's failure, he wrote to William: 'I had the sense of knowing terribly little about the kind of life I had attempted to describe ... I was afraid of the reproach (having seen so little of the whole business treated) of being superficial and cheap.'[16] Significantly, this is exactly the charge he had made against Daudet's *L'Evangéliste*. And it is true that Daudet seems often to be writing a polemic instead of a novel; he even goes so far as to give supporting footnotes from John Chapman's *History of Christian Revivals* and Mrs. Trollope's *Domestic Manners of the Americans*.[17] Perusal of James's novel does not reveal such factitious attempts to achieve authenticity. Probably the only way that James can be found fault with in this connection is that some of his characters seem too theatrical for their surroundings, like the Baroness Eugenia in *The Europeans*. It was as if James was trying to make up in liveliness what he lacked in certainty about these American types. Even allowing for this, he wrote one of the very few American novels of the nineteenth century to deal concretely with a social movement. In this respect, *The Bostonians* began where *The Blithedale Romance* left off.

The novel does, however, have faults of which James seems to have been unaware. Part of the trouble is structural. The absence of the hero for long stretches of the novel upsets the dialectic of forces on which it is based. In addition, the centrifugal force of James's interest in the queer manifestations of Boston reformism is often at work to deflect the forward march of the narrative. A greater part of the trouble seems to stem from the influence of Daudet on the novel, an influence that was, fundamentally, alien to James's genius. In adopting the kind of critical and ironic attitudes towards his characters that James found in Daudet, he forfeited the compassion and imaginative identity with them that we find in his best work. Although they are drawn with great care, the characters of *The Bostonians* do not, somehow, deeply involve the reader. Even the terrible pathos of Olive's situation is not fully realized. Verena sees in her qualities of an Electra or an Antigone but, although Olive has the will and strength of these tragic figures, she has little of their selflessness and nobility.* As a result of James's lack of emotional commitment to his characters, such as he gave to his more romantic heroines like Daisy Miller and Isabel Archer, the novel does not quite live up to its own high promise. The whole is less than the sum of its parts. The reader is finally left vaguely dissatisfied by Ransom's hollow victory over the forces of feminization.

On the other hand, the technique of literary impressionism and the naturalistic approach to character and event which James derived in large part from Daudet enabled him to see American life afresh, to grasp it more firmly and write about it more realistically than he had ever been able to do before. It enabled him to project a concrete sense of place without condescending to its lack of beauty or interest and also to identify Boston imaginatively with the lives lived in it.

In all his later years, James never lost his sense of disappointment at the injustice meted out to this book. In one of his last letters, written in 1915 to Edmund Gosse, he discussed the exclusion of the novel from the New York Edition. He lamented the fact that he had lost the opportunity to re-issue it and write a preface. The novel, he remarked to Gosse, was 'probably rather a remarkable feat of objectivity ...'[18] No doubt he would have amplified this view in his preface and, freed from the immediate soreness at its reception, particularly in Boston, gone on to comment that the situation in a sense crowned his whole endeavour. The Bostonians, in rejecting this wonderfully incisive and witty novel, had proved the main point about their awful moral earnestness. Their queerness, as he had pointed out in the earlier story, *A New England Winter*, was not individual, but supremely collective.

*Cargill has amplified this allusion to the *Antigone* by pointing out the resemblances between the action of *The Bostonians* and Sophocles' play (128–9). Similarities there are, but the Jamesian reference should not be taken too seriously, since he put it into the mouth of the naïve and unlettered Verena.

· 12 *·*

English Years
and
American Letters

It is well known that James's next novel, *The Princess Casamassima*, was no better received by the public than *The Bostonians*. As he complained to Howells, the two novels, between them, reduced the demand for his work to zero.[1] Like *The Bostonians*, *The Princess Casamassima* has come in for its share of revaluation lately. It now appears to have a central place in James's development as a novelist and thus must be given some treatment here.

As in *The Bostonians*, he was making an experiment in realism. Once again he uses the techniques of literary impressionism to present vivid pictures of London streets and interiors. Just how far he consciously went towards the impressionist techniques is shown by an unpublished letter that he wrote to Norton about his friend the painter, Burne-Jones, on 25 March 1889: 'He goes on working at (I believe) a great many large allegorical designs, in which his abundance and beauty of imagination are as striking as they have ever been, but which seem to me less and less in the direction in which painting becomes most interesting and most *itself* – more and more away from the open air of the world and the lovely study of the aspects and appearances of things and the real – or at any rate to me the fascinating – problems of the painter's art. He might paint exactly as he does if there were *no* open air, no light, nor atmosphere, nor aspects, nor appearances – nor moving, flushing, changing, larking ambient life.'[2] In the kinetic response to appearances that the impressionist theory emphasized, James found his favourite way of representing the changing face of life.

At first the action of *The Princess Casamassima* is presented externally and from an omniscient point of view. Like the naturalists, James shows how the environment has played its large part in forming the character and consciousness of his little bookbinder hero, Hyacinth Robinson. Leon Edel records how James went to visit Millbank prison so that he could use the place as the scene for Hyacinth's mother's death.[3] James also records in his preface to the novel how his habit of walking in all parts of London qualified him to represent Hyacinth's environment. Against this background James projects Hyacinth's consciousness of his aristocratic father to create in him the sense of betrayal and exclusion from society that would lead him to join the anarchist movement.

But whereas in *The Bostonians* James had diffused his narrative among several characters, in *The Princess Casamassima* he created a central figure with whom he could feel far more sympathy than he could towards any of his Bostonians. As the novel progresses and Hyacinth reaches maturity, James moves increasingly into the consciousness of the bookbinder and devotes less and less space to representation of the external world. In his preface to the New York Edition of the novel, he elaborately justified this treatment: 'This in fact I have ever found rather terribly the point – that the figures in any picture, the agents in any drama, are interesting only in proportion as they feel their respective situations; since the consciousness, on their part, of the complication exhibited forms for us their link of connexion with it.' The interest for James was mainly in characters who were, like Hamlet and Lear, 'finely aware and richly responsible.'[4] Hyacinth is, in fact, the first of the many Jamesian heroes whose consciousness becomes the theatre of action of the novel. This is the case particularly after he has received his little legacy from Miss Pynsent and goes to Paris and Venice to begin the education of his perceptions which ends only with the rejection of his assassin's role and his suicide.

In his article 'The Princess Casamassima: Its Place in the James Canon,' Mr. Walter Dubler has suggested that the second part of the novel is the turning point of James's career as a novelist. In entering Hyacinth's consciousness in Book IV, he claims, James created a new sense of immediacy. 'It is an immediacy,' he writes, 'growing out of an intricate intertwining of background threads weaving their way into a single consciousness and being magically rewoven into something entirely new. In each case cited, the external situation becomes part of the background, one of the factors which make possible that which occurs in the foreground. And the foreground consists entirely of the momentary drama of perception ... For the reader, now, the external "place" ceases to exist, except as it is recreated within the new center of consciousness.'[5] Mr. Dubler further claims that the change marks James's rejection of dramatic gesture in favour of symbol. The particular symbol that organizes Hyacinth's awareness of Paris is the guillotine, with all its penumbra of meanings as a creative as well as destructive image. This leads James, Mr. Dubler points out, towards the great organizing symbols of his later works – like the spoils, the dove, and the bowl.

Mr. Dubler has oversimplified the complexities of James's development in order to strengthen his case. The main point that he misses is that James was not yet quite convinced of the adequacy of the technique in the second part of *The Princess Casamassima*. In several chapters he deserts Hyacinth and presents scenes involving other characters. At other times he speaks in the persona of the omniscient author. All the same, Dubler's contention is valid – that James was expanding on the technique that he had used for the first time successfully in chapter forty-two of *The Portrait of a Lady*. With a few exceptions, his future fiction was to deal not with objective settings and characters but with a dramatized perception of scene and characters from the point of view of one or more characters in the novel. In other words, his work was to become increasingly involved with what goes on behind the eye of the recording observer.

This change was to have far-reaching consequences for his own fiction and the art of the novel in general. It also released him from some of the limitations of the literary schemata that he had applied to the formation of both setting and character in his previous fiction. By moving into the consciousness of a central character, by projecting himself empathetically into a different identity, James was able quickly to free himself from the limitations of many of the schemata he had derived from earlier writers. It was no longer a case of being 'outside of his ingredients' or 'objective to his own vision,' as he had described Daudet, and as he himself had been in *The Bostonians*; in using the point-of-view character, James becomes, like Tennyson's Ulysses, a part of all he has met. The traditional identity of the omniscient author, who tends to represent the norm of his society and to be a fixed part of the literary convention, is dissolved, and the persona of the novel recreates everything anew in 'the momentary drama of perception,' as Mr. Dubler aptly calls it. Seeing the world from another point of view was a familiar enough device in the English novel. What was new in James's method was re-interpreting all experience, sense-data, emotions, concepts, and intellectual processes to re-create the drama of perception from a variety of widely differing view-points.

In his ability to do this, James showed the fundamentally American nature of his imagination. The European novelist of James's day confronted a fairly static society and tended to use a concomitantly static narrative viewpoint. For example, in George Eliot's country towns, Thomas Hardy's Wessex, and Flaubert's provinces, the heroes seem to push more or less hopelessly against the seated physical and social realities that confront them. From Emerson onward, the American writer, on the other hand, has felt reality to be uncertain, and he has often taken a more personal, even more eccentric, view of society. Following this, in the nineteenth century at least, the American artists were often more experimental than the European, as in the case of Whitman in poetry, Winslow Homer in painting, and Charles Ives in music. The lack of a fixed class structure in the United States had a great deal to do with this situation, of course. In all the years that James lived in England, he never lost the sense of being outside the class system. E. S. Nadal recounts that a woman of the English middle class had said to James, apparently *à propos* of some discussion of manners: ' "That is true of the aristocracy, but in one's own class it is different," meaning, said James, "her class and mine." He did not wish to be confounded with the mass of English people and to be adjudged a place in English society in accordance with English standards.'[6]

Accordingly, James could project himself into the mind and posture of his little bookbinder and completely realize his world from that depressed point of view. It is worth noting that almost at the same time, Mark Twain was creating the recording consciousness of Huck Finn, to which he had worked through trying on the various masks of frontier raconteurs. Twain found a vernacular form which perfectly suited his talent, whereas James remained tied to a more traditional literary English; but, at the deepest level, their work reflects the same concern: to reinterpret reality through the perceptions of an innocent and alienated consciousness. Hyacinth is the first of the long line of sophisticated innocents that were to figure in James's work from then on – Maisie, the governess in *The Turn of the Screw*, Lambert Strether of *The Ambassadors*, Maggie of *The Golden Bowl*, and Gray Fielder of *The Ivory Tower*.

Tony Tanner has characterized the dominant American literary stance as that of wonder. He relates this emotion to the American writer's desire to excise the past and live in a constantly created present.[7] Wonder is certainly felt by these Jamesian heroes. James, however, unlike Emerson and Twain, did not deny the past, but attempted instead to incorporate the sense of it into the consciousness of the present in his characters. Hyacinth writes from Venice to the Princess about his awareness of the totality of the place as: 'the monuments and treasures of art, the great palaces and properties, the conquests of learning and taste, the general fabric of civilisation as we know it, based if you will upon all the despotisms, the cruelties, the exclusions, the monopolies and the rapacities of the past, but thanks to which, all the same, the world is less of a "bloody sell" and life more of a lark ...'[8] The various forms of the past and the schemata that they had supplied James for his fiction enrich the consciousness of his characters in novel after novel. Mark Twain, on the other hand, like so many American writers, could not sustain the quality that he had, with almost as much luck as skill, displayed in *Adventures of Huckleberry Finn*. His attempt to re-create the past, in a novel like *A Connecticut Yankee in King Arthur's Court*, resulted in sentimentality and confusion as well as comedy.

In the preface to *The Princess Casamassima*, Henry James insisted that he could not see the leading interest of any situation 'but in a consciousness ... subject to fine intensification and wide enlargement.'

This did not prevent that consciousness from feeling bewilderment – which is often a kind of wonder – but that bewilderment is backed in James's later characters by an intelligence and sensitivity that responds to the complexities of life not by merely 'slashing out' at them. He felt he had succeeded in creating Hyacinth's consciousness effectively, even as to his 'subterraneous politics and occult affiliations.' There was the danger that this representation might be challenged by readers with a greater knowledge than his, and he had to admit that he, along with society in general, did not know what went on 'irreconcileably, subversively, beneath the vast smug surface' of London. James had expressed the same doubts about his knowledge of Boston for his previous novel. He did not appear to think, however, that this ignorance vitiated *The Princess Casamassima*. He wrote at the end of his preface: 'What it all came back to was, no doubt, something like *this* wisdom – that if you haven't ... the sense of life and the penetrating imagination, you are a fool in the very presence of the revealed and assured; but that if you *are* so armed you are not really helpless, not without your resource, even before mysteries abysmal.'[9] In creating Hyacinth, James had found his method of best using his sense of life, of penetrating surfaces and grasping realities that had hitherto eluded him. Given this technique he would, in time, sound even the 'mysteries abysmal' of American life.

For the time being, however, he believed that America was closed to him as a field for fiction. He settled happily back into the warm, thick stream of London life and addressed himself exclusively to English subjects. He resented editors' requests for stories on the international theme which had made him famous. In a letter to William written in October 1888, he wrote: 'I am deadly weary of the whole "international" state of mind – so that I *ache*, at times, with fatigue at the way it is constantly forced upon me as a sort of virtue or obligation. I can't look at the English-American world, or feel about them, any more, save as a big Anglo-Saxon total, destined to such an amount of melting together that an insistence on their differences becomes more and more idle and pedantic ...' He wished to write so that no one could tell whether he were English or American. 'The great thing,' he added, 'is to be *saturated*.'[10]

As his years in England rolled away, any illusions or romantic notions that he might have once held about the country gradually disappeared. Van Wyck Brooks was quite wrong when he insisted that James's vision was always fogged by the glamour of Europe. In a letter to C. E. Norton, written in 1889, he complained about 'this frumpy old England, where things are getting to be as slipshod from a want of freshness as they have long been with us from an excess of it. The things I am more particularly thinking of, those of the mind – or the higher parts of it – don't impress me here any longer so much with the ancient superiority that the imagination has always lent them. In a word, the glamour, the prestige and the mystery have – subjectively no doubt – been much rubbed away from the visage of the old England; she doesn't strike me as so very "distinguished" and I am, I fear, glaringly conscious of the ugly and clumsy sides of what she has to show – the vast miseries and meannesses of London, e.g. – which have been suffered to grow so myriad-headed – rather than of the rich and beautiful characteristics.'[11] As a result of this disillusioned view, James was able to write, in *The Tragic Muse, The Spoils of Poynton, What Maisie Knew, The Awkward Age*, and many short stories, some of the most penetrating and ironic studies of English social life in existence.

As the nineteenth century drew to its close, however, James, who had been unable to get away from England even as far as France for some years, began to have vague nostalgic yearnings for his native land. In June 1897, he wrote to an American friend, Frances Morse, to thank her for a letter shining with 'good solid vivid Boston truth' and 'full of interesting substance as always and of things no one else has the imagination or the inspiration to tell me.' He had recently seen a magazine picture of the new bas-relief by Saint Gaudens of Colonel R. G. Shaw and the 54th Massachusetts, the regiment of Negro troops in which his brother Wilky had served, which had been installed opposite the State House in Boston. It made him reflect to Miss Morse that since he had left America a whole generation had grown up for whom the Civil War was 'as alien as the battles of Alexander.' It gave him a prospect of a new revivifying force in American life. In closing the letter, he could not resist comparing his 'smoky London stuffiness' with the *milieu* of the Morse's home at Beverly, in 'the element of wide verandahs, cut peaches – I mean peaches and cream, you know – white frocks and Atlantic airs.'[12] For a time, however, this incipient home-sickness was quelled when James acquired, in that same summer, Lamb House, Rye, the weathered, red-brick Georgian house that was to be his much-loved home for the rest of his days in England.

His interest in America seems to have revived on the visit to England of his old friend William Dean Howells, in November of 1897. In January 1898, he wrote to thank Howells for his 'admirable counsel and comfort' during that period. It had made all the difference to him and left him with 'an exciting, absorbing feeling of occupation and preoccupation ...'[13] According to Leon Edel, Howells was able to arrange for the serial publication of some of James's work in the United States. Their discussions must also have touched on American literature, for soon afterwards James agreed to write a series of 'American Letters' to the newly-founded English periodical *Literature*, to which Howells also contributed. For one who had been so long out of America, it was an odd assignment. Moreover, it was the first time that he had agreed to write articles on any regular basis since his last contribution to the *Nation* in 1879. He appears to have been given *carte blanche* to review any kind of American book. His first paper, *The Question of the Opportunities*, appeared in the first issue, 26 March 1898. From then on his essays appeared almost every week until 9 July of that year.[14]

James started off by discussing the growth of an immense American reading public and the influence that 'a great common-schooled and newspapered democracy' could exert on the production of literature. He noted that, in spite of all other temptations, English was emerging as the great mill for grinding all the diverse elements of the nation into unity. He had realized by this time – as Tocqueville had pointed out long before – that the literature that would emerge from these conditions was bound to be different from that of previous ages. Critics, he observed, had to beware of 'the foregone conclusions and narrow rules.' The new masses not only gave wide opportunities for the production of literature: they also provided the possibility of the emergence of special publics, 'shoals of fish rising to more delicate bait,' who would 'assist individual genius or save individual life ...'

Puritan culture, he concluded, had exhausted its opportunity. The

New England voice was no longer predominant. Two books he had read, Mrs. Field's life of Harriet Beecher Stowe and John Jay Chapman's *Emerson and Other Essays*, appeared to refer to a past already far behind. 'The American world of today,' he asserted, 'is a world of combinations and proportions different from those amid which Emerson and Mrs. Stowe could reach right and left far enough to fill it.' Knowing as we do how limited James had thought this world to have been, we can understand his pleasure at this prospect.

One novelist whom he thought to be taking advantage of the new field of opportunities was Owen Wister. In his novel about cattle-punching, *Lin McLean*, 'the manners of the remoter West' were worked into the American air at large. Plenty of other subjects suggested themselves to James that could be seized upon by young American writers. One that immediately came to mind was the comparatively untouched businessman, whose possibilities worked James up to a wonderful proliferation of clauses and mixture of metaphors: 'He is,' he wrote, 'often an obscure, but not the less often an epic, hero, seamed all over with the wounds of the market and the dangers of the field, launched into action and passion by the immensity and complexity of the general struggle, a boundless ferocity of battle – driven above all by the extraordinary, the unique relation in which he for the most part stands to the life of his lawful, his immitigable womankind, the wives and daughters who float, who splash on the surface and ride the waves, his terrific link with civilization, his social substitutes and representatives, while, like a diver for shipwrecked treasure, he gasps in the depths and breathes through an air-tube.' It was essentially he, James maintained, who had fought the Civil War, and, having won it, had gone back to his business, 'with an undimmed capacity to mind it.' This fact, along with his magnanimous abasement before the opposite sex, touched him 'with the romance of fact ... that quite puts to shame the romance of fiction.' In the field of letters, too, women exercised the predominant role, as they did in so many things in America. There is more than a trace of irony in the way he celebrated his 'sense of sport' in looking forward to 'how *they* took their vast opportunity.'

His second letter, *The American Novel*, is equally remarkable for its enthusiasm for recent American writing. Although rather hostile to a new 'international' novel by Gertrude Atherton, he is warm in his praise for the midwesterner Hamlin Garland, whose work must have been introduced to James by Howells. Fiction from the United States was most interesting, he observed, when it was most local, 'even abjectly passive to surrounding conditions.' 'Saturation,' as he called it, was of more value to the novelist than mere talent. He could call Hamlin Garland, with all honour, 'the soaked sponge of Wisconsin.' In this essay, James revoked his own prophecy of 1881 that for fifty years at least the American novelist would have to deal with Europe. Garland's example, indeed, made him feel nervous that American talent should wish to sail eastward. Discussing another regional novelist, he remarked: 'On the day Miss Mary Wilkins should "sail" I would positively have detectives versed in the practice of extradition posted at Liverpool.' It was a curious statement for the inveterate expatriate to make, and it indicates that James was, once again, thinking about the consequences of his own decision of twenty-five years before.

Henry James's re-awakened sympathy for his native land is shown most clearly by his review of two books which in earlier years he would have passed over in charitable silence. The first was a selection of General Grant's letters, mostly written on his post-presidential European tour, and the second was the Calamus letters of Walt Whitman. He enjoyed the former, even though they were 'as hard and dry as sandpaper,' and quoted with approval some of Grant's statements that sounded 'the old American note.' The tone and style of these letters reminded James of 'an old, dry portrait,' or 'an old angular piece of furniture' that affected the 'historic, not to say the aesthetic, sense.'

Whitman's letters appealed to neither of these so much as to the democratic sense. The new book would appeal mainly, James thought, to 'the Whitmanite,' whom he defined as one for whom 'the author of *Leaves of Grass* is, with all his rags and tatters, an upright figure, a *successful* original.' James now appeared to number himself among these, for, in a remarkable switch from his stand of thirty years before, he praised these letters as being 'vividly American.' They had, he thought, 'a thousand images of patient, homely, American life' and a strong natural beauty, 'the man's own overflow in the deadly dry setting, the personal passion, the love of life plucked like a flower in a desert of innocent, unconscious ugliness.' His was an audible New Jersey voice. 'The reader,' James added, 'will miss a chance who does not find in it many odd and pleasant human harmonies.' In spite of all the drawbacks placed on it by the environment, the record remained 'positively delightful.' The reason why was a neat riddle 'for the sphinx of democracy to offer.' The riddle, however, was surely not propounded by that sphinx, but by James's own re-awakened sense of his native land. Whitman had not changed, but James had. This fact is underlined by his sympathetic review, three weeks later, of Whitman's letters to his mother, collected under the title *The Wound Dresser*. To James this volume held up its 'jagged morsel of spotted looking-glass' to 'the suffering and sacrifice of the American people' during the Civil War, without 'unhappy verbiage or luckless barbarism.' In other words, James had learned to see that various kinds of voices and visions could represent American experience in literature other than the strictly belletristic forms by which he had judged Whitman's work in the 1860s. The liberation he had found in his ability to represent various points of view in his work extended also to his being able to perceive virtues in writers who, twenty years before, were anathema to him.

The geniality that James had shown in the early essays was sorely tried by some of the American books which he discussed in the later. Novels by George Eggleston, Paul Leicester Ford, R. W. Chambers, and others left him gasping equally at their ineptitude and their sales. Of Chambers' *Lorraine: a Romance*, he asked, 'Why in the world operetta – operetta, at best, with guns?' A novel by the fecund Winston Churchill intended satire but, in James's opinion, achieved 'mere slashing at the wall.' Another by Bret Harte showed him still working his exhausted Western mine. A spate of dialect novels merely proved 'how little the cultivation of vulgar linguistics is a guarantee of the cultivation of any other truth.' All these were sharp tests for his theory about the development of special publics. How could books like these develop anybody? In the hopes of finding more fruitful guides to modern American thought, James turned increasingly to non-fiction: to travel literature, history, criticism, political science, even to the magazines.

In a backward reference to magazines read in his youth there is a tantalizing reference to Herman Melville as a contributor to *Putnam's*. Melville published *Israel Potter* and 'Benito Cereno' there, among other things; James, however, mentions only his prose style, 'as mild and easy as an Indian summer in the woods ...'

The modern magazines, James granted, were an educative influence on their mass audience. Although there was a lot of poor stuff in them, they were always on the march into barbarian territory. 'They mostly love dialect,' he concluded, 'but they make for civilization.' The same could not be said, however, about Theodore Roosevelt's book *American Ideals*. James thought of himself as a loyal American, yet he recognized how little he himself fitted the definition that the great nationalist insisted on. The mindless chauvinistic patriotism that Roosevelt required was appalling to James. 'The best he can do for us,' he wrote of the future President, 'is to turn us out, for our course, with a pair of smart, patent blinders.'

The penultimate 'American Letter' deals with some works on education and a book called *Unforeseen Tendencies of Democracy*, by the editor of the *Nation*, James's old friend, E. L. Godkin. He had read no more interesting volume than this in his recent strenuous bout of reviewing. The author had the benefit of 'intense saturation' in his subject; he was 'mercilessly lucid' and good-humoured. Obviously he provided James with insights into American life that he had looked for in vain among most of its novels. Godkin devoted most of his space to pointing out problems in legislation and administration that had not been foreseen by those who had initiated democratic government in America. Among other things, he discusses the nominating system, the decline of the legislatures, and the corruption of municipal government. Many of his strictures were as harsh as those of James's fictional Tory M.P., Sir Rufus Chasemore, in *The Modern Warning*, written fifteen years before. Godkin's conclusions were, however, quite different from those of Sir Rufus. James quoted one of them in full: 'Is the situation then hopeless? Are we tied up inexorably simply to a choice of evils? I think not. It seems to me that the nomination of candidates is another of the problems of democracy which are never seriously attacked without prolonged perception and discussion of their importance ... Every one of them looked hopeless in the beginning; but the solution came, in each case, through the popular determination to find some better way.'

James was excited to find that a man of Godkin's intelligence and experience could be so optimistic. He commented: 'What indeed may well give the book a positive fascination for almost any American who feels how much he owes it to his country that he is what he may happen to be is the way in which the enumeration of strange accidents – and some of the accidents described by Mr. Godkin are of the strangest – modifies in no degree a final acceptance of the huge democratic fact. That provides, for such a reader, an element of air and space that amounts almost to a sense of aesthetic conditions, gives him firm ground for not being obliged to feel mistaken, on the whole, on the general question of American life.'

A reading of Nicholas Murray Butler's *The Meaning of Education* confirmed this optimism and gave James a sense of 'the great things that, from quarters so interspaced, may more and more find themselves gathered together under the wide wings of the language.' These and other comments on American life and letters in this series of essays indicate an enthusiasm of the kind that James had not felt since his youth. There is even something of Whitman's *éclat* in his acceptance of the 'air and space' of democracy. In the past it had seemed to him mostly to encourage all the powers of ugliness. Now, with the help of a new generation, the old American values of freedom and opportunity, he felt, had been revivified.

It was about this time, also, that James re-evaluated the American writer who had always influenced him most – Nathaniel Hawthorne. The rather grudging respect that he had paid him in his English Men of Letters study of 1879, gave way to generous praise and heightened appreciation in an essay he wrote on his work in 1897 and in the long letter he sent to the Hawthorne Centenary celebrations in 1904. In the essay, an introduction to selections of his work in an anthology, he said nothing about Hawthorne's provincialism or of the limitations of his environment. On the contrary, he pointed out that Hawthorne's 'distinguished mark' was in his 'feeling for the latent romance of New England, which in summary form is the most final name to be given, I think, to his inspiration.' His imagination had been equal to the task of working up stories from his environment, and by his ability to 'go behind' for the suggestive idea and the expressive motive. He had made most of all, James remarked, of 'the great complication ... the pressing moral anxiety, the restless individual conscience.' In the Centenary letter he concentrates on Hawthorne's saturation in 'the blissfully homogeneous community' of Salem in the eighteen-forties and fifties. Unlike so many romanticists, he had not found it necessary to go 'outside' for his subjects, but had remained true to place even while he cast a romantic spell over his readers.[15]

This is a far distance from James's position in *Hawthorne*, in which he had in large part blamed the *milieu* for the romancer's artistic inadequacies. The lack of 'paraphernalia' placed, he thought, an intolerable limitation on the novelist and, at least by implication, the 'aridity' of American life in general made artistic excellence almost impossibly hard to achieve. In his re-evaluation of Whitman and Hawthorne, James was placing the onus where it belonged: on the artist rather than on his *milieu*. Both men, he believed, had been strong and original enough to triumph over the lack of social and artistic amenity. They had *made* the interest by their particular means of perceiving reality in America and converting it into poetry and romance.

When James returned to the United States again for the setting of a story, it was precisely to make something out of the theme of deprivation. '*Europe*,' published in 1899, fourteen years after his last American story, is intensely American because of the intensity with which three spinster sisters yearn to get to Europe, the promised land. Its theme is one that he had recently judged to be at the heart of Hawthorne's work: 'the pressing moral anxiety, the restless individual conscience.'

The story begins: 'It's a memory of the American time, which revives so at present – under some touch that doesn't signify – that it rounds itself off as an anecdote.' That American memory supplied James with the imagery and characters of the tale, and the faint, ironic nostalgia with which it is invested.

To gauge the distance that James had moved in his ability to write short stories over a twenty-year period, it is profitable to compare '*Europe*' with *Four Meetings*, an analogous tale, published in 1877. *Four Meetings* is told by a narrator who meets the spinster schoolmistress heroine for the first time at the house of a friend's mother in North Verona, a village somewhere in New England. He shows her photographs of Europe, from which he has just returned, and discovers her deep, quiet yearning to go there. The second and third meetings take place in the Havre. The narrator discovers that she has just landed for her long-anticipated grand tour. However, she is met by her good-for-nothing cousin who tells her that he needs money as he is in debt and has secretly married a countess. The schoolmistress gives him all her money and then leaves by the next boat for the United States. The fourth meeting is in the schoolmistress's little house back in North Verona. The narrator finds that the so-called countess is living with her, for her husband, the cousin, has died and she has come to live off the person she claims is her only relative – thus ending for all time any hopes of another trip to Europe for the schoolmistress. The story is told episodically and chronologically; the narrator is hardly characterized at all, and acts merely as the channel through which the story flows. He makes the appropriate remarks when the little schoolmistress is deprived of her dream, cheated of her savings, and exploited by the widow.

'*Europe,*' on the other hand, is all contained within the retrospective consciousness of the narrator, as the quotation from the beginning of the story indicates. The meetings of the narrator with the ancient Mrs. Rimmle and her three daughters all take place in the parlour of the house in the 'almost pastoral sweetness of the good Boston suburb' of Brookbridge. The tone of the story, its setting, and the characters are finely unified through the perception of the sophisticated, travelled, humorous New Yorker who is the narrator. 'It was another world,' he writes, 'with other manners, a different tone, a different taste; a savour nowhere so mild, yet so distinct, as in the square white house – with the pair of elms, like gigantic wheat-sheaves, in front, the rustic orchard not far behind, the old-fashioned door-lights, the big blue-and-white jars in the porch, the straight bricked walk from the high gate – that enshrined the extraordinary merit of Mrs. Rimmle and her three daughters' (ANS, 747).

The narrator pieces the story together on the basis of a series of visits that he makes to the house over many years. Far back, he relates, not long after Waterloo, Mrs. Rimmle had gone to Europe with her husband, a famous orator. Ever since then, and long after the orator's death, the daughters, Becky, Maria, and Jane, had looked forward to retracing their parents' path to Europe, the source of so many of their mother's memories and mementoes. But each time the trip appears imminent, the old lady falls ill and they never leave. After many years, the youngest, Jane, finally makes the break and gets away, never to return. The old lady, who, after this, begins to fail of lucidity, eventually pronounces her dead. The eldest daughter, Becky, not only sympathizes with Jane but also supplies her with money. Under the strain of deceiving her mother, however, she dies. The old lady, now little more than a mummy, is left alone in the house with the middle daughter, Maria. Mrs. Rimmle gaspingly asks the narrator on his final visit if he knows where Becky has gone. The narrator has an inspiration. 'To Europe?' he asks. 'To Europe,' says Mrs. Rimmle.

The mind of the narrator becomes the scene where the drama is played out, an echoing chamber of all that he hears. In the earlier *Four Meetings*, the narrator, while showing the schoolmistress some pictures of Castle Chillon, misquotes some lines from Byron. The story goes on: 'She fanned herself a moment and then repeated the lines correctly, in a soft, flat, and yet agreeable voice. By the time she had finished, she was blushing. I complimented her and told her that she was perfectly equipped for visiting Switzerland and Italy' (CT, IV, 90). In *'Europe'* the narrator also refers to Switzerland and the Italian lakes – ' "Como, Bellaggio, Lugano." I liked to say the names to them.

"Sublime but neither bleak nor bare – nor misty are the mountains there!" Miss Jane softly breathed, while her sister looked at her as if acquaintance with the poetry of the subject made her the most interesting feature of the scene she evoked.'

The direct quotation and its reported effect are immensely more effective than the indirection of *Four Meetings*. The poetry illuminates a great deal more than yearning for Europe. It dramatizes also the helpless, adoring quality of the relationships between the sisters. At the same time, the complacent superiority of the narrator is given a delicate rebuke.

By such devices *'Europe'* suggests wide ranges of feeling and nuance. The narrator rapidly becomes aware that old Mrs. Rimmle is holding her age and her potential ill-health like a sword above the heads of her devoted daughters. But her tyranny is seldom directly alluded to; it is represented by the imagery that the narrator uses about her. She is 'perched like a vulture' over them; she is 'a subtle old witch.' He also delicately shows the daughters' growing awareness of their mother's vicious power over them, and their pathetic attempts not to betray this knowledge as the narrator keeps calling on them, himself with a cat-like curiosity to see the end of this death-struggle.

The villains in *Four Meetings* are clearly the cousin and his bogus countess widow. In *'Europe'* the evil is more subtly distributed. The old lady is often described as 'magnificent' by the sisters and the narrator, although he has, mentally, to draw the line when one of them describes her as being better than Europe. Her magnificence, however, is all in her grim determination to hang on to life at the expense of the lives and hopes of her aging daughters. On his penultimate visit, the narrator reflects that her intensely aged face and her dauntlessness 'might have been that of some immemorial sovereign, of indistinguishable sex, brought forth to be shown to the people in disproof of the rumour of extinction' (ANS, 759). She is death in life, and she can tyrannize over her daughters just so long as she has the advantage over them that she has been in Europe and they have not.

The trip to Europe is seen again, as in the earlier stories, not only as an education but also as a form of life-giving experience. When Jane finally makes her dash, the Hathaways who go with her and have to return without her, say that 'She has tasted blood.' Once having done so, there is no prospect of her returning to the thin experience suggested by the name of Brookbridge. So Mrs. Rimmle pronounces her dead, for she has lost that control over Jane that is the source of her own predatory vitality. Becky, finally sucked dry by this tyranny, dies before her mother. Becky can therefore be allowed her 'trip' to 'Europe,' for her mother has won that battle.

The final image of the house containing the mummylike figure of the old lady and the third sister, Maria, who now looks as old as her mother and who can never go to Europe, is a picture of Gothic horror almost as effective as Faulkner's 'A Rose for Emily.' The narrator sees everything, yet he states nothing. Everything is implied by the language and gestures of the characters and assembled in the ironic, sympathetic, and almost diabolically prescient vision of the New Yorker. *'Europe'* is the quintessence of the New England idea of duty and conscience. Between them these deadly virtues destroy whatever instinct and desire for life remain in Becky and Maria. Only Jane is away in Europe trying to make up for all the years of life she has missed while looking after her mother in Brookbridge. This is the theme, of course, that James was to take up so effectively in *The Ambassadors*.

The sense of liberation that Europe brings, which James expresses in the figure of Jane, was not incompatible with a nostalgia for America. This appeared to grow in James as the century neared its end. As William's two sons, Harry and Billy, grew up and became immersed in varieties of American life, Henry could not help comparing their experiences with those of his own childhood. In a letter to his brother written in April 1899, he wrote: 'Nothing you tell me gives me greater pleasure than what you say of the arrangements for Harry and Billy in the forest primeval and the vision of their drawing therefrom experiences of a sort that I too miserably lacked (poor Father!) in my own too casual youth.'[16] He urged William to conjure his sons to 'contract local saturations and attachments,' to strike roots into their *'own* great and glorious country.' Looking back on his own life from the vantage point of his fifty-six years, he felt that the international jaunts on which Henry James, Sr., had led his children had been one of the chief causes of his own alienation from America.

This reviving sense of the opportunities and promises of his native land surely had a great deal to do with his revived interest in the international novel at the turn of the century. The sense of creative tension that had animated the earlier novels on that theme came back to suggest the subjects for the three great novels of the major phase, *The Ambassadors, The Wings of the Dove,* and *The Golden Bowl.* Although a discussion of these novels lies outside the scope of this study, it should be noted in passing that many critics have observed in them a tendency towards fable or romance. In *Anatomy of Criticism,* Northrop Frye, discussing the forms of the novel and the romance, points out a rule that bears directly on James's situation at this time. 'The novelist deals with personality,' he writes, 'with characters wearing their personal or social masks. He needs the framework of a stable society, and many of our best novelists have been conventional to the verge of fussiness. The romancer deals with individuality, with characters *in vacuo* idealized by revery, and, however conservative he may be, something nihilistic and untamable is likely to keep breaking out of his pages.'[17] As a generalized description of the novels of the major phase, this could hardly be bettered, for in them, James combined the stable European society and often fussily depicted conventions of the novelistic tradition with idealized American characters of romance to produce a conflict that is often only just contained short of disintegration. Witness, for example, the confrontation of Sarah Pocock and Madame de Vionnet in *The Ambassadors*, Maggie Verver prowling around the house in which the other characters of the novel sit playing cards in *The Golden Bowl*, and the storm-lashed Venice in which Millie lies dying in *The Wings of the Dove*.

Although the imaginary towns of Woollett, Massachusetts, and American City are symbolically suggestive of restriction, narrow conscience, and remorseless duty, they are still seen as sources of moral spontaneity and integrity. By contrast, the stable hierarchical societies of London, Rome, and Paris often seem almost melodramatically sinister. The conflict between the American and European characters frequently becomes idealized and takes place in the rarefied atmosphere of romance. There is interesting evidence that Henry James himself was unaware of this process. Edith Wharton, commenting on how these later novels seem 'more and more severed from that thick nourishing air in which we all live and move,' relates that she asked the Master: 'What was your idea in suspending the four principal characters in *The Golden Bowl* in the void? What sort of life did they lead when they were not watching each other, and fencing with each other? Why have you stripped them of all the *human fringes* we necessarily trail after us through life?'

After a pause of reflection, James replied: 'My dear – I didn't know I had!' and Edith Wharton realized that the question had 'turned his startled attention on a peculiarity of which he had been completely unconscious.'[18] Mrs. Wharton may have underestimated the quality and amount of novelistic detail that lends weight to these books, but she certainly seized on the romantic characteristics with which James, nostalgically remembering his native land, had endowed these international novels.

A year or two after the turn of the century, Henry James determined to visit America again. In order to prepare himself, physically and financially, he refused several invitations to visit Europe. In reply to one invitation, he wrote to the wife of Paul Bourget: 'Europe has ceased to be romantic to me, and my own country, in the evening of my days, has become so; but this senile passion too is perhaps condemned to remain platonic.'[19]

He broached the projected visit to William in April 1903, and was surprised at the strong objections that his brother raised against the idea. 'I should hate,' William perceptively wrote, 'to have you come and, as a result, feel that you had now *done* with America forever, even in an ideal and imaginative sense, which after a fashion you can still indulge in.' The only crumb of encouragement that William offered Henry, after a list of dire warnings, was that there might be some benefit in seeing the South and far West, even Hawaii. He recommended that he should avoid the '*banalité*' of the eastern cities.[20]

This opposition was enough to rouse Henry to a long and eloquent letter in justification of his tour, ending with the insistence, aimed at his brother's pragmatism, no doubt, that his primary idea was 'absolutely economic ... '[21] William withdrew his reservations on receipt of this appeal, and replied, with a note of malicious humour, 'I augur a great revival of energy and internal effervescence from the execution of your project. Drop your English ideas and take America and Americans as they take themselves, and you will certainly experience a rejuvenation.'[22]

A rejuvenation seemed to take place in James's spirit even before the voyage started. It spurred him on to tremendous efforts at the writing-table and long letters to his friends in the United States to prepare them for his coming. Among these was John Hay, now Secretary of State. James had talked about Hay with the Cabot Lodges who had visited him at Lamb House in the summer of 1903. In recent months Hay had had some spectacular diplomatic successes with his 'Open Door' policy in China and the Hay-Pauncefote Treaty which was to prepare the way for the construction of the Panama Canal.

In a letter written in December, James expressed his wonder and appreciation at his friend's achievements. '[The Cabot Lodges] greatly added to the desire I feel to make my way to America somehow or other, as it were (even, that is, as a stoker or a steward or a lecturer), in the course of the approaching year. Nothing is at all lucid about this design, as yet, *but* the desire; but I cling tight to that as to my little all. If it floats me over I shall feel engaged in a gorgeous romance: no moment of which will be more romantic than that of my knocking at your door. Please give orders, in time, that I shall be "shown in." '[23] Every aspect of his proposed return seemed to glow with a romantic light. One of the most significant remarks about it was made to another correspondent, Mrs. Francis Child, the widow of the Harvard folklorist. Speaking of his plans to go to Chocorua, William's summer home in New Hampshire, he wrote: 'I think with a great appetite, in advance, of the chance once more, to *lie on the ground*, on an American hillside, on the edge of American woods, in the manner of my youth – which is not the manner of this damp, enclosed, non-trespassing country.'[24] Invoking the myth of Antaeus, he sought symbolic contact with his native soil so that he could revitalize the sources of his life and art.

Just before he sailed, near the end of August 1904, he confided to C. E. Norton his apprehensiveness as well as his eagerness. He was quaking a little at the thought of the 'Formidable Country,' and felt more conscious than ever before of his 'intensely English corner' and his attachment to it. 'This seems familiar and native, really, and the adventure almost terrific. So I see, and you will see, that it is high time I should break so uncanny a spell.'[25]

His steamer, the *Kaiser Wilhelm* II, arrived in Hoboken on 29 August. It is tempting to picture the portly, dignified James, in his sixty-first year, descending to the dockside. He had been away for over twenty years and in that time the port of New York and the city had changed out of all recognition.

His impression of the place was recorded, with rich elaboration, in *The American Scene*. In a letter to a friend he branded it, more simply, 'appalling, fantastically charmless and elaborately dire ...'[26] Before he went up to New Hampshire he made a brief stay at the home of the publisher, George Harvey, with whom he had already made arrangements to publish his impressions of America. George Harvey had taken over *The North American Review*, which had serialized *The Ambassadors*. Referring to the stay in an unpublished letter to his literary agent, J. B. Pinker, James mentioned, in a parenthesis that makes the reader gasp at a precious lost impression, that a fellow-guest had been 'poor dear old Mark Twain.'[27]

After a few weeks of saturation in the American environment James felt that he could do full justice to the series of articles he had promised Harvey. Writing to him in October from Edith Wharton's house in Lenox, Massachusetts, he apologized for the delay in sending off the first instalment and asserted: 'I am very glad to be able to say that the stuff of them, the impulse toward them, gathers force and volume in my mind every day and every hour; so that, verily, I am moved inwardly to believe that I shall be able not only to write the best book of social and pictorial and, as it were, human observation ever devoted to this country, but one of the best – or why "drag in" *one of*, why not say frankly *the* Best? – ever devoted to any country at all ... I can't "knock off" things – and I want to produce a work of art, and shall. If Thomas Hardy hadn't long ago made that impossible I should simply give the whole series of papers the title of *The Return of the Native*. But as that's out of the question I have found myself thinking of, and even liking better – *The Return of the Novelist* – if that doesn't seem too light and airy or free and easy. It *describes* really my point of view – the current of observation, feeling etc., that can float me further than any other. I'm so very much more of a Novelist than of anything else, see all things *as* such. But this determination isn't final.'[28] Apt as the title would have been, James finally decided against it. It may have been too free and easy; more likely he rejected it because it failed to convey the quality of the essays he completed for *The North American Review*. Dramatic, comprehensive in its vision, large in conception and achievement, the book fully lives up to the title he finally chose – *The American Scene*.

❊ 13 ❊

The Restless Analyst
of the
American Scene

The American Scene, published in book form in 1907, has undergone a long ostracism from the critics until recent years. Ezra Pound's powerful plea for it in *The Little Review* in 1920 had no appreciable effect, and it did not get any extensive critical discussion until 1948. In that year, W. H. Auden wrote a discriminating short introduction for a new edition. Since then it has gradually grown in reputation. James was, perhaps, a little too sanguine about this book but, with the exception of Tocqueville's *Democracy in America*, it is hard to think of a more subtle and penetrating study of American life. There is no gainsaying, however, that it presents problems to the reader. The turns and twists of James's extraordinary imagination produced some of the most labyrinthine sentences he ever wrote. One recent critic, the novelist Wright Morris, quotes extensively from the book, praises it ecstatically, but in the end seems to abdicate the critical function in the face of its encompassing complexity and irony. Throwing up his hands in delighted despair, he writes 'James is simply too much for us.'[1]

The American Scene is, however, not inaccessible. Beneath its closely textured surface lies a wonderfully organic and coherent structure; unifying its intricacy is the rod of purpose. From the outset, James rejected the form of the conventional travel-book with its patchwork of unrelated observations, facts, and figures. In reviewing one such some years before, he had remarked, 'I have a habit that

qualifies me but scantly for reporting lucidly on definite results ...'
Nothing was so interesting to him in reading books of travel as the
' "psychology" they may suffer to be read into them – to say nothing
of the amount of personal impression and visible picture.'[2] In writing
The American Scene James brought to bear all the psychological
penetration, the intense analytical consciousness and the sophistica-
tions of form that he had perfected in writing the three great novels
of the major phase. As a travel book it has no predecessors. It is true
that he did profit from reading Hyppolyte Taine's two volumes
Voyage en Italie (1866), in which the French author had attempted
to paint a psychological portrait of Italy after a six week tour. But, as
James informed a friend, his book was to be 'immeasurably more
mature' than Taine's.[3]

The chief challenge that the United States made to James's
imagination was that, unlike Italy, or any other land with a long
history, there were few objects of art or architecture to make use of.
The observer had to fall back on his inner resources from which to
create his narrative. As James reflected to himself after observing the
blankness of Richmond, Virginia, 'It's a bad country to be stupid in
– none on the whole so bad. If one doesn't know *how* to look and to
see, one should keep out of it altogether. But if one does, if one *can*
see straight, one takes in the whole piece at a series of points that
are after all comparatively few. One may neglect, by interspacing
the points, a little of the accessory matter, but one neglects none of
the essential. And if one has not at least learned to separate with due
sharpness, pen in hand, the essential *from* the accessory, one has
only, at best, to muffle one's head for shame and await deserved
extinction' (AS, 368). As he well knew, he had no need to muffle
his head. At this point in his career, he had above all that 'grasping
imagination' that he had yearned for long ago. He had also a fund of
organic awareness, which enabled him to see relationships everywhere. 'It came back again,' he wrote in the Richmond chapter –
'it was always, after this fashion, coming back, as if to make me
extravagantly repeat myself – to the quantity to be "read into" the
American view, in general, before it gives out an interest. The
observer, like a fond investor, must spend on it, boldly, ingeniously,
to make it pay ...' (AS, 372).

The elderly novelist had no shortage of imaginative funds. Quite the reverse. 'I became aware soon enough ...' he wrote in the preface to the book, 'that these elements of the human subject, the results of these attempted appreciations of life itself, would prove much too numerous even for a capacity all given to them for some ten months; but at least therefore, artistically concerned as I had been all my days with the human subject, with the appreciation of life itself, and with the consequent question of literary representation, I should not find such matters scant or simple' (AS, vi). Very soon, in fact, James found himself engaged in an heroic battle to select from the abundance of impressions what he should use for his book.

As a novelist, he found his tools ready to hand. 'Without much foreshortening,' he wrote, 'is no representation,' and this is the principle on which *The American Scene* is built. Everything is representative; nothing is merely descriptive, isolated, or inorganic. In order to represent, of course, James had to find his window from which to observe; in other words he had to dramatize the persona who sees and orders the experience. This projected character of the returned novelist soon emerges. The narrative voice is in the first person singular, or sometimes, plural, but James keeps reminding the reader of the mental stance, if not the physical aspect, of his major character. He is 'the ancient contemplative person,' 'the charmed visitor,' 'the returned expatriate,' 'the chronicler,' 'the fond critic,' but most of all, and again and again, the 'brooding,' or 'restless analyst.' The implied image of the narrator is central to the meaning of the book. The style of *The American Scene* does much to establish that image. The narrative voice is bland, sophisticated, urbane, unshockable, and invincibly ironic. The narrator is not omniscient. Indeed, part of his power lies in his ability to be surprised and bewildered, a capacity only matched by his power to overcome that bewilderment and to relate each new observation to his schema, to 'compose' the fresh detail or the new colour with his picture. The metaphor of painting is seen throughout the book; even the title implies it. There are numerous references to landscape painters – Claude, Turner, the Japanese water-colourists, Whistler, the Hudson River School, the French Impressionists. The last-named school of painters is surely the most influential on the method of *The American*

Scene. The French painters' methods of seizing on characteristic details and emphasizing them in terms of light, of using strong colours, of analytically representing the social scene, are all used by James in his book. He blends these values with the styles and manners of other schools quite frequently to emerge with a pastiche which yet is overpainted with his own characteristic manner.

An excellent example of this technique is seen in the New England chapter of *The American Scene*. In a description of a lake he refers explicitly to the Hudson River School, which had done so much to form the artistic schema of the region, but touches up the picture with some typical impressionistic details: 'The question of the encircled waters ... larger and smaller – that again was perhaps an ado about trifles; but you can't, in such conditions, and especially at first, resist the appeal of their extraordinarily mild faces and wooded brims, with the various choice spots where the great straight pines, interspaced beside them, and yielding to small strands as finely curved as the eyebrows of beauty, make the sacred grove and the American classic temple, the temple for the worship of the evening sky, the cult of the Indian canoe, of Fenimore Cooper, of W. C. Bryant, of the immortalizable water-fowl. They look too much alike, the lakes and the ponds ... all save the pick of the family, say, like George and Champlain; the American idea, moreover, is too inveterately that woods shall grow thick to the water. Yet there is no feature of grace the landscape could so ill spare – let alone one's not knowing what other, what baser, promiscuity mightn't oppress the banks if that of the free overgrowth didn't. Each surface of this sort is a breathing-space in the large monotony; the rich recurrence of water gives a polish to the manner itself, so to speak, of nature; thanks to which, in any case, the memory of a characteristic perfection attaches, I find, to certain hours of declining day spent, in a shallow cove, on a fallen log, by the scarce-heard plash of the largest liquid expanse under Chocorua; a situation interfused with every properest item of sunset and evening star, of darkening circle of forest, of boat that, across the water, put noiselessly out – of analogy, in short, with every typical triumph of the American landscape "school," now as rococo as so many squares in ingenious wool-work, but the remembered delight of our childhood. On *terra firma*, in New England, too often dusty or scrubby,

185

the guarantee is small that some object at variance, cruelly at variance, with the glamour of the landscape school may not "put out." But that boat across the water is safe, is sustaining as far as it goes; it puts out from the cove of romance, from the inlet of poetry, and glides straight over, with muffled oar, to the – well, to the right place' (AS, 17–18).

It must be very seldom that an artist uses schemata so self-consciously and humorously as this. Yet, given all James's implied sense of the limitations of writer, poet, and painter that he has drawn on, and even of the limitations of the variety of landscape in America, there is still so much richness of perception and harmony of composition that the resulting picture is far from being hard, dry, and thin, as New England had always seemed to be to him in the past. Nostalgia colours the scene, a complex memory deepens the background, the added complexity and richly evocative imagery of James's prose style itself lends finish to the picture. Far from being meagre, the landscape now appeared to be that 'happy and charming thing, feminine,' similar, in fact, in many respects to Italy, which was, James reminded himself, in the same latitude as New Hampshire.

Henry James as central actor, the endlessly reflecting consciousness at the heart of the book, moves through the scenes, composing them and making sense of their appearances and implications. He convinced himself, first of all, that what he saw did make sense, and kept on reminding himself of this through all the difficulties that bristled for him: 'To be at all critically, or as we have been fond of calling it, analytically, minded ...' he observed, 'is to be subject to the superstition that objects and places, coherently grouped, disposed for human use and addressed to it, must have a sense of their own, a mystic meaning proper to themselves to give out' (AS, 273). He was better able to convey that sense when he had had prior experience, twenty, thirty, even forty years before, of the places that he saw. The echo chamber of his mind never failed of a reverberation on a revisit. The implicit image that he used for this process is that of Rip Van Winkle, awakening to America after twenty years of European sleep. 'I woke up,' he writes in the first chapter, 'by a quick transition [via New York], in the New Hampshire Mountains, in the deep valleys and the wide woodlands, on the forest-fringed slopes, the far-seeing crests of the high places, and by the side of the liberal streams and the lonely lakes; things full, at first, of the sweetness of belated recognition, that of the sense of some bedimmed summer of the distant prime flushing back into life and asking to give again as much as possible of what it had given before ...' (AS, 13). America was now romantic to him, as Europe had been years before. This fact he felt was 'like the rifle of a keen sportsman, carried across his shoulder and ready for instant use' (AS, 366).

The first thing was to select the most important targets, and James set out on the hunt with the richest arsenal of imagery that any traveller hunting for generalizations ever brought to America. The first target was 'the huge democratic fact' which James, like Tocqueville before him, adduced as the vital principle of American life. The dramatic metaphor with which he introduced the idea shows Democracy as the chief actor in the drama staged on the American scene, the Faustian hero-villain that dominates the play: 'The great presence that bristles for him on the sounding dock, and that shakes the planks, the loose boards of its theatric stage to an inordinate unprecedented rumble, is the monstrous form of Democracy, which is thereafter to project its shifting angular shadow, at one time or another, across every inch of his field of vision. It is the huge democratic broom that has made the clearance and that one seems to see brandished in the empty sky.' Democratic consistency determined 'manners, feelings, communications, modes of contact and conceptions of life ...' (AS, 54-5). James never lost sight of this clue wherever his feet or his imagination took him. It is the figure in the carpet of *The American Scene.*

Everything fitted so well into this grand design that even an 'ancient contemplative person' occasionally gasped 'before the assault of the quantity of illustration.' The behaviour of 'the rustic cynically squalid,' who insisted on being received at the front door of his brother's New Hampshire house, the shrieking summer girls on top of the coach from Jackson, N.H., the acquiescence of towns and villages to the railway, the absorption of the men in business, the solitary eminence of women in the social sphere, the assurance of the immigrant, the rise of the skyscrapers, the suppression of the past, the corruption of the cities, even (strangely enough) the phenomenon of the Country Club – all testified to the supremacy of the democratic dogma. Perhaps, best of all, for James's purpose, even 'the aching void of appearances,' so often to be encountered, testified also to 'the democratic intensity.' The broom often swept very clean indeed.

The American Scene is so rich and perceptive in its multitudinous insights and illustrations that any commentator can take only a small sample from its widespread plenitude. In order to follow the main thread that runs through the book it is necessary to snap off short most of the wondrous chains of association that James, with exquisite art, so carefully linked to it along the way. It must be noted at the outset that James used throughout the book the social order of Europe, generally England, as an implicit standard of reference. When he writes of 'the absence of forms,' he usually means English forms. His underlying assumption is that American society derived itself from England. Probably without being aware of the fact, James subscribed to the 'germ theory' of history, so favoured by historians of the period. For him, the chief modifier of the original social arrangement had been the democratic spirit. While it had infused American society with a tremendous social dynamic, that spirit had at the same time, he concluded, impoverished its culture. This simplified view of the historical process is a limitation of the book. From an artistic point of view, however, it is an invaluable unifying force.

The great difference, for example, between the old England and the New England village was the consequence of 'the suppression of the two great factors of the familiar English landscape, the squire and the parson' (AS, 23). This made the aesthetic difference as well as the social and spiritual. The shabbiness and untidiness of the New England village indicated that no one cared sufficiently for the appearance of the whole. The summer people were too transient to have much effect; the others too disorganized to operate effectively. Society in the village, as elsewhere in America, was unstable and heterogeneous. This was brought home to James by an encounter he had with a labourer while out walking in New Hampshire. The man could speak none of the languages that James addressed to him in quest of directions and they parted in mutual incomprehension. He ran into this situation again and again during his stay. Whenever he asked his way, he was bound to be encountered with blank looks or strange accents from the 'flagrant foreigners.'

It is not surprising that the immigrant question was the most importunate that James had to face. The first decade of the twentieth century saw the peak of unrestricted immigration to the United States. During the period of James's visit, over a million people, mainly from central and southern Europe, poured in. James himself remained blissfully unaware of the extent and nature of this infusion until he made a trip out to Ellis Island. His guide while there was the Commissioner of Immigration himself, F. P. Sargent. From the tenor of Sargent's annual reports to Congress, one must assume that he was by no means an unprejudiced guide. Year after year he made ominous prophecies about the possible effects of such an immigration policy. All the same it is unlikely that James needed much help to arrive at his own conclusions. He was shaken to the roots of his being by the sight of the thousands of immigrants going through the Island's procedures. There they were 'marshalled, herded, divided, subdivided, sorted, sifted, searched, fumigated,' before they left to enter the stream of American life. No sensitive citizen, James thought, could look on this spectacle and remain unchanged. 'He has eaten of the tree of knowledge,' he went on, 'and the taste will be for ever in his mouth. He had thought he knew before, thought he had the sense of the degree in which it is his American fate to share the sanctity of his American consciousness, the intimacy of his American patriotism, with the inconceivable alien; but the truth had never come home to him with any such force.' James's metaphor is rich with associations. We are reminded that he had used the same image in connection with the Civil War. That had been for him the first American fall from innocence. Mass immigration was a second fall. It was, of course, quite different and much more incalculable in its effect. After such knowledge, the old American had a new look in his face, a chill in his heart. 'So is stamped,' he wrote, 'for detection, the questionably privileged person who has had an apparition, seen a ghost in his supposedly safe old house' (AS, 84–5). James shared, with many cultured Americans of his generation, fears about the effects of racial intermixture. The apprehension was in a few years to lead to restrictive legislation against uncontrolled immigration.

On the score of James's attitudes to the aliens, Maxwell Geismar has a case against James's snobbery and 'nightmarish fantasies of prejudice and doom.'[4] There is an aristocratic disdain in James's race-consciousness that makes these pages of *The American Scene* unpleasant reading. He seemed to take the flood of immigrants almost as a personal affront. No doubt they did add to the sense of dislocation and dispossession he had expressed as soon as his ship docked in the United States. Looking at the varieties of social types and linguistic backgrounds, he believed at first that the social fabric of America, already loose, was in danger of complete disruption. After further investigation, however, he changed his mind – a fact which Geismar, with his typically highly selective use of James's work, disregarded. James finally came to the conclusion that the scale of national machinery for transforming the immigrants' children, if not the immigrants themselves, was so immense that American society could absorb even this enormous inclusion. The question of what sort of national character was emerging from the process, however, left him baffled.

With astonishment, he noted the speed with which the American vat bleached the national colours out of the incoming aliens, even though that colour had taken centuries to produce. Some races, he observed, still held out. James writes some of his richest pages about the ghetto on New York's East Side. Geismar vastly exaggerates James's anti-Semitism in this section, which he arrives at after ingeniously quoting out of context. What James was most seeking to represent in this part was the energy and the prosperity of what he called, with ironic reference to his father's ideas, this 'New Jerusalem.' With some friends he went on a tour of the East Side's tenements, cafés, and Yiddish theatres. As a literary man, he appeared most to fear the fate of the English language in Jewish New York, as an index to what would happen to English in a United States becoming increasingly alien. The East Side cafés struck him as 'the torture room of the living idiom.' 'The accent of the very ultimate future,' he went on, 'in the States, may be destined to become the most beautiful on the globe and the very music of humanity (here the "ethnic" synthesis shrouds itself thicker than ever); but whatever we shall know it for, certainly, we shall not know it for English – in any sense for which there is an existing literary measure' (AS, 139).

James was astonished at the extent to which the alien had permeated the parts of American life that he had always felt to be the most personal to himself and representative of his heritage. Finding them by their thousands in Central Park was to be expected, but seeing them flooding over the brow of Mount Vernon Street in Boston, in Hawthorne's Salem, and in rural New England made him feel that they sounded the *real* American note more than anyone else. He could see that they had become essential to the country economically and that politically, through 'the exotic boss,' they were becoming a force to be reckoned with. While they were creating and sharing in the general prosperity, it was also true that the rising tide of wealth on which they floated made possible the growth of trusts and 'new remorseless monopolies.' One of the freedoms the immigrants had gained, he noted, was the 'freedom to grow up to be blighted' (AS, 137). For the present, however, they had been democratically accepted into the thriving business activities of the country, and they showed it in their appearance, from their shiny boots to their gleaming teeth.

James, in his 'fatally uninitiated state,' was unable to comment any more specifically on the effects of trusts and monopolies. But he could, and plentifully did, comment on the appearances that the business-world made. The most obvious of these was in downtown Manhattan, where the skyscrapers raised their 'towers of glass' like the jagged teeth of a broken comb. In the absence of other traditional or hereditary occupations for the men of the country, the businessman, with his pervasive standard of money-values, called the tune and set the tone for society.

In *An International Episode*, James had mentioned 'a light ornamental structure' ten stories high, from which Lord Lambeth had looked out at the weather-vane on top of Trinity Church on Wall Street. James's view of the rise in power of business and the increased scale of its importance in American life in the twenty-five years since then may be judged by comparing this to his description of the skyscraper in *The American Scene* that overhung 'poor old Trinity to the north' like 'the mountain-wall that drops the Alpine avalanche, from time to time, upon the village, and the village spire, at its foot ...' (AS, 83). These towers of Mammon had symbolically as well as physically extinguished the church. James commented balefully: '*They*, ranged in this terrible recent erection, were going to bring in

191

money – and was not money the only thing a self-respecting structure could be thought of as bringing in?' (AS, 94). As I have pointed out elsewhere, James was one of the first critics of the skyscraper as a form.[5] His reason for subjecting it to such scrutiny was that it was the only claim to consideration, 'other than the merely statistical,' that 'the resounding growth of New York' merited.

The restless 'money-passion,' as James called it, found other outlets in the constant destruction and rebuilding of the city and its upward thrust beyond Manhattan. It had ruined the fine opportunity presented by the river-front, and had turned the upper regions, nearer the park, into opulent residential areas which had the temporary look of painted stage-sets. Beyond the city, money expressed itself in the conspicuous consumption of the large, tasteless shore houses on the Jersey coast, or, further off, in the huge 'white elephants' along the Ocean Drive at Newport and, finally, in the gross and extravagant hotels of Florida.

But it was in New York itself that the passion found its best expression and was transformed into something which even James recognized with a kind of awe and exhilaration as something 'lately and currently *done*, done on a large impersonal stage and on the basis of inordinate gain.' Returning from Washington by train to Boston, his carriage was shipped aboard a barge on the Jersey side and taken round to the tip of Manhattan up the East River to Harlem where it resumed its journey. The trip inspired James to a vision of the power of New York which, I believe, is unexcelled as a piece of descriptive writing about the city. The imagery appears not only to reflect the Impressionists, but also to anticipate Fernand Léger. 'The aspect the power wears then is indescribable; it is the power of the most extravagant of cities, rejoicing, as with the voice of the morning, in its might, its fortune, its unsurpassable conditions, and imparting to every object and element, to the motion and expression of every floating, hurrying, panting thing, to the throb of ferries and tugs, to the plash of waves and the play of winds and the glint of lights and the shrill of whistles and the quality and authority of breeze-born cries – all, practically, a diffused, wasted clamour of *detonations* – something of its sharp free accent and, above all, of its sovereign sense of being "backed" and able to back. The universal *applied* passion struck me as shining unprecedentedly out of the composition; in the bigness and bravery and insolence, especially, of everything that rushed and shrieked; in the air as of a great intricate frenzied dance, half merry, half desperate, or at least half defiant, performed on the huge watery floor. This appearance of the bold lacing-together, across the waters, of the scattered members of the monstrous organism – lacing as by the ceaseless play of an enormous system of steam-shuttles or electric bobbins ... commensurate in form with their infinite work – does perhaps more than anything else to give the pitch of the vision of energy. One has the sense that the monster grows and grows, flinging abroad its loose limbs even as some unmannered young giant at his "larks," and that the binding stitches must for ever fly further and faster and draw harder; the future complexity of the web, all under the sky and over the sea, becoming thus that of some colossal set of clockworks, some steel-souled machine-room of brandished arms and hammering fists and opening and closing jaws. The immeasurable bridges are but as the horizontal sheaths of pistons working at high pressure, day and night, and subject, one apprehends with perhaps inconsistent gloom, to certain, to fantastic, to merciless multiplication. In the light of this apprehension indeed the breezy brightness of the Bay puts on the semblance of the vast white page that awaits beyond any other perhaps the black overscoring of science' (AS, 74–5).

As a piece of poetry and prophecy, as well as of description, this is unmatched among the many impressions that New York has evoked. It demonstrates how much appearances could yield to the restless analyst and how he could use the incomparable rhythms of his sentences to evoke a similar response in a sympathetic reader. This is indeed the 'sense' of New York and it shows more, perhaps, than James realized, far more, certainly, than the 'money-passion' which he thought it supremely exemplified. It shows also the restless will, the reckless drive, the complex skills, the heady power and joy of a city which has mercilessly multiplied, as James predicted, but kept its energy, its brightness, its young, unmannered, ruthless giganticism.

The image of the young giant is, of course, identical with the huge figure of democracy that James introduced in the opening pages of the book. New York, the Faustian metropolis was, in fact, for him a comprehensive symbol of the new America that he found on his return. Its innumerable immigrants, its soaring skyscrapers, its resounding noise, its ceaseless change, its rough and ready manners, its boundless energy staggered and stimulated his rich imagination. It was for him 'the American beauty rose,' with an interminable stem, and the irony of the phrase does not completely undercut his admiration.

Henry James devoted four of his fourteen chapters to New York, seeking in it everywhere representative symbols of the American condition. One which fascinated him was the New York hotel, particularly the Waldorf-Astoria where, he thought, American private life had become most triumphantly public and innocently promiscuous. It made him fairly hold his breath to find a society's ideal of life so magnificently realized. Hundreds of people circulated in the great over-heated corridors and in the imitation Versailles and Trianon rooms, walking and talking, eating and drinking, listening and dancing to music, buying and selling. In 'the element of ingenuous joy below and of consummate management above' Henry James found 'the American spirit most seeking and most finding itself.' With a delightful irony, James describes the rich synthetic details of this 'paradise,' and whips up a fantastic *mélange* of observations on conventions and club meetings into a 'gorgeous golden blur' (AS, 105). His research into 'the hotel-spirit' was continued in the Royal Poinciana in Miami, where the company came from 'all-over,' from every prosperous corner of the country. There, on a strip of land between sea and jungle, the hotel was in exclusive possession. Among the expensive hotel-shops, the lofty rooms and verandahs, the ornate gardens and terraces, James felt that he would have the best opportunity to study Society. But his notebook yielded a blank; there were no types, only *a* type. The discovery brought him back ruefully to his starting point. The products of the 'business-block' and their indulged ladies were exclusively the patrons. They constituted a neutrality of respectability that might have been figured 'by a great grey wash of some charged moist brush causing colour and outline, on the pictured paper, effectually to run together' (AS, 455).

From the monotony of the business world James often found himself thrown back to the variety of his own American past. In fact the juxtaposing of his own schemata of this silent past, now inconceivably remote, with the loud present gave him some of his most fruitful pages. Many things in the American present were alien to him, but the past contained warm memories of a more complex and interesting order. So he made the inevitable pilgrimage back to his birthplace near Washington Square. The changing face of the area was first indicated by the new, unsupported, and unaffiliated 'lamentable little Arch of Triumph.' Hope revived when he found that the shabby red-brick house in Waverley Place where he had gone to dame-school was still there, along with other houses of the period. But he received a rude snub in Washington Place. There he found that his birthplace had been torn down and replaced with 'a high, square, impersonal structure.' He felt then that he had been amputated of half his history. It made him realize how absurd it would be to place on New York buildings those commemorative mural tablets that are so much a feature of the London scene. What was the point of putting one anywhere when the chances were that the building would be pulled down? How could a former dweller in a skyscraper apartment, moreover, be commemorated so that anyone could see his tablet? It was another testament to New York's future as 'a huge, continuous fifty-floored conspiracy against the very idea of the ancient graces ...' (AS, 92).

He went searching for his past again in Boston and at first found some pleasant echoes of it. Mount Vernon Street was so good, as it wandered up to the rear of the State House, that he was conscious of not having done justice to it in the past. The same was true of Charles Street which, although somewhat fallen in the social scale, still had the same house with the same drawing-room that he had used in *The Bostonians*. He even found that pleasant old house in Ashburton Place where he had spent two vibrating and crucial years at the close of the Civil War and had felt 'the very young man's earliest fond confidence in a "literary career." ' He was disturbed, however, to see that there were already signs of demolition in that area of winding streets, one of the few *not* merely rectangular city layouts in America. The supreme shock of James's tour came when he returned a month later for another whiff of the fragrant past. By the strangest chance, he had been there before on the eve of demolition. The house in

Ashburton Place had been levelled. 'It was as if,' he wrote, 'the bottom had fallen out of one's own biography, and one plunged backward into space without meeting anything' (AS, 229). It was an emblem of the severing of his old connection with Boston and the closing of another chapter in the history of his American life.

Since the body of his own past had been so mutilated, Henry James then turned to the literary heritage for some consolation from the ravages of the present. In two cases he was lucky. He made a trip from New York up to Washington Irving's old home, Sunnyside. Although the old state road to Albany bristled with 'the cloud-compelling motor' (in 1904!) and Sleepy Hollow in general was somewhat qualified by modernism, the house itself yielded a rich draught of the past. It retained the sense of Irving's ' "command" of the admirable river and the admirable country, his command of all the mildness of his life, of his pleasant powers and his ample hours ...' It recalled a past that now seemed legendary, and he was catching 'the last faint echo of a felicity forever gone' (AS, 157).

Concord yielded more felicity and gave rise to some of the most exquisite writing in *The American Scene*. It happily combined history, 'the little old Concord fight,' with literary history. Super-imposed over it all was James's vivid memory of Emerson. Concord went straight back to a pre-Civil War, pre-lapsarian America, and had now all the air of a classic site. James called it, with some justice, 'the American Weimar.' The battle by the bridge was to 'determine the future in the way we call immortally.' It was also 'the large firm nail, ringingly driven in, from which the beautiful portrait-group' of Emerson, Hawthorne, Thoreau, and the rest was to hand. Naturally the place was most redolent of Emerson, 'the first, and the one really rare, American spirit in letters,' as James called him. Concord had given Emerson half his images and his 'nearest vision of life.' James ends the piece with a sentence that captures at one and the same time the melancholy and silent beauty of a New England November day and the ghostly presence of its most distin-guished son: 'If one had reached a "time of life" one had thereby at least heard him lecture; and not a russet leaf fell for me, while I was there, but fell with an Emersonian drop' (AS, 264–5).

There was little hope that such a clear note of the past could be sounded a third time. The next pilgrimage that James took, to Hawthorne's Salem, was a sad disappointment. Since his last visit, many years before, the place, he discovered, had been invaded by 'smoky modernism' and the 'ubiquitous alien.' His search there for the 'New England homogeneous' collapsed on the spot. The witch-house looked 'incorrigibly and witlessly innocent,' and the place reported to be the prototype of the House of the Seven Gables was a mere 'weak, vague domiciliary presence' (AS, 271). Hawthorne's ladder at Salem had been knocked away, just as his own had been in New York and Boston.

In Newport, however, James found at least a few fragments left, shreds of a memory of the 'pure Newport time' that he had commemorated in the *Nation* article of 1870. 'The Old Town' still retained some of its fine colonial buildings and there was still the breath of silvery air, the glint of bright sands, and the breeze of the cliff-walk. It all brought back the social summers when a little band 'who confessed brazenly to not being in business' gathered together to sacrifice 'openly to the ivory idol whose name is leisure.' It made James remember the time when it seemed possible that the artistic society that America had not yet succeeded in producing might at last flourish here. Its members had been, James recalled, 'a collection of the detached, the slightly disenchanted and casually disqualified, and yet of the resigned and contented, of the socially orthodox: a handful of mild, oh delightfully mild, cosmopolites ...' (AS, 222). The impossibility of the survival of such a group was made immediately apparent to James when he caught sight of the ugly new mansions crowded together over the cliffs, the results of the avalanche of new wealth into Newport since his last visit. 'What an idea,' James nostalgically concluded, 'originally, to have seen this miniature spot of earth, where the sea-nymphs on the curved sands, at the worst, might have chanted back to the shepherds, as a mere breeding-ground for white elephants! They look queer and conscious and lumpish – some of them, as with an air of the brandished proboscis, really grotesque – while their averted owners, roused from a witless dream, wonder what in the world is to be done with them. The answer to which, I think, can only be that there is absolutely nothing to be done; nothing but to let them stand there always, vast and blank, for reminder to those concerned of the prohibited degrees of witlessness, and of the peculiarly awkward vengeances of affronted proportion and discretion' (AS, 224–5). James must have mused wryly over the memory of his old *Nation* article in which he had celebrated the triumph of the natural atmosphere of Newport over the destroyer and reformer. This was the answer to his hopes for a revival to the architectural art and his trust in the increasing discrimination among the *villegianti* of Newport. The white elephants had trampled ruthlessly on this idyllic vision. The spoiled resort proved to be another broken link with the past.

James paid one more visit to the remembered past before he started on his tour of unknown America. He went to Washington, where he was hospitably received by his old friends Henry Adams, Oliver Wendell Holmes, and John Hay. He was introduced to President Roosevelt, whom he found, contrary to the impression gained from reviewing one of his books, 'extraordinary and rather personally-fascinating.'[6] Under the aegis of such powerful friends, his whole visit was tinged with privilege. A 'charming government launch' took him down the Potomac to Mount Vernon, on a private view, as it were, with all the 'prowling ghosts' of the fellow-pilgrims of his previous visit conveniently laid. He had never come so close to feeling positively wrapped in the folds of the star-spangled banner. He found himself, like his own Count Vogelstein of *Pandora*, falling under the spirit of the place, and the 'little hard facts' cohered themselves under 'the rich interference of association' into a sovereign impression of the man Washington, and 'the resting ... consciousness of public service consummately rendered' (AS, 337).

The city presented itself again in its two faces. The first was the public and official, 'overweighted by a single Dome and overaccented by a single Shaft.' This was 'the immense painted, yet unfinished' backcloth. The other was the private foreground, the little society 'perpetually engaged in conversation.' Washington was still the one place in America where men were solidly, vividly present on the social scene, although as in the past not many of them were from the Senate and fewer still were from the House. It was the only place where the omnipresent businessman did not prevail and, accordingly, where his womenfolk did not rule the roost. Men had talked themselves back into the picture and had re-established a balance in the relations between the sexes. Pandora could still hope for preferment here, as she had done in James's story in the 1880s, but the lid was on the box of misfortunes that she released by her dominance in the social life of the rest of the country.

James's revisit to the Capitol found him more sympathetic than the remarks of his surrogate the Count had revealed twenty years before. He found it 'a builded record of half the collective vibrations of a people; their conscious spirit, their public faith, their bewildered taste, their ceaseless curiosity, their arduous and interrupted education.' He even looked with ironic sympathy at those remarkable busts that used to be ranged around the circumference of the hall under the Congressional Dome. These were the 'terrible artistic tributes from and scarce less to, the different States – the unassorted marble mannikins in particular, each a portrayal by one of the commonwealths of her highest worthy, which makes the great Rotunda, the intended Valhalla, resemble a stonecutter's collection of priced sorts and sizes' (AS, 361). He looked forward to a great sacrificial fire of this lot, which would be proportional to the grand possibilities of the American future. The relegation of these busts to a lower level of the Capitol since James's visit is perhaps a decent compromise with this exalted vision. The Capitol itself appeared to James as a kind of national democratic symbol, 'the warm domestic hearth of Columbia herself.' Her various marble fronts raked the national futures. They were commensurate with the size of the continent so that 'their marble embrace appears so the complement of the vast democratic lap' (AS, 363).

·ᪧ· 14 ·ᪧ·

Undiscovered America

It was 'the pressed spring' of the past, as James was fond of calling it, that always yielded the richest treasures to his imagination and provided the schemata against which he could project his renewed vision. The last third of *The American Scene*, which consists of chapters on areas that James had never seen before, is not as memorable as the first. For the most part, he concentrates on the meaning to be read into the *absence* of signs and forms. The general blankness of cities like Baltimore, Richmond, and Jacksonville, Florida, became portentous to the restless analyst, the more portentous the less they had to show. Even Philadelphia, surely one of the more interesting American cities, affected him mostly as the place 'that didn't bristle.' In the neat plan and order of the streets – William Penn '*must* have laid them out,' he wrote, 'no one else could possibly have done it so ill' (AS, 280) – it seemed to him to be wonderfully homogeneous, with its rows of houses like 'a double file of grizzled veterans' and its comparatively few aliens. Quaker society had made it so orderly and serene; it was a 'society in which every individual was as many times over cousin, uncle, aunt, niece, and so on through the list, as poor human nature is susceptible of being' (AS, 279). From this calm surface, he received no glimmer of its underside, however, the most lurid case, he was amazed to discover, of corruption in city government in the United States. In the end, though, this information only confirmed his main hypothesis and explained the immense sociability of the place. Its society was like an *ancien régime*, all in the same boat, in which they 'would either float merrily together or (almost as merrily) go down together.' The risk, the vague danger posed by the pestilent administration was 'the very music of the excursion' (AS, 286). This is a wondrous example of how James could work all the elements of his perception into the pattern of a main idea.

Philadelphia was also fortunate in having something historically and aesthetically first-rate to which to relate itself. This was Independence Hall, which became the object of one of James's finest fancies. He imagined some clever man of the period looking around at its admirably proportioned, wainscoted chambers and taking the hint: ' "*What* an admirable place for a Declaration of something! What could one here – what *couldn't* one really declare?" And then after a moment: "I say, why not our Independence?" ...' (AS, 292). It needed only the image of Benjamin Franklin, with his 'aged, crumpled, canny face,' to complete the picture. It was he who had put the original stamp on the soft local wax, started the conversation, and left his genial memory to succeeding generations.

Baltimore, without such distinguishing marks, struck him as a remarkably blank and vacant city. In the golden June light it seemed to him 'a perversely cheerful little city of the dead.' Such blankness tested his ruling theory that 'there is no such thing as an unrelated fact, no such thing as a break in the chain of relations' (AS, 312). The theory did not fail, though, even in Baltimore. The reason for such blankness, he concluded, was the ghostly presence of the Civil War. Baltimore, he recalled, had been the 'particular bloodstained patch' of shadow across the path of the North. The muse of history accordingly spoke to him there of the burial of the past and the long convalescence of the patient city, which accounted for its 'fine warm hush.'

One of the most cherished parts of James's original plan had been to spend part of his American winter in the warm South. But that season in 1904–5 was an unusually severe one. The winter preceded him southward so that where he had banked on 'the reign of the orange grove,' he had found instead 'the usurpation of the snow-bank.' This was one more illustration of the law that 'it is the genius

201

of the American land and the American people to abhor, wherever it may be, a discrimination.' The spread of the 'wash of winter' had to him its analogy 'in the vast vogue of some infinitely-selling novel, one of those happy volumes of which the circulation roars, periodically, from Atlantic to Pacific and from great windy State to State, in the manner ... of a blazing prairie fire; with as little possibility of arrest from "criticism" in the one case as from the bleating of lost sheep in the other' (AS, 305–6).

The weather did at last moderate and he found the South he was looking for. In all the romance of his return to America nothing had appeared to him to have more promise than what he called 'the latent poetry of the South' (AS, 368). The name of Richmond, for example, had, from the outbreak of the War, been for him full of the most 'lurid, fuliginous, vividly tragic' associations. The old Confederate capital represented above all others 'the supreme holocaust, the final massacres, the blood, the flames, the tears.' His first walk in the quiet town, however, produced in him only a sense of mystery. He asked himself incredulously: 'This then the tragic ghost-haunted city, this the centre of the vast blood-drenched circle, one of the *most* blood-drenched for miles and miles around, in the dire catalogue aforesaid?' (AS, 369–70). The town looked simply void and blank. Even this set-back to the historic muse did not, however, disconcert James for long. His grasping imagination reached beyond the appearance to a cause. What did it all testify to but the 'very essence of the old Southern idea – the hugest fallacy, as it hovered there to one's backward, one's ranging vision, for which hundreds of thousands of men had ever laid down their lives.' The appearance of the city revealed to his mind the grotesque folly of the idea of the self-contained slave state and also the isolation and solitude of the South which was the consequence.

The result had been a pathetic provincialism and backwardness that revealed itself to James in every aspect of the city. To aid in this hypothesis, Henry James called on the work of the historian James Ford Rhodes, who had analyzed the mind of the South at mid-century to show 'the conception that, almost comic in itself, was yet so tragically to fail to work, that of a world rearranged, a State solidly and comfortably seated and tucked-in, in the interest of slave-produced Cotton' (AS, 373). The resulting public tone of legislation, political speeches, and journalism seemed to James to be 'as artlessly perverse, as untouched by any intellectual tradition of beauty or wit, as some exhibited array of the odd utensils or divinities of lone and primitive islanders.'

The case was amply illustrated to James by a visit to the Museum of the relics of the Confederacy in Jefferson Davis' former 'White House.' There the spirit of the old slave state descended and was expressed in 'the very nudity and crudity, the historic, the pathetic poverty of the exhibition' (AS, 384). But while he was at the Museum he encountered a young southerner who was gazing raptly into one of the glass cases. It contained some antique regimentals that corresponded with those the young man's father had worn in the Civil War. He recounted to James an adventure in which his father, effecting his escape, had smashed the skull of a Union soldier. He cheerily affirmed that he would be ready to do the same things all over again himself. James saw that this southerner would not in fact hurt a northern fly, *as* northern, but his consciousness would have been 'poor and unfurnished without this cool platonic passion.' Then it came to him, after some further conversation with the young southerner that, although he would not have hurt a northern fly, there were things he would have done to a southern Negro. There were horrors enough beneath the bland surface of the South to James's penetrating gaze.

He travelled further south to Charleston, which he hoped would give him a glimpse of the ante-bellum South in its hey-day. But, charming as it was, it seemed to suffer a 'deficiency of life.' Charleston, for him, was a handsome, pale beauty, 'prepared for romantic interment, stretched in a fair winding-sheet, covered with admirable flowers, surrounded with shining tapers' (AS, 409). James had shown in *The Bostonians* a North feminized by the War; the male element had all been supplied by his leonine southerner, Basil Ransom. He was disconcerted to find a South that had suffered even more from feminization. The ancient order there had seemed to him all 'masculine, fierce and mustachioed,' whereas the present one was 'at the most a sort of sick lioness who has so visibly parted with her teeth and claws that we may patronizingly walk all round her' (AS, 417).

His impressions of the deeper South were in no way to change this conclusion. Savannah, Jacksonville, and Miami had neither the richness of historical association nor the beauties of nature that James needed for his best effects. The attempts of St. Augustine to capitalize on and, if necessary, to fake Spanish relics he found pathetic. Later, James travelled westward with high hopes of finding rich veins to work there, but the brief glimpse that he gave us of the West, in *The American Scene*, shows how badly let down he felt about it. Even the fabled California was disappointing, although not because of the lack of natural beauty, which was as 'aristocratic' as anything that American conditions permitted. The beauty of the state struck him as a kind of instinct on the part of Nature 'to brace herself in advance against the assault of society so much less marked with distinction than herself' (AS, 412).

Henry James intended to record his impressions of California and other parts of the West in a second volume to be entitled *The Sense of the West*,[1] but illness and other tasks prevented this. The best summary of his reaction is contained in a letter, previously unpublished, that he sent to a friend in England, Jocelyn Persse. It was written from the Hotel Van Nuys, Los Angeles, on 25 March 1905. The notepaper had at its head a large and unattractive picture of the hotel, beneath which James began: 'Be patient with my distressing paper, which is the most convenient to my hand and which may express for you a little the extreme and the awfully ugly (for the most part) exoticism (so far as it's artificial) amid which I move ... I came hither, to Southern California, a day or two ago, by a prodigious straight journey from Chicago, an endless dreary weary run of three nights and three days, in a wondrously appointed train, but through desperate "alkali" deserts of Kansas, New Mexico and Arizona. This country is too *huge* simply, for any human convenience, and so unutterably empty that I defy any civilization, any mere money-grabbing democracy, to make on it any impression worthy of the name. It has made none yet, save that of the three or four long transcontinental railways. Yet this extraordinary California at the end of the awful dusty grind, this great blooming *garden-realm*, enclosed between the giant mountains and the Pacific is, so far as nature goes, a fair reward for the pilgrimage ... Everything is larger, intenser, braver, with a kind of conscious insolence of success; everything in contrast makes one's (or at least *my*) poor little English gardening a meagre dusky show.'[2]

California was, James wrote in *The American Scene*, an 'unconscious and inexperienced Italy, the primitive *plate*, in perfect condition, but with the impression of History all yet to be made' (AS, 462). He had an unhappy vision of how that history *might* be made, however. The vision took the form of a prophecy which ended his book. These pages, five of them, were, significantly enough, not printed in the Harper's edition published in New York. That closed with some remarks on the natural beauty of 'Florida adorable.' I do not know whether the publisher or James himself wished to spare the American readers his last judgment. It was certainly not one to please the strident patriot. The alternate pages of these five are headed, in Chapman and Hall's London Edition, 'The Last Regret,' 'The Last Question,' and 'The Last Answer.' The regret was at having to leave the warmth of Florida for 'the ugly, wintering, waiting world' to the north and west. The question was: 'To what extent was hugeness, to what extent *could* it be, a ground for complacency of view, in any country not visited for the very love of wildness, for positive joy in barbarism?' During these long, transcontinental journeys, the Pullman wheels seemed to rumble repeatedly at him: 'See what I'm making of all this – see what I'm making, what I'm making!'

Henry James's last answer was: 'I see what you are *not* making, oh, what you are ever so vividly not ...' The railway seemed to him to be a symbol of the power, ruthlessness, and irresponsibility of American commercial exploitation. It had dispossessed 'the painted savages' and ravaged the beauty and solitude of the wilderness. In its place, with a violence that seemed to make the face of the land bleed, it was setting down at intervals across the great lonely country crude, hideous 'places,' which nobody noticed, cared about, or suffered from. 'Is the germ of anything finely human,' James wondered, 'of anything agreeably or successfully social, supposably planted in conditions of such endless stretching and such boundless spreading as shall appear finally to minister but to the triumph of the superficial and the apotheosis of the raw?'

The answer to this final rhetorical question is self-evident. No wonder that he had ended the letter to Jocelyn Persse already quoted by saying: 'I am well-nigh *rotten* with the languishment of home-sickness.' The plain fact was that his long, quiet years in England had not prepared him for these interminable train journeys, quick visits, strange faces, and wildly fluctuating temperatures. It may be that these arduous conditions darkened his view of the West, which he had instinctively distrusted anyway from his earliest years. James certainly made too few allowances for a civilization that was still in process of formation and for a development that had been so rapid that aesthetic considerations had gone by the board. Yet, on the other hand, it is no use denying the relevance of his criticism of most western towns, nor can one help deploring with him the terrible exploitation and destruction of so much natural beauty in the wake of the rapid post-Civil War westward movement.

The western journeys confirmed in James the belief that the restless money-passion, released like the genie from the lamp of democracy, had gained control of American development. In the immense national future that he had gazed at from the steps of the Capitol he could not foresee where the passion would take the country, but looking at its products in the West, he could not feel very hopeful. The large pattern of *The American Scene* is not made explicit. It is, perhaps, deliberately concealed in the elaborate and subtle weavings of his prose, but I believe that it can be roughly summarized in the following terms. Without the control of an hereditary aristocracy or the sanctions of an established church, American democracy had chosen its own course with that freedom of action and movement that was one of the country's supreme characteristics. In New England the Puritan theocracy, and its residuum the Puritan ethos, had supplied a restraining force and also an aesthetic from which had flowered the most characteristic and best American art. The South had pursued its own course in its forlorn and romantic dream of a slave-holding state. The Civil War had seen the downfall of both states of mind; it had been the original sin, the eating of the apple representing the loss of an innocent, if provincial, America. In that War many of the best and most promising spirits of the age had died. From the War, the businessman and his creed had emerged triumphant. He had gained control of the South and opened up the West to exploitation. His restless passion had led to the enormous upsurge and use of power, best symbolized by the devouring railroad. Aesthetically, the business ethic found its expression in the skyscraper, which had demanded the sacrifice of the 'old' New York and Boston that had commemorated much of his country's, and his own, more innocent past. Its excess wealth had gone into extravagant and impractical consumption, as in the resort houses of New Jersey and Newport. The release of this restless energy had created a demand for labour. On democratic principles the gates of the country had been opened wide to mass immigration from alien cultures. This constituted for James the second 'Fall,' which meant the end, for him, of the American consciousness as he had known it. Most of the pleasure which he found in this return trip came from nostalgic glimpses of the places in his own American past, in the Hudson Valley, at Concord, in Washington, which were all the more poignant because he felt that these places too were on the brink of harsh change.

This summary certainly emphasizes how much James disliked twentieth-century America, and there are many more reasons for this dislike to be found in the pages of *The American Scene*. The country often seemed to instil in him a kind of fear, a fear that became evident in his encounter with new developments in American life, and in response to areas that he had never visited before. This may be because he had no schemata with which to control his reactions to such new experience. He seemed to fear, too, the naked power that giant of a country was now displaying in so many areas, particularly in its commercial and industrial endeavour. The fear evidenced itself often in criticism of new developments and in a fastidious rejection of much American taste. On the other hand, there are passages in the book in which the encompassing irony of his criticism breaks down in the face of his sense of the staggering achievements of the United States, in which the heroic, almost daemonic, element in the national life is given its due.

Whitman thought of America as 'essentially the greatest poem'; James seems to have thought of it as potentially a great novel, one which he himself, and perhaps no one else could ever complete. *The American Scene* is in some respects a scenario for later short stories and his unfinished novel, *The Ivory Tower*, and many other fictions that he did not live to write. The astonishing thing is that James, who had lived for so long in another country, under such totally different conditions, and who had been so innocent of American developments, could have taken such an encompassing view of the country. His passion for perception, so deeply committed to penetrating appearances and finding underlying patterns, enabled him to derive from surface realities clues to deep motivations and national drives. Consequently he was able to reconcile contradictions and explain anomalies that had baffled many other observers.

James found, however, that it was for him difficult to work, impossible to live, in America. Not that it was without blandishments. In America, he discovered, he could make up to $500 per hour lecturing to 'female culture clubs,' as he called them, and other groups. The ready acceptance of his articles by *The North American Review* and by *Harper's Bazar* also indicated that he could find a market for his work about America. He knew that he could share in the general prosperity if he decided to stay on. 'But I would rather live a beggar at Lamb House,' he told Edmund Gosse. 'Let my biographer, however, recall the solid sacrifices I shall have made.'[3] At last, too, he found that he was not without honour in his own country. Harvard, at which he delivered his lecture on Balzac, gave him an honorary degree. Bryn Mawr College asked him to give the Commencement Address. To do these things he had to delay his return to England. He had cause to regret this, for in June the customary heat-wave struck. One of the few reliefs he could find was in being whirled around the New England countryside in Edith Wharton's car. But on 4 July 1905, he gained his independence from these intolerable conditions, and sailed from Boston back to England and his 'little downward burrow' in Rye.

❧ 15 ❧

In the Finer Grain

One of the prime reasons for Henry James's return to America in 1904 was, as he explained to William, to gather material for new fiction. His 'too monotonised grab-bag' of English experience was yielding, he thought, fewer and fewer good situations and themes to his imagination.[1] In this respect, at least, the American journey was an unqualified success. He came back brimming over with ideas and images for which he needed only time and good health to pour into fiction. Dorothea Krook suggests that it took some time for all the painful and unpleasant implications of his American visit to emerge into James's consciousness. While *The American Scene,* she notes, 'is dominated by the thrill, the excitement, the absorbing interest of it all,' the later fiction increasingly reflects the darkness and bitterness of unhappy retrospection.[2] Certainly James's physical and psychological health became uncertain in these years, and he was plagued by periods in which he was unable to work. These late stories with American settings are all, in their various ways, retrospective. *The Jolly Corner, Crapy Cornelia, A Round of Visits,* and *Julia Bride,* all have an explicit or implicit reference to an earlier American order – an order which he felt had been transformed or destroyed by recent developments. For these stories, *The American Scene* acted as a kind of expansive notebook from which he took characters, settings, and themes.

Three interconnected concerns, recurrent in *The American Scene,* all appear in these stories. The first is what James called 'the money-passion,' the phrenetic quest for wealth which he had found had touched and corrupted almost every aspect of American life; the second is the destruction of the past, not only in terms of the actual pulling down of buildings but also in terms of the rapid change of consciousness that the American lack of concern with history and the ceaseless flood of immigrants had accelerated; the third is the search for the meaning of the self. In a country in which values so rapidly changed, James saw that the very nature of identity was thrown into question. All the protagonists of his late American stories confront the self in some form, and investigate the values by which it lives; the result is either traumatic or pathetic. Only in the case of *Crapy Cornelia* is the consequence comic; in that story, the protagonist in effect completely rejects the present in order to live in the past with his Cornelia.

Crapy Cornelia and another story of this group, *A Round of Visits*, were later collected in the volume called *The Finer Grain* (1910). The title is an accurate summation of James's effect in all this late, short fiction. Although in the American stories he worked as close to life as he ever came in terms of observed detail and characterization, he painted these fictional pictures with the finest grain of consciousness and the richest compositional effect. Each is written from the point of view of an intelligent and perceptive observer, sensitive not only to the vibrations of the minds of other personalities but also to the meaning of the experience for himself. This is true even of the flighty young protagonist of *Julia Bride*. The main trouble with James's previous American fiction is that he had presented his characters objectively or satirically or had used their points of view as ironic devices with which to underline their limitations. In these later stories, with his developed ability to identify himself even with characters unsympathetic to himself and then to dramatize their perceptions, he could use various types of grasping imaginations to present aspects of American life without resorting to patronage.

Probably the first written and certainly the most impressive of this group of stories is *The Jolly Corner*.[3] Its origins go back to *A Passionate Pilgrim*, in which Clement Searle looks for and, in his madness, becomes the *alter ego* who grew up and lived in England while he remained marooned in Saragossa, Illinois. In *The Jolly Corner*, Spencer Brydon looks for the self who stayed behind in New York, while he spent his time in Europe. The story is a clear example of how the United States had become 'romantic' for James in his later years, as Europe had been for him in his earlier. Of course, *The Jolly Corner* is infinitely more complex in theme and treatment than *A Passionate Pilgrim*. It is not surprising that it had a lasting effect on another American expatriate, T. S. Eliot. Not only is it a search for a lost national past, but also a quest for identity and of the meaning of selfhood, one of the most recurrent of contemporary artistic themes.

The biographical elements in the story are clear enough. Brydon, like James, has returned to New York, the place of his birth and childhood, after a lapse of many years – thirty-three in Brydon's case, twenty-two in James's. Brydon expresses a concern that had exercised James for some time before his return to the United States in 1904. What would he have been like if he had stayed on there all those years ago instead of settling in Europe? In effect, James was asking Brydon's nagging question: 'What would it have made of me?' when he was reviewing books in the 'American Letters' of 1898.

The immediate source for *The Jolly Corner* seems to have been the shock that James felt when he returned to Washington Place in search of his birthplace, only to find a high, impersonal structure where the house once stood. Later in his American tour, he had visited the soon-to-be-demolished house in Ashburton Place, Boston, which recalled for him the tension-filled years the family spent there during the Civil War and his own beginnings as a writer. There, on the spot, he had heard 'some echo of ghostly footsteps – the sound as of taps on the window-pane heard in the dim dawn.'[4] The destruction of the two old family houses was a significant symbol of his loss of home and of the American past which had done so much to create his own identity. On the ruins of that past rose the skyscrapers of commercial endeavour. Yet another apparition appears in *The American Scene* which may be reflected in *The Jolly Corner*. On his visit to Ellis Island, he believed that he had seen 'a ghost in his supposedly safe old house.' In this case, the house was his American consciousness which had been invaded by the spirit of the 'inconceivable alien.'

All these fears, questions, and images find their way into the texture of *The Jolly Corner*. Perhaps above all is expressed James's failure to predict all that had happened to his native land during his long absence. Brydon reflects: 'He *had* supposed himself, from decade to decade, to be allowing, and in the most liberal and intelligent manner, for brilliancy of change. He actually saw that he had allowed for nothing ... proportions and values were upside-down; the ugly things he had expected, the ugly things of his far-away youth, when he had too promptly waked up to a sense of the ugly – these uncanny phenomena placed him rather, as it happened, under the charm; whereas the "swagger" things, the modern, the monstrous, the famous things, those he had more particularly, like thousands of ingenuous enquirers every year, come over to see, were exactly his sources of dismay. They were as so many set traps to his displeasure, above all for reaction, of which his restless tread was constantly pressing the spring' (ANS, 792).

The Jolly Corner is not, however, a biographical story, any more than *A Passionate Pilgrim* was. Reading it as biography has, as usual with James, been the main source of critical confusion about it. A glaring example of this is Maxwell Geismar's crass assertion that the ghost in the house on the jolly corner is 'the Jamesian unconscious.'[5] From the start, Brydon is represented with considerable ambiguity. Like Clifford Searle, he is in many ways a weak and ineffectual man. The fact that a good many of his impressions about the United States coincided with those of Henry James should not blind us to the differences between the character and his creator. Moreover, the reader must be on his guard against believing everything that Brydon sees or says. James's subtle technique dramatizes all the information about and all the perceptions of the main character. With one exception that will be discussed later, James makes everything *subjective* to Brydon's vision.

Until his return from Europe, Brydon has been living on the rents of the house on the jolly corner and another, less good, which he owns, 'two bristling blocks westward.' These rentals have provided him with sufficient money to live comfortably abroad. Now he has the opportunity to increase his income considerably by having the two old houses pulled down to make way for two blocks of flats. The lesser of the houses has already been removed and construction com-

menced when the story begins. The other remains. It has strong
sentimental associations for him as it represents 'the ineffaceable
past' of his parents and favourite sister, all long since dead, and of his
own childhood spent there. To pull this house down would mean
destroying the symbol of that past. Miss Alice Staverton, a friend
from his New York past, and his constant resource for conversation
since his return, puts her finger on his self-indulgent feelings when
she says: 'In short you're to make so good a thing of your sky-scraper
that, living in luxury on *those* ill-gotten gains, you can afford for a
while to be sentimental here!' (ANS, 797).

Alice accompanies Brydon to the site of the construction of the new
apartment block. While there, Brydon vigorously reproves the representative of the building firm which had undertaken the work
over a failure to observe 'some detail of one of their noted conditions.'
Alice tells Brydon, later, that he had neglected a real gift. 'If he had
but stayed at home he would have anticipated the inventor of the
sky-scraper. If he had but stayed at home he would have discovered
his genius in time really to start some new variety of awful architectural hare and run it till it burrowed in a gold-mine' (ANS, 795).

This observation chimes with one of Brydon's own 'most disguised
and most muffled vibrations.' This 'wanton wonderment' represents
itself to him 'very much as he might have been met by some strange
figure, some unexpected occupant, at a turn of one of the dim passages of an empty house.' In other words, Brydon converts Alice's
reference to the rich man he might have become into the image of a
ghost in a haunted house. With this clue, Brydon starts on the hunt
for his *alter ego*. The first stage is merely theoretic, a discussion with
Alice about what he might expect that other self to be like. He
believes that he may have missed some 'fantastic, yet perfectly possible,
development' of his own nature. There was in him, he feels, 'a strange
alter ego ... as the full-blown flower is in the small tight bud ...' In
going to Europe he transferred this bud to a climate 'that blighted
him for once and for ever.' Miss Staverton believes that the flower
would have been 'quite splendid, quite huge and monstrous.' Brydon
adds that it would also have been hideous and offensive, but Alice
replies that he does not really believe that. She does believe that he
would have had power. Under Brydon's repeated question, she admits

213

that she would have liked him that way too because she has already seen the *alter ego* in a dream.

The chase itself begins when Brydon begins to haunt the house on the jolly corner every night, trying to locate his *alter ego* in the great, empty rooms. There follows a brilliantly narrated ghost story, but it is far more than that. At the same time, it is the exploration of a consciousness and the education of a perception. For Brydon, prowling the house becomes his real life, 'the life that, as soon as he heard behind him the click of his great house-door, began for him, on the jolly corner, as beguilingly as the slow opening bars of some rich music follows the tap of the conductor's wand' (ANS, 803). This image of the beginning of some fine artistic enterprise is balanced by another which reveals the mercenary side of Brydon's nature: 'He knew what he meant and what he wanted: it was as clear as the figure on a cheque presented in demand for cash.' He is relentlessly after that other self, who he feels sure is somewhere in the house. He likens his quest to a search for some savage beast of the forest, yet it comes over him, more and more, that he himself is the beast, and he acquires the faculty, 'like some monstrous stealthy cat,' of seeing in the dark. He wonders what effect he would have upon 'the poor hard-pressed *alter ego*' if he should find him. As he returns night after night to the house, he feels that he is cultivating his perception to a higher and higher pitch. In fact he seems to be gradually creating the consciousness that he hunts, and the turns and twists of the chase reflect the different projected aspects of personality that he attributes to or intuits in the *alter ego*. Later on, he gets in his turn the sense of being the hunted. 'It worried, it finally quite broke him up, for it proved, of all the conceivable impressions, the one least suited to his book' (ANS, 806).

At the beginning of his last visit to the house, he feels that his *alter ego* is 'the fanged or the antlered animal brought at last to bay.' It produced in Brydon 'a prodigious thrill' and dismay, but at the same time 'the most joyous, possibly the next minute almost the proudest, duplication of consciousness' (ANS, 806). Brydon has in fact achieved what he has for so many weeks been trying to do. He has created that other consciousness so vividly that it can take form and appear to him. Brydon is very close to insanity at this point, so complex and contradictory are his feelings, and in this part of the story there are strange dislocations in time and feeling as James portrays a consciousness on the edge of the abyss. Finally, Brydon locates the *alter ego* behind a closed door that he knows that he has left open. Out of fear, compunction, or whatever, Brydon grasps at discretion, and instead of pushing the door open, he stands in front of it, renounces his quest and asks the *alter ego*, also, to let him rest. Then, in a state of dread, Brydon, after waiting for hours for dawn to throw a dim light into the house, begins to descend the staircase in order to leave the house. He has decided that the wreckers can come in as soon as they like.

He gets almost to the bottom of the last flight of stairs when he observes that the inner door of the two leading to the street is open. He is quite sure that he had left it closed. Then he begins to make out a shape. 'He saw, in its great grey glimmering margin, the central vagueness diminish, and he felt it to be taking the very form toward which, for so many days, the passion of his curiosity had yearned. It gloomed, it loomed, it was something, it was somebody, the prodigy of a personal presence.' Brydon discovers him to be what he had expected from the start – one of the types 'who have been hammered so hard and made so keen' by American conditions. But this creature is far more ravaged and sinister than the one he had expected. The *alter ego* is in evening dress like himself, but has thick spectacles instead of the monocle that Brydon carries, and has two fingers missing from his right hand. He is obviously a rich and powerful creature, the product of the 'rank money passion.' Brydon sees him so clearly that 'no portrait by a great modern master could have presented him with more intensity ...' But Brydon denies that the bared identity of the *alter ego* could be his own. He was too hideous, 'unknown, inconceivable, awful, disconnected from any possibility – ! He had been "sold," he inwardly moaned, stalking such game as this: the presence before him was a presence, the horror within him a horror, but the waste of his nights had been only grotesque and the success of his adventure an irony. Such an identity fitted his at *no* point, made its alternative monstrous.' This was the face of a stranger. Then the *alter ego* advances on Brydon, like 'one of those expanding fantastic images projected by the magic lantern of childhood.' Brydon

215

falls back before the apparition and loses consciousness before 'the hot breath and the roused passion of a life larger than his own ...'

When he regains consciousness, he finds his head in the 'ample and perfect' lap of Alice Staverton. He is certain that he has returned from death. It transpires that Alice has seen the *alter ego* again in a dream, has accepted him and pitied him. She implies that her pity has saved Brydon from destruction. Brydon continues to assert that the *alter ego* was none of him, 'even as I *might* have been.' It is quite clear that Alice does not believe that, but, as a mother would comfort a hurt child, she plays along with his delusion and, as the story ends: ' "And he isn't – no, he isn't – *you*!" she murmured as he drew her to his breast.'

Her love has overcome the division between the two egos and has accepted – as she had been ready to all the years – the flawed personality of Brydon. For his part, he can remain convinced that the brute that confronted him at the door of the house was none of him, and can remain protected from this knowledge by the maternal bosom of Alice Staverton.

The Jolly Corner has aroused almost as many interpretations as it has readers. Like many of the later works, however, it will continue to elude definitive elucidation because of the ambiguity of its technique. Perhaps the most complicated view of the story is that of Floyd Stovall, who maintains that there are not two but three egos – Spencer, the ghost on the fourth floor behind the closed door, and the one inside the door to the street. The real self, he maintains, is released by Alice's love; the false self is the one that has overlaid his true self for the thirty-three years of his European past – the ground-floor ghost. The self that he might have been had he never left New York is the one on the fourth floor.[6] While this explanation does rather happily explain some of the problems of dislocation in the story, it does add what seems to be a needless complication. What happens to that poor ghost left up on the fourth floor? More essentially, why is it necessary to posit a third ghost at all, given the notorious resourcefulness and adaptability of spirits? Surely explanations have to be sought that reconcile two selves in the story, since no others are mentioned.

The Freudian critics have of course made hay with *The Jolly*

Corner as the two selves seem to fit so neatly with the division of the personality into id and ego functions. In addition, these critics cite the womb and birth symbols in the text, and see it as a story about the symbolic death and rebirth of the protagonist. Saul Rosenzweig, the most ingenious of this school of critics, in his essay, 'The Ghost of Henry James: a Study in Thematic Apperception,' relates *The Jolly Corner* to James's first American tale, *The Story of a Year*. He maintains that 'the obscure hurt' that James suffered in the first year of the Civil War is related to the wounds that Ford suffers and to the *alter ego's* missing fingers. Rosenzweig claims that James was trying to rectify the past in returning to the United States in 1904–5. He came back to confront his unlived life, heal old wounds, overcome old barriers and pass beyond them. Alice Staverton, he goes on, is the counterpart to Lizzie Crowe but whereas Lizzie had been faithless, Alice had always remained ready to accept her lover as he was and is. Rosenzweig even maintains that *The Jolly Corner* was intentionally written as a counterpart to James's first American story.[7]

A closer look at the evidence makes it easy to demolish this theory. Ford and Brydon are completely different characters in very different situations. Ford is a selfless, heroic figure who fights bravely on the battlefield and is brought back to his New England village in a terribly weakened state. When he returns, he realizes that Lizzie has ceased to love him. She becomes the sinister Venus figure familiar in James's early stories. Ford in the face of her betrayal turns his face to the wall, like Millie in *The Wings of the Dove*. This is a specific gesture of renunciation, not the act of one who has never lived. Nor is Brydon one of those Jamesian heroes, like Marcher in *The Beast in the Jungle*, who finds out too late that he has not lived. Brydon has lived; the point is that he has not lived 'edifyingly.' He has been selfish, frivolous, and scandalous, 'followed strange paths and worshipped strange gods.' Unfortunately, he had been too self-absorbed to notice that Alice had loved him all his years. That love in the end saves him from annihilation by the *alter ego*. The difference between the roles played by Lizzie Crowe and Alice Staverton is one index to James's changed attitude towards women, which is reflected most distinctly in his portrayal of Madame de Vionnet in *The Ambassadors*.

There seems to be no reason why the reader should not accept

Brydon's own view of the *alter ego's* maimed state, instead of reading psychological wounds into it or, as some biographically-oriented critics have done, interpreting the wounds as the loss of artistic power that James would have suffered had he stayed in the United States. Brydon points out that it would have been absurd to sport a monocle – the very symbol of English snobbery – downtown. The missing fingers seem to him to be the result of a gunshot wound. As a more generalized symbol, this wound may represent the violence that James saw everywhere in American life.

Another critic, Edward Honig, suggests that the death and rebirth symbols in the story are related to the Dionysian myth of the destruction of the god's old self and the rebirth of the new.[8] There are certainly signs of rebirth at the end of the story, but in the light of the *alter ego's* victory in the hall, it does not seem that the old god has been destroyed. The story does, as Honig claims, contain imagery of the quest legend. Brydon himself sees in his search 'an image almost worthy of an age of greater romance,' but the story's development ironically undercuts this motif. Before Brydon senses the presence of the *alter ego* behind the door on the fourth floor of the house, he believes that he has in a sense already encountered and faced up to it. He pictures himself at that moment proudly descending the stairs brandishing his dignities like a parchment scroll and bearing in his other hand a drawn sword. After the actual encounter with the ghost's presence, this heroic image is destroyed, and he descends the stairs in something resembling panic. Certainly the discretion which he assures himself he possesses instead of his former valour seems an inadequate defence against the presence on the ground floor, who looms up at him like some 'black-vizored sentinel guarding a treasure' (ANS, 814). If Brydon is the white knight, he seems to be defeated by the black in this particular romance. The imagery suggests his inability to come to grips with the evil – perhaps even the original sin – in his own personality. 'The black and white squares of his childhood' of the floor of the hall underscore this imagery, and also suggest that the story is like a game of chess, an imaginary duel of dialectical opposites. Brydon loses the game, but he wins the match, for Alice comes to him and brings him back to life with 'the cool charity and virtue of her lips.' This is an inversion of the familiar Jamesian romance theme of the sleeping beauty.

Putting aside, then, the Freudian overtones and Dionysian dimensions, the story seems to make most sense as an account of the effects of environment upon personality. The two Brydons are the 'perfectly possible' developments of that tight bud born in the New York house. The two environments, American and European, change the form of these developments, but not their essential nature. Brydon refuses to accept this fact even though he has to admit that Alice is right in seeing the latent tycoon in his treatment of the contractor's representative in the building of the new apartment block. As Brydon's character is presented in the first part of the story, it is perfectly possible that he should have become the rich, powerful presence who appears to him in the doorway.

In this way, as I suggested above, *The Jolly Corner* resembles *A Passionate Pilgrim*. Clement Searle, as he declines towards death, imagines himself to be a man who was born and educated in the England where he is now preparing to leave his bones. The idea is a perfectly natural one, after all, for an expatriate to consider, and James took it up once more in the uncompleted novel, *The Sense of the Past*. There is evidence that the theme was also in the back of his mind when he wrote *The Ghostly Rental*, the story about the haunted New England farmhouse, shortly after he went to live in England in 1876. The rejected daughter who has been acting the part of the ghost to terrorize her father is in turn confronted by the actual ghost of her father. She drops her candle and flees in fear. The house burns down behind her. The colonial New England house with its ghost suggests both the tradition and the past that James left behind in coming to Europe. In *The Jolly Corner*, it is as if James sent a representative to confront that ghostly figure left behind, in order to lay a spirit that had haunted his consciousness in all the years of his absence.

In discussing the story, however, the critic should not forget that the schema of the encountered *Doppelgänger* was a popular one in late nineteenth-century literature. R. L. Stevenson's *Dr. Jekyll and Mr. Hyde* (1886) is only the most famous example of a theme that many explored, from Oscar Wilde in *The Picture of Dorian Gray* to Joseph Conrad in *The Secret Sharer*. James and Conrad saw in the *Doppelgänger* theme an immensely more complex *donnée* than the earlier writers, and brought to it a psychological penetration and

219

technical adroitness that made it yield a wealth of meanings. For both of these writers, consciousness was a complicated state; double consciousness was almost immeasurably complex. For both, the essence of the theme depends on the question: what would a given character have been like if he had been placed in a different, but analogous, situation? The captain in *The Secret Sharer* comes to see in the fugitive officer the image of what he could easily have become; just as Brydon pursues what is really his unrecognized self.

Even more than Conrad, however, James seems to move *inside* a consciousness rather than creating another character. The house on the jolly corner, like the House of Usher, becomes the emblem of a mind. As he enters it, Brydon feels that the place is like 'some great glass bowl, all precious concave crystal, set delicately humming by the play of a moist finger round its edge' (ANS, 803). This description is reminiscent of James's definition of experience, in *The Art of Fiction*, as 'an immense sensibility, a kind of huge spider-web of the finest silken threads suspended in the chamber of consciousness ...' James also frequently uses the image of a house to represent the mind. As Brydon penetrates deeper and deeper into the house, particularly into its darker regions, the nearer he comes to the 'duplication of consciousness' that is to result in the actual creation of the *alter ego*. The house thus becomes a projection of all the fears, as well as all the possibilities, of the Brydon he would have been had he stayed at home in America. As mentioned earlier, James only once steps completely outside Brydon's consciousness to record his own view of the process, and this in the face of his own felt inability to portray the subtlety of the moment when Brydon knows that his *alter ego* has 'turned' and is ready to meet him. 'There came to him, as I say – but determined by an influence beyond my notation! – the acuteness of this certainty' (ANS, 806). Apart from this, he stays tenaciously with all the complex shifts and turns of Brydon's consciousness as it goes through the terror of facing the ghost that he has himself created.

At all points, James is careful to keep the double aspect of the story in the mind of the reader; the house is also a mind, the ghost is also Brydon. The whole story is double, too, just like Poe's story 'A Descent into the Maelström,' for it is a metaphor for the descent into the hell of one's self. Surely T. S. Eliot was doing much the same thing when he had Prufrock inviting his other self to go with him through 'half-deserted streets' to the 'overwhelming question.' Prufrock, it is true, never quite gets to the question, and drowns in human voices. Brydon *does* ask the question; this is his courage. He is not, however, brave enough to face the answer, and only another's love can save him.

Crapy Cornelia also came directly out of James's experience in New York. It lacks the intensity of *The Jolly Corner* as the *donnée* is thin and the tone sophistically ironic, almost flippant. The situation, of a man who goes to propose to a woman and changes his mind at the last moment, is a comic cliché, a device for getting to the heart of the matter – the contrast between the mind of the old and the new New Yorker. The hero is called White-Mason, an interesting revival of the name of the sensitive young Civil War colonel, Ferdinand Mason, in *A Most Extraordinary Case* (1868), who also had failed to propose and had shortly afterwards died. This is a correspondingly older, a 'white' Mason, another sensitive hero, who is out of his depths in the harsh competitive world of twentieth-century New York. He has proposed three times before to different women, but had on each occasion been turned down because he did not 'charming as he was, cause himself to be superstitiously believed in; and the lapse of life, afterward, had cleared up many doubts' (ANS, 821–2). Now, White-Mason, with the aid of his 'somewhat extended means, of his possibly augmented charm, of his certainly improved mind and temper' was more sure of success.

For settings of the story, James used his old stand-by, Central Park (although now it is crowded with 'the overwhelming alien'), and the new residential areas east of the Park which he had described in metaphors of the theatre in *The American Scene*. He uses the same metaphors again, this time for the interior of one of the houses, the drawing-room of the polished and prosperous widow, Mrs. Worthingham – a later version of Mrs. Beck of *Guest's Confession* and Mrs. Luna of *The Bostonians*. She is surrounded by Dresden china shepherdesses, and looks like one herself, with her 'charming complicated yellow tresses.' In her rococo, pink, white, and gilded Louis Quinze drawing-room (reminiscent of the 'period' reproductions in the New York hotels of *The American Scene*), White-Mason feels that the curtain is rising 'to the first act of some small and expensively mounted comic opera.' The exterior of the house has already been described in an image that figures in most of James's later fiction about the United States; it has 'that gloss of new money, that glare of a piece fresh from the mint and ringing for the first time on any counter, which seems to claim for it, in any transaction, something more than the "face" value' (ANS, 822).

The metaphor functions soon enough when, in the scene that follows, White-Mason comes to realize that he has over-rated the value of Mrs. Worthingham. He does not propose because someone is already on the scene before him. It is not a rival, but 'a small black insignificant' woman who is wearing a 'frumpy, crapy, curiously exotic hat ...' The juxtaposition of the two women, one in all her knowing modernity and the other so obviously belonging to a past order, throws White-Mason off his balance and purpose. The change is brilliantly dramatized by James's play of figures. For example, he represents White-Mason's view of Mrs. Worthingham's outlook as 'a great square sunny window that hung in assured fashion over the immensity of life.' Even as he looks at the view, he seems to see her 'light gemmed hand' touch a spring that drops 'half across the scene a soft-coloured mechanical blind, a fluttered, fringed awning of charmingly-toned silk ...' (ANS, 825). White-Mason knows that, once married to her wealth and high detachment, he would be on the balcony above the swarming plaza, beyond the burden and worry of life, and shaded from its harsh lights. Into this agreeable picture juts the unfashionable, incongruous, crape-covered, black hat that comes nearer and nearer to his vision 'after the manner of images in the kinematograph.' (This is a remarkable example of how James could adapt new technologies to his imagery of consciousness and rapidly adapt a schema from another art form for his fiction.)

To White-Mason's surprise, he finds that the hat belongs to a friend of former days, Cornelia Rasch. She is poor, but she is honest *old* New York, with none of the pampered confidence and essential ignorance of Mrs. Worthingham, who comes, White-Mason surmises, from one of those parts of the country that 'New Yorkers of his approved stock and conservative generation' would have 'naturally figured to their view as "God-forsaken" and generally impossible'

(ANS, 830). Cornelia, on the other hand, is rich in associations dear to White-Mason. Later on he visits her. She has a small flat in a new apartment building that James, with his devastating eye for New York detail, calls 'The Gainsborough.' But her rooms are furnished in 'the serene and sturdy' style of the 1860s, and they are full of photographs of mutual, now mostly dead, friends. In the face of these mementoes, he realizes all that Mrs. Worthingham does not have, even though Cornelia assures him that the lady is eager to marry him. He determines to spend the rest of his time with Crapy Cornelia. He will not marry her even though, like Maria Gostrey with Strether in *The Ambassadors,* she practically proposes to him. He will merely live with her in continual visits to her fireside and share the 'glow of her little household altar.' As Sister Corona Sharp has suggested, Cornelia is to perform for the Prufrockian White-Mason the function of extending his own consciousness.[9] He shies away from the threatening face of marriage, content to realize that he is old (although he is in fact only forty-eight).

The story is an excellent example of how James could work all kinds of social and moral aspects into a basically simple, comic plot, and of how he could squeeze a little subject to make it yield the last drop of general significance. Mrs. Worthingham and Cornelia represent the contrasting lives and manners of the present and the past. An infinitely more attractive and dangerous merry widow than Mrs. Luna, Mrs. Worthingham is dramatized not only through her gleaming personage, but also through her house, her drawing-room, and her style. James makes the reader feel in the end, as White-Mason feels, that her exterior is everything, her interior non-existent. She is counterfeit money, a stage-setting, style without substance, like her Dresden-shepherdess figure and her imitation period furniture. White-Mason comes to feel that the most impertinent thing about her is her confidence that 'every blest thing ... was somehow matter for her general recreation.' This 'innocent egotism' and 'overflowing anarchism' was her 'rabid modern note.' With a sentence that captures the Park Avenue *nouveau riche* with deadly accuracy, James describes her manner as the 'music of the future – that if people were but rich enough and furnished enough and fed enough, exercised and sanitated and manicured and generally advised and advertised and made "knowing" enough ..., all they had to do for civility was to take the amused ironic view of those who might be less initiated' (ANS, 829). Mrs. Worthingham symbolically represents all the 'taste' that the new acquisitive society could muster, for whom the expensively-bought present made up for a non-existent past, for whom 'the riot of the raw' is the substitute for 'the tone of time.'

In contrast to the iridescent widow, Crapy Cornelia reminds White-Mason of 'the old brown surface and tone as of velvet rubbed and worn, shabby, and even a bit dingy, but all soft and subtle and still velvety ...' (ANS, 834). She refers to the almost legendary past of New York, when 'the best manners had been the best kindness, and the best kindness had mostly been some art of not insisting on one's luxurious differences, of concealing rather, for common humanity, if not for common decency, a part at least of the intensity or the ferocity with which one might be "in the know." '* These are, in fact, the manners of an aristocracy, or at least an *élite* in a democratic society. In the end, White-Mason rejects the luxurious present and grasps at the remnant of the old New York that Cornelia represents, with all its treasures of shared experience. He sits down with her at the considerable glow of 'her little household altar.'

A sociologist, in discussing sacrifice in primitive societies, has written: 'There obviously is continuity, biological and cultural, between the living and the dead. We are partly formed by the past, even the distant past. Sacrificial offerings for ancestors symbolically recognize this. Further, those who remember their dead together, and share the same dead, also of necessity emphasize their living relationships among themselves: commemoration of the ancestor is affirmation of the range of relationships he created among the living, a holding together of all those who account him important in their past.'[10] This

---

*Marius Bewley, as part of his adverse criticism of this story, observes that 'Crapy Cornelia is not sufficiently realized ... to enable her to carry those values of life and society that James would endow her with.' (*The Eccentric Design: Form in the Classic American Novel* (London, 1959), 233.) Mr. Bewley has overlooked two significant aspects of the story: firstly the many small but significant details that do characterize her (i.e., 'her oddly unassertive little rotund figure ... (like) a black satin ottoman treated with buttons and gimp'; 'Cornelia gasped and wriggled – she practically giggled ...' etc.) ; secondly that the images deliberately emphasize her obscurity in relation to the showy elegance of Mrs. Worthingham.

same belief is the basis of *Crapy Cornelia,* as it is of a similar story, *The Altar of the Dead.* In New York, James had been touched on a deep psychological spring by the destruction of the past, by ruthless, unthinking modernity and by the infusion of all the new and alien elements into his native city. White-Mason, in choosing Cornelia, is symbolically asserting his own identity by accepting his age and rejecting a future in which he would have become an acquisition of Mrs. Worthingham, another of her expensive reproductions. For she neither knows nor cares that he is a genuine relic of an older order, and this is perhaps the thing that hurts the fastidious White-Mason most.

Crapy Cornelia also presents James's later view of the process of perception and its value as moral as well as aesthetic experience. Without a sense of the past – one's own rather than an historical past – one's perception of the present is a barren thing. With Mrs. Worthingham, White-Mason would have been condemned to present time and surface knowledge only. To the Jamesian observer-character it is the pressed spring of memory, to use an image recurrent in *The American Scene,* that releases the richest flow of images and creates the strongest felt experience. The danger of this view of life, and it is common to many of James's later heroes, is that it means the rejection of the present, with the threats that it poses particularly in the form of sexual encounter. James's earlier fear of women in general seems in these later years to have been transferred to younger women who still present the fascination but also the menace of the Vénus d'Ille. He turns instead to older women for his heroines, Alice Staverton and Cornelia, for example, because they present no threat, only the warmth and safety of the mother-image.

Mrs. Worthingham bears certain resemblances to Mrs. Connery, the mother of Julia in *Julia Bride.* Mrs. Connery is less successful and more frequently married, but has the same sort of hard, artificial, iridescent beauty. Her hair is in 'arranged silver tendrils which were so like some rare bird's nest in a morning frost ...' (ANS, 768). She bears most of the responsibility for making Julia what she is, just as the hypochondriac and helpless Mrs. Miller has a good deal to do with the nature of Daisy Miller. *Julia Bride* was, in fact, intended by James as a companion-piece for *Daisy Miller.* The two stories, along with *Pandora,* give us a picture of the evolution of characteristic American girlhood over three decades.

In both *Daisy Miller* and *Pandora,* James had taken the absence of the male members of the families for granted. On his return to America in 1904, he found to his consternation that, except in Washington, the absence of the male had become the law of social life. The American girl was now left in a completely uncorrected and unrelated state. She was expected to supply, as he put it in *The American Scene,* all the interest that was not the mere interest on the money. She had been abandoned and betrayed by the male parent and brothers and cousins until she was, James thought, practically lost.

More of the background for *Julia Bride* can also be found in the essays on the speech and manners of American women that James contributed to *Harper's Bazar* in 1906–7.[11] His conclusion, in these articles, was that no witness who had been enabled to compare the manners and speech of American women as they were at this point in the twentieth century with what they had been twenty years before could fail to notice the deterioration. One of the obvious sources of this falling-off was to be found in the women 'with hard faces and harsh accents' who populated the great hotels. It seemed to him that they illustrated some statistics that he had seen on the rising rate of divorce. They were the natural products of a system that made divorce cheap and easy, and he speculated about the type of training that they might be giving their 'terrific bedizened little girls.'

Julia Bride was meant to chronicle his sense of the change, to present a hypothetical product of such a mother. It was to be the last evoking of the creature who had appeared so frequently in his fictions and who had had to bear the burden of so many of his references to American life. In the preface to the tale, in volume XVII of the New York Edition, he imagined her coming once more onto his artistic scene; ' "Here we are again!" she seemed, with a chalked grimace, to call out to me, even as the clown at the circus launches the familiar greeting; and it was quite as if, while she understood all I asked of her, I confessed to her the oddity of my predicament. This was but a way, no doubt, of confessing it to myself – except indeed that she might be able to bear it. Her plea was – well, anything she would; but mine, in return, was that I really didn't take her for particularly important

226

in herself, and would in fact have had no heart for her without the note, attaching to her as not in the least to poor little dim and archaic Daisy Miller, say: the note, so to call it, of multitudinous reference.' Julia's note had been struck again and again by the American girls he had seen during his recent visit. 'What if she were,' he wondered, 'the silver key, tiny in itself, that would unlock a treasure? – the treasure of a whole view of manners and morals, a whole range of American social aspects?'[12]

Having to carry this burden, Julia can have nothing to do with 'pure poetry,' which was James's description of Daisy and his attribution to Pandora. She is instead a symbolic figure who embodies many of James's ideas about social change in America in the twenty years that he had been absent from the country. She was designed to be a focus for criticism of the new society. Just as Daisy was, as one critic has said, 'an archetype of American innocence.'[13] So Julia was intended as the type of American experience. James uses *Daisy Miller* as his own schema for *Julia Bride*, but the story is told from Julia's point of view, which in itself is a significant difference; Daisy would have had a point of view so restricted as to be quite colourless. Julia anticipates Scott Fitzgerald's flappers in her brightness as well as her beauty. There is nothing in the air that she fails to feel. The education of her perception is the dramatic development of the tale.

It is a story of deceit and intrigue. Julia and her mother have between them 'nine nice distinct little horrors': six broken engagements for Julia and three nullified marriages for her mother. Julia, as the story opens, is trying to extricate herself from her compromised past in order to marry the rich and fearfully respectable Basil French, of 'the serried Frenches.' She sees her ex-step-father, Mr. Pitman, in the Metropolitan Museum, where she has been with Basil, and rushes back to ask him to assure Basil of the innocence of her mother in their divorce case. She promptly discovers to her consternation that Mr. Pitman wants her to vouch for the *guilt* of her mother in the same case to his *fiancée*, a rich widow, Mrs. Drack. It is clear that two conflicting testimonies will not do and that the genial Pitman would be quite inadequate for his task anyway. She tells him that she will have to look elsewhere, to attempt to clear her own past instead of her mother's. As it happens, Mr. Pitman has recently seen the most plausible of Julia's ex-*fiancés*, Murray Brush, whom Julia had thought was abroad. She determines to ask him to vouch for her. At this point, Mrs. Drack turns up. She is a vast, bland woman, of 'a large complacency, a large sentimentality, a large innocent elephantine archness,' with a 'huge hideous pleasant face.' Julia rises to the occasion, magnificently vouches for Mr. Pitman's innocence and floats away leaving the couple to 'be happy together' (ANS, 780).

Later on she meets Murray Brush in Central Park. He promises to 'lie like a gentleman' to Basil French about their relationship. But then he demands his own *quid pro quo*. He has just become engaged again, and he wants Julia, should his part of the bargain be fulfilled, to help him and his girl, Mary Lindeck, to rise to the level of the society to which Julia would be elevated by her marriage to Basil French. He suggests that Julia invite Mary and himself to have tea with Basil French and herself. Julia has by this time felt the cold waters of her social doom rising towards her throat but she resignedly agrees to this arrangement and then hurries away to her room in the 'horrible flat which was so much too far up and too near the East Side.' Once there she gives way to the 'long lonely moan' of her conviction that Basil would not for one moment be deceived and that her whole design is doomed to failure.

Most of the characters in *Julia Bride* are the natural products of a society that takes a system of 'cheap and easy divorce' for granted. The exception is Basil French, who is a glamorous symbol to the rest of them of wealth and social prestige. Julia, having a mother with one impending and two past divorces to her credit, had naturally gone in for 'the young *speculative* exchange of intimate vows,' as James called it in his preface to the story. Her plight, like that of Daisy Miller, was the fruit of ignorance. Julia's half-dozen engagements and disengagements were of no more account to her than Daisy's numerous trysts with Giovanelli in Rome. Only after she has come to know Basil, who is 'cultivated, earnest, public-spirited, brought up in Germany, infinitely travelled, awfully like a high-caste Englishman,' does she see that there might be something shabby about her past and a real need for glossing it over.

Murray Brush disposes of the possible objections of Basil by putting him in the category of those 'who are not in sympathy,' as he puts it, 'with the old American freedom.' Daisy Miller, brought up, like Julia, in an extremely haphazard manner, had simply taken for granted this freedom of association with the opposite sex. She was never able seriously to consider any alternative mode of behaviour, and retains this outlook to her early death. Julia, in contrast, comes to see that 'the disgusting, the humiliating thing' was that her mother had allowed her to assume all along that 'her own incredibly allowed, her own insanely fostered frivolity' had been the natural career for a young girl. She has to attempt to sever herself from this career by sordid intrigue.

Julia, by realizing that she has been caught irrevocably in the tangle of her own false upbringing, at least reaches a degree of self-knowledge. The other characters in the story remain enmeshed in deceit, snobbery, and 'money-passion.' Mr. Pitman, speaking of his desire to marry Mrs. Drack, says simply, 'Julia, she has millions' (ANS, 774). He announces proudly that she too 'disapproves of divorce quite as much as Mr. French.' Murray Brush has also taken the precaution this time of getting engaged to a girl who is 'not, thank goodness, at all badly off, poor dear' (ANS, 790). His calculated effort to climb socially makes the snobbery of Winterbourne's aunt in *Daisy Miller* look almost charitable by comparison. In this respect, incidentally, the subjects of *Julia Bride* and *Pandora* are the same. Julia, Murray, and Mr. Pitman are, like Pandora, all trying to better themselves socially and financially. The circumstances of each tale, however, make a directly opposing impression on the reader. Pandora's method of self-advancement, given the nature of the American political system, is direct and honest. The methods of the characters of *Julia Bride* are devious and sordid.

Julia Bride is so rich in wit, and its implications and overtones are so various, that no paraphrase can convey what James in the preface called 'its note of multitudinous references.' This note is quite lacking in the flat texture of tales like *Daisy Miller* and *Pandora*. James sought to explain the difference by saying: 'A whole passage of intellectual history, if the terms be not too pompous, occupies in fact, to my present sense, the waiting, the so fondly speculative interval ...' In that time, James had been hanging around, as he whimsically termed it, like 'an irrepressibly hopeful artistic Micawber,' on the chance that something would turn up out of the situation of this repeatedly presented fictional type, the American girl. In *Julia Bride*, he believed it had turned up at last. In this strictly foreshortened story, he was trying to make 'a full-fed statement ... – the imaged résumé of as many of the vivifying elements as may be coherently packed into an image at once.' He felt the necessity for making the statement through the vehicle of a story like *Julia Bride* because, as he explained yet again, 'the world down-town' was closed to him. His sheer ignorance of any detail of business operations disbarred him from making any fictional representation of it.

He was confined for subject matter to 'the minor key' of the uptown world. 'To ride the *nouvelle* down-town,' he wrote wistfully, 'to prance and curvet and caracole with it there – that would have been the true ecstasy.' But he knew that one spill, such as he might easily have had in Wall Street, or wherever, would have prevented him, for very shame, from ever mounting again.[14] The only way, then, that he could portray what he considered to be the most important aspect of American life was by implication. It was, once again, the method he had brilliantly used in *The American Scene*. Acting on what he knew, he projected his consciousness into the blankness of what he could only deduce. In *Julia Bride* he uses the genre of the comedy of manners and the symbolism of the business world. It is as if he caught the image of the downtown world in the small mirror of uptown. He did this by the pervasive use of imagery of financial transactions and animals.

All the characters have their appropriate correlatives in terms of cash values. Poor Mr. Pitman, although not shabby, has written all over him the 'business slackness' that caused Julia's mother to dispense with him. Mrs. Drack, when she appears in the Museum, conveys her value by 'the whole metallic coruscation' of her personality, her lustrous black brocade, her 'enhancements, of every description, that twinkled and tinkled,' all of which represent 'the large figure of her income, largest of all her attributes' (ANS, 777). Julia herself exults in the items of her own beauty as if they were investments in a rising market. '*Le compte y était* ...,' she thinks, 'this sum of thumping little figures.' But she also feels the investor's qualms. 'Nobody knew better than Julia that inexpressible charm and quoteable "charms" (quoteable like prices, rates, shares, or whatever, the things they dealt in downtown) are two distinct categories; the safest thing for the latter being, on the whole, that it might include the former, and the great strength of the former being that it might perfectly dispense with the latter' (ANS, 780). Julia plays the marriage market by attempting to realize on her quoteable charms, having sold off cheaply her blue-chip charms of delicacy, innocence, and reputation. She discovers, however, that the quotable charms of beauty, elegance, and grace, will not make up for the inexpressible ones. She realizes that the prospective buyer will back away when he discovers their inflated value. In the end, talking to Brush, she declares she has 'no margin' and like an overreaching speculator, she faces certain ruin.

The shadier aspects of the story's personal transactions are emphasized by another series of monetary images. Mr. Pitman and Julia, meeting in the Metropolitan Museum, are like 'a pair of pickpockets comparing ... their day's booty.' Murray Brush and Julia in 'the paths and favouring shades' of Central Park are like 'Nancy and the Artful Dodger ... talking things over in the manner of "Oliver Twist." ' Julia realizes when she sees her ex-*fiancé* how little he is 'of metal without alloy.' His charity towards her, all bogus as it is, 'is like a subscription of a half a million' (ANS, 786). Even the opening setting, the Museum, plays its ironic part in the financial ambience of the proceedings. Its great shining rooms and marble steps, 'its mockery of art and "style" and security,' represent all the things that Julia is vainly after. The ambiguity of the word 'mockery' in this context is enriched by a knowledge of James's comments on the Metropolitan in *The American Scene*. It signified for him 'acquisition,' and the word, of course, connotes not only the paintings magnificently collected and the Museum sumptuously built but all the gathered cash that these things represented. 'There was money in the air,' he wrote, 'ever so much money – that was, grossly expressed, the sense of the whole intimation. And the money was to be all for the most exquisite things – for *all* the most exquisite except creation, which was to be off the scene altogether; for art, selection, criticism, for knowledge, piety, taste.'[15]

The imagery of birds and animals, particularly of zoo specimens, runs parallel to the financial imagery. Reflecting on the penalties that she and her mother had paid for their ruinous prettiness, Julia comprehends that people had regarded them 'as if they had been antelopes or zebras, or even some superior sort of performing, of dancing, bear' (ANS, 769). Having 'cleared' Mr. Pitman of responsibility in his divorce case with her mother to the 'elephantine' Mrs. Drack, Julia floats 'swanlike' away through the halls of the Metropolitan. Thus the animal imagery is linked with another series of images of water, symbolic of Julia's consciousness. She floats elegantly and supremely in the consciousness of her beauty at the beginning of the story, but the more she realizes how she has been compromised by her past the more she feels 'the cold swish of the waters' rising to engulf her. At the end of her interview in the Park with Murray Brush she is completely demoralized by the obvious hopelessness of her case, but rather than let him see that, 'she would have hurled herself publicly into the lake there at their side, would have splashed in her beautiful clothes, among the frightened swans, rather than invite him to that ineptitude' (ANS, 789).

Although *Julia Bride* is a wonderfully dexterous social comedy, its 'imaged résumé' of New York financial and social life is an extremely harsh one. It reflected James's belief that 'the old American freedom' based on self-reliance and individualism, had been corrupted in these latter years into a strategy of selfishness and self-aggrandizement. American women, having been forced to run the social game unaided, had nevertheless tended to take their cue from the financial game played downtown. Many felt that manners, delicacy, stability, honesty, all could be sacrificed in order to gain better prizes in the marriage market. Some, like Julia's mother, regarded one marriage simply as a stock investment, to be sold as soon as a better prospect appeared. The children brought up in such a *milieu* paid the penalty for this folly.

Julia Bride has another dimension missing from both *Daisy Miller* and *Pandora*. Mr. Miller, supplying the cash that makes the action possible, remains behind in Schenectady, and is a cipher in the tale. Pandora's parents appear only fleetingly in her story, on board the liner from Europe to America. They sit all day in their steamer chairs, closing their eyes whenever Pandora approaches, like 'a pair of household dogs who expect to be scratched.' Julia's real father does not figure at all in *Julia Bride*, yet so strong are the overtones of the story that there is no sense of missing connections or motivations. Julia's life has a 'full fusion,' as James puts it in his preface, 'with other lives that remain undepicted, not lost.' The other lives form part of Julia's consciousness: her mother's ex-husbands, her numerous ex-*fiancés*, the 'serried Frenches,' even the spiteful Mrs. Maule, mother of four eligible 'kittens,' who is seeking to turn Basil's mind against Julia. They are all, in turn, representatives of a range of American manners and aspects. The flat quality that James ascribed to Daisy thus disappears in *Julia Bride* under the pressure of 'the other lives ... [that] press in, squeeze forward, to the best of their ability.' Daisy is a pathetic figure, for she dies wronged and innocent, but since she has little comprehension of the causes of her fate, can hardly arouse deep feelings of sympathy. Julia, on the other hand, sees more and more as the story progresses that she is the victim of a mistaken upbringing, the unfortunate scapegoat of her own reckless career. She views the society around her from a new perspective and judges it accordingly.

The freedom of the relations between the sexes that James had accepted as a desirable American norm – at least *in* America – in *Daisy Miller* came in for a critical re-appraisal in *Julia Bride*. Julia's generation had played fast and loose with the idea and stretched it in order to cover all kinds of irresponsible behaviour. James thought that it needed evaluation and criticism from those who stood most to lose by laxness. He achieved this by making the girl herself the centre of the rich consciousness of the tale. Julia thus misses nothing of the process of her failure. In her 'certain ruin' she has the 'grim lucidity' to see and appreciate the man, Basil French, who has the money and power to create such a social appetite in others. The 'whole passage of intellectual history' between *Daisy Miller* and *Julia Bride* thus records both James's achieved mastery of the foreshortened and tightly packed nouvelle and the transition of the consciousness of a characteristic type of American girl from innocence to experience and from ignorance to knowledge.

The idea of fraud and deceit that had been central to James's imaginative projection of American business since the beginning of his career turns up once more in his last American, indeed his last published, story, *A Round of Visits* (1910). The germ of this story had hung around for some time, in various stages of development, in James's notebook before it reached its final form. In 1899, James sketched in the situation quite fully, setting it in 'the great heartless preoccupied' London. When he came finally to write it, however, he changed the setting to New York in wintertime. This gave him the opportunity to work in some of his wondrous glimpses of the hot hotel world there as well as his recollection of a 'blinding New York blizzard.' This stark contrast of atmospheres underlines the theme of the story – the gulf between appearance and reality. The hotel-setting acts as an 'imaged résumé' of New York society as well as supporting the theme. It is named 'The Pocahontas,' but its internal furnishings are carried out 'largely on "Du Barry" lines.' In threading its labyrinth, the hero, Mark Monteith who has just arrived from Europe, passes 'from one extraordinary masquerade of expensive objects, one portentous "period" of decoration, one violent phase of publicity, to another' (ANS, 847).

With its luxuriant vegetation, its tropical heat, its 'vociferous, bright-eyed, and feathered creatures,' the hotel strikes him as a great jungle. This suggests an ironic parallel with Upton Sinclair's *The Jungle*, written three years before, but the Chicago stock-yards are no more heartless than the self-absorbed hotel-world. Monteith, sick and lonely in his room, like Colonel Mason of the Civil War story *A Most Extraordinary Case*, has no one to whom he can turn for help, even to lighten his consciousness of the wrong he has suffered at the hands of the man, Phil Bloodgood, whom he has entrusted with his 'poor dividends.' He cannot imagine telling the hotel-doctor that Phil Bloodgood is the matter with him. The doctor, he felt, could have much more pertinently confessed his own burden of miseries seen in hotel practice. When Monteith is on his feet again, the one person he knows in the hotel, who has also been swindled by Bloodgood, is so full of herself that he cannot bear to talk with her about his own losses and, what is more important, his own increasing sense of what Bloodgood must have suffered.

At last he meets a pretty girl at a crowded, lonely lunch who tells him that he must look up an old acquaintance, her brother-in-law, Newton Winch, who is badly laid up. It need only be remembered that Mrs. Luna's terrible little son in *The Bostonians* was called

Newton to make us realize what associations the name had for James. This would be, therefore, a grown-up version of that 'insufferably forward and selfish lad.' Monteith remembers Newton, 'from college years and from those two or three luckless and faithless ones of the Law School as constitutionally common, as consistently and thereby doubtless even rather powerfully coarse, clever only for uncouth and questionable things ...' (ANS, 856). He goes to see him only after the other resources of comfort have failed, as the last stop on his round of visits to self-absorbed friends. But he soon discovers that, although Winch lives in a luxurious studio-apartment that has something of the Pocahontas-Du Barry aspect about it, he has undergone, since Monteith has last seen him, 'some extraordinary process of refinement' – as if 'he had suddenly and mysteriously been educated.'

In the fine scene that follows, in which no subtle shade of perception and emotion is missed, Monteith feels the burden of his need to tell slip gradually away while his sense of Newton's suffering grows and, with that, his sympathy with the feelings of the man who has cheated him. With his sensibility tuned to the highest pitch, Monteith makes out that Newton's trouble is similar to that of Bloodgood, and, moreover, that his arrival had interrupted the conclusion of it by 'a small neat weapon he had been fingering in the low luxurious morocco chair ...' The process of his new-found friend's education now becomes clear to him: 'It had been, in its immeasurable action, the education of business, of which the fruits were all around them.' Newton confesses that he is probably worse than Phil Bloodgood. Unlike Phil, however, Newton, as he says, has stayed to 'take it.' To Monteith's question, 'To take what?' there comes as an answer the peal of the doorbell.

Mark, at Newton's request, goes out to the hall to answer it. Two policemen step in without a word. As they do so, there is the crack of a pistol, and the sound of a great fall. All three rush into the apartment. As one policeman bends over Winch's body, the other asks Monteith if he might not have prevented the act. Mark replies: 'I really think I must practically have caused it' (ANS, 866). In the policeman's question, a hundred things had come to him. What they are, James leaves to the reader's ingenuity, for at that point the story ends.

When Mark had rung Winch's bell earlier, he had caught him, he later in the interview surmises, with the revolver in his hand. Why had Winch not shot himself then? It would seem that he had been unable to find the courage to end his life at that moment. Mark's sympathy and understanding of Bloodgood and so, by analogy, with Winch, had helped him find courage again to end the affair without the squalor of a trial, to 'take it' with a bullet. This is surely what Mark means when he tells the policeman that he practically caused the suicide.

Krishna Baldev Vaid has suggested that, like *The Jolly Corner*, *A Round of Visits* is a *Doppelgänger* story.[16] Bloodgood and Winch represent what Monteith would have become had he stayed in New York instead of going to Europe. This is going rather too far, but the theory does underscore the link that can be established between Monteith and the two swindlers. Monteith is another of James's gentlemen who has steered absolutely clear of business and all innocently trusted his affairs to a friend. He had been, as he expresses it to Winch, 'a client temptingly fatuous,' even after he had been warned of the possibility of fraud. As such he has become a representative of the trusting ignorance that has, presumably, also tempted Winch to his undoing. This subtle theme of the guilt of an injured party, and consequently of the identity of the cheated with the cheater is present in James's work as early as *Guest's Confession*, published in 1868. It was to be the major theme of *The Ivory Tower*. In *A Round of Visits* it is implied more than developed. Winch himself certainly recognizes Mark's representative guilt of ignorance and trusting innocence, and it may be that Winch intends to make him pay for this, or at least recognize it, by drawing him into the affair by shooting himself while Mark goes to the door. A further subtlety is that Mark appears to recognize this ruse, but goes anyway in order to give Winch the opportunity to end it quickly. But these questions and surmises are all left in the complex air after the shot. The one certain thing is that this suicide is not the act of a man unhinged by worry and hopelessness, like that of Nora's father in *Watch and Ward*, but a considered act of resignation, even of expiation of fraudulent practices.

It is the familiar theme of Hawthorne, of education by sin and suffering, that James has used here, but there is, in the case of *A*

Round of Visits, a more direct source. In a penitentiary that James had visited on the outskirts of Philadelphia, during his American visit, James had met a reprieved murderer. Recording this incident in *The American Scene,* James had noted the man's urbanity and lucidity as a result of the 'refinement wrought in him by so many years of easy club life' in the prison, and half-expected to see him ring for coffee and cigars.[17] Winch's 'education' was somewhat less ironic than the convict's. It fully expressed, however, James's exaggerated sense of the menace of business life, a sense that had increased in these later years of his career until it reached its fullest expression in the vision of a practically total financial corruption in *The Ivory Tower.**

Inevitably, James's centres of consciousness in these late stories had to share or come to share James's vision of the corruption, inanities, disproportions, and vulgarities of much of contemporary American life, for these things supplied the *données* of all the tales. They learned and suffered from the knowledge of the power, the money-passion, the frivolity, the very note of *modernity* which James found so little to his taste on his American visit.

In his 'American Letters' of 1898, James had wondered why there were so few 'studies of the human plant under cultivation' in contemporary American literature. The answer to that question, he had written then, might lie in the circumstances under which the plant actually *was* under cultivation. These late stories both partially filled the gap he had noted and show us what he thought of the conditions of cultivation. Indeed the horticultural image appears several times in the stories. Most notably it is used in his references to hotel-civilization, the most complex and most typical symbol, James thought, of American life. Monteith imagines the hotel doctor's life in the monstrous place in images reminiscent of Baudelaire. He thinks of its 'flowers of oddity, flowers of misery, flowers of the monstrous, gathered in current hotel practice' (ANS, 846). The hotel itself, is, of course, a

---

*Marius Bewley, as part of his blanket criticism of these later stories, writes of *A Round of Visits*: 'It is possible to bring deviously subtle interpretations to one's reading of this story, but James's answer is categorical and blunt enough. Newton Winch has become a swindler and has been "refined" by dishonesty' (*The Eccentric Design,* 243). It is a curious fact about certain critics of James that they wish to rule out of court forever any interpretation of James's fiction other than their own.

symbol of luxuriant, uncontrolled jungle growth, a place where human relations have lost scale, harmony, and taste, all symbolized by the sham 'period' decor. In sum, James seems to have thought that the conditions for cultivation in American life were those of a hot-house, where the delicate plant of the social was forced, as so many things he thought were forced, by the desperate pace of life. This was the reason for his belief in getting back to his 'poor little English gardening,' where he could feel that, in spite of some dark moral undergrowth, these things were kept under more or less temperate control and cultivation.

❧ 16 ❧

The Fresh Start
and the Broken Link
The Ivory Tower

In *The American Scene,* James advanced the theory that most Americans wanted to make large sums of money so that they would not have to 'mind' the inconvenience, the desperate pace, and the bad manners of the national life.[1] This theory helped explain for him the intensity of the money-passion and also the abortive attempts that Americans made to create retreats from the world of business. The 'white elephants' of Newport struck him most forcibly as the symbols of what the money-passion did to aesthetic taste and social discretion, just as they reminded him, by contrast, of the shy little Newport of his own youth. Then it had harboured a small group of cosmopolites who seemed to have had all the leisure in the world to write and paint and talk, and stroll together on the empty sands.

So Newport was the logical choice for the opening scenes of his last American novel, which he wanted to write as soon as he got back to England. He was, as he told Edmund Gosse, like a 'saturated sponge,' eager to wring himself out into new projects.[2] After the completion of *The American Scene,* the revision of his novels, and the writing of prefaces for his New York Edition, which took far longer than he had expected, he found time, however, only to write the shorter pieces discussed in the previous chapter. He made a start on the novel in late 1909, calling it, in his notebook, 'The K.B. Case.'[3] This attempt was interrupted by a long illness. After that he was hit hard by William's death. This resulted in the writing of the autobiographical volumes which began as a kind of expansive biography of his brother, although they turned into something quite different. It was not until the early summer of 1914, that he could really settle down to his long-delayed novel. He was too late; what he left of the novel, *The Ivory Tower*, is merely a fragment, an incomplete construction of little more than three of the ten books which he planned. He did leave, however, in addition, the blueprint for the rest, the long scenario that James customarily drew up for his later novels. The notes to *The Ivory Tower* are invariably printed after the fragment of the novel but it is better in a way to start with them, for, although they do not reveal the complete story line, they do indicate the structure and part of the meaning of the intended whole. Moreover, by comparing these notes with the completed part of the novel, the reader can watch a great artist in the very process of shaping his work from an outline, bowing to the necessities of his form and to the demands of his creative imagination.

The notes reveal how strongly many aspects of twentieth-century America had acted as a spur to James's energy, although they had at the same time galled his sensibilities. 'Well before me surely too,' he wrote, 'the fact that my whole action does, can only, take place in the air of the last actuality; which supports so, and plays into, its sense and its portée. Therefore it's a question of all the intensest modernity of every American description; cars and telephones and facilities and machineries and resources of certain sorts not to be exaggerated; which I can't not take account of' (ANS, 1035). What modern America, with its power, its pressures and its gadgets, was making of its people was to be the basis of the story.

The structure of the novel was carefully planned. Like *The Awkward Age*, *The Ivory Tower* was to be composed according to James's law of successive aspects. Each book was to present a different aspect of the central situation by concentrating on the experience of one character. In an unpublished section of the notes to books three and four of *The Ivory Tower* now in the Houghton Library at Harvard, James explained in some detail how he intended to work the aspects out in the novel. He was not going to enter the consciousness of, or 'go behind' as he called it, any character except his hero, Graham, or Gray, Fielder. Even the second most important character, the billionaire's daughter, Rosanna Gaw, is represented externally, though he noted that it might appear otherwise. 'I give her appearances and aspects and semblances and motions there [in the first two books], but at no point speak as from myself for what is actually beneath; and this I keep up for all the rest of the business.' In other words, all but the Gray sections of the book were to be enacted as drama; the Gray sections were to be drama plus consciousness. In sketching out the action for books three and four in the unpublished notes he speaks of 'lines' as if they were lines of dialogue – 'the Rosanna-Davey lines,' the 'Horton-Cissy and Cissy-Horton lines.' 'For the rest,' he added, 'I stick to my luminous difference [that is, Gray's consciousness]; keeping my Gray-and-his-uncle, my Gray-and-Miss Mumby lines, my Gray-and-Rosanna lines (as distinguished from any Rosanna-and-Gray) for the beautifully applied law. So there it is. Absolutely organic.' Gray's consciousness, it seems, was to become the reflector of all the others in the book, the organic centre of awareness, if not of action. In this way, James was going to attempt a fusion of the methods of *The Awkward Age*, which is almost totally dramatic, with those of *The Ambassadors*, which is largely a record of consciousness.

Another organic factor in the novel was to be in the time scheme, which James carefully worked out in the notes printed in the volume to be just over a year, like his first American story. He planned to make the temporal cycle concentric with the cycle of adventures of Gray from his arrival in the United States until his departure. Books I through III take place in late summer in Newport where he comes from Europe to inherit a fortune. Books IV through VIII are set in New York. The climax takes place in the empty city in 'a more or less torrid mid-August,' where he discovers that he has been swindled of his money. This, it will be remembered, is the setting which F. Scott Fitzgerald, with a similar artistic insight, chose for the climax of *The Great Gatsby*. James's conclusion, Books IX and X, is in the fall of the year, as was Fitzgerald's, in 'the admirable Indian Summer' of the 'New England mountain-land' of the Berkshires. Here Gray renounces the whole business and decides, the notes indicate, to return to Europe (ANS, 1030–5).

The notes also make plain that ill-gotten money was to be the essence of James's subject, both as foreground and background. The

241

fraud that is practised on the hero is a counterpart of the many frauds that constitute his inheritance. James intended to permeate his novel with the dark moral atmosphere in which the American moguls operated. Part of Gray's education in America is to be his gradual realization of what James called 'the black and merciless things that are behind the great possessions.' He is concerned not only with the ways in which his hero will come to the consciousness of his 'damnosa hereditas,' but also with the ways he is to consider expiating the guilt attaching to it. One possibility, James noted, is that he should feel inclined to hand over 'great chunks of his money to public services and interests, deciding to be munificent with it, after the fashion of Rockefellers and their like ...' But Rosanna Gaw points out to Gray the flaw in this procedure. Rosanna has also inherited vast sums of money, and she hates every cent of her fortune. The source of her unhappiness is that she feels her possessions are so dishonoured and stained and blackened at their very roots that they carry their curse with them. She wonders what 'application to "benevolence" as commonly understood, can purge them, can make them anything but continuators ... of the wrongs in which they had their origin' (ANS, 1012).

James took enormous pains to visualize his characters in his notes and to work out their personalities. Pelham Edgar justly claimed: 'James has never, I think, been more firmly possessed of his characters, nor launched them to better effect.'[4] Gray Fielder was, James desperately recognized, another in the long series of his 'intelligent' heroes, 'another exposed and assaulted, active and passive "mind" engaged in an adventure and interesting in *itself* by so being ...' (ANS, 1027). He is of American parentage, but has been raised in Europe. With Gray, James reversed the theme which had supplied him with the subjects for his greatest novels: he brought the European to America; he confronted an innocent from the old world with the experience and evil of the new. Just as James's earlier heroes were ignorant of the forms and values of Europe, so Gray was to be ignorant of the forms, or rather the formlessness, of American society and the money-values which James believed largely governed it. He intended Fielder to be what he called 'an out and out non-producer ... an anomaly and an outsider alike in the New York world of business, the N.Y. world of ferocious acquisition, and the world there of enormities of expenditure and extravagance ...' (ANS, 1025).

Rosanna Gaw was to be Gray's one true friend. 'The big, the heavy daughter' of a billionaire, she is also, James noted, '*morally elephantine*' (ANS, 1010). Since her tastes are correspondingly disproportionate, she is to be unable to communicate satisfactorily with Gray, at least on aesthetic grounds. Before the action of the novel begins, she is to persuade Gray's rich, estranged, and dying uncle to leave his fortune to his nephew because he has not been corrupted either by the accumulation or the possession of wealth. The man who embezzles Gray's money is another friend, the genial, crew-cut Horton (ironically nicknamed Haughty) Vint. He is one of those desperate people, as James saw them, with rich friends and expensive tastes, but no means of keeping up with either. Gray's ignorance of and distaste for money matters causes him to hand over the entire management of his fortune to Haughty, who is in business, unsuccessfully, in New York. He thus holds out, James noted, 'an enormous and fantastic opportunity and temptation' to his friend. Haughty has an additional reason for needing money, in the shape of a beautiful young American girl, with whom he is in love, Cissy Foy. She too is poor. Although she is fond of Haughty, she agrees with him that without funds there can be no question of marriage for them. The notes suggest that she is also to become involved with Gray Fielder, probably as a decoy for Haughty's purposes. The other major characters are Davey and Augusta, called Gussy, Bradham, organizers of guests and parties and conspicuous consumers. But even with these characters, James adds the complication that they are not as prosperous as they seem, so that it is in their interest to cultivate Gray and Rosanna as much as they can.

In sketching out his story, James was not content merely to delineate his characters; he also arranged their associations antecedent to the action of the novel. All the major characters except Gray and the Bradhams have known one another before in some connection, so that their relationships in the novel are to be superimposed over a whole range of remembered facts, emotions, and expectations. Formally, this was a means by which James could avoid unnecessary exposition and clear the ground for the immediate intimacy of his characters. More important, it was one of the ways in which he could heighten the tension and moral ambiguity of his action. In the world of this novel no act can be divorced from its context of personal history, no decision can be made that is not coloured and influenced by predisposition. The choice between right and wrong, the nature of good and evil, was thus to be in *The Ivory Tower*, as in life, shrouded in ambiguity. 'The beauty,' James said of his situation, 'is in the complexity of the question ...' (ANS, 1028).

The further James worked into his notes, the more he realized that he was, as he put it, 'rather as usual, offering a group of the personally remarkable ... all round.' Given the nature of the problems of the novel, they could scarcely be anything else. For his characters, particularly in his late fiction, perception is the primary function. James, in fact, depends completely on their subtle insights into the nuances of personal relationships in order to convey the moral complexities of his action. His characters watch one another, reflect, theorize, intrigue, and, above all, exercise that freedom of will on which all the later novels so much hinge. In the economy of action which James planned, there could be, moreover, no superfluous, flat characters. 'That they are each,' he wrote, 'the particular individual of the particular weight [is] ... the essence of my donnée' (ANS, 1008).

The notes do not reveal how *The Ivory Tower* would have ended. Speculation on this topic has been one of the major concerns of critics of the novel; it has been a fruitless occupation. By the time James had completed sketching eight of his projected ten books, he had the action of the last two so firmly in his mind that he felt no need for further discussion. As in most of James's novels the choices are so open that we can, on hints from the author, predict only one development – that Gray will renounce the whole matter and refuse either to prosecute or even question the man who has cheated him of his fortune. 'He feels ...,' James wrote, 'after what he has learnt about the history of the money, [it is] the most congruous way of his ceasing himself to be concerned with it and of resigning it to its natural associations' (ANS, 1006). He will then return to Europe and the modest patrimony on which he has previously lived.

The richness of the notes goes a long way towards making up for the loss of the completed novel. There are in all literature few more rewarding glimpses into an artist's workshop. They show how James adjusted and readjusted proportion and relationships as he went along, saw deeper and deeper into his subject, puzzled and pondered, let himself go, pulled up, worried, and fussed until the whole lucid and complex design was complete in his mind. 'That brings me round,' he wrote near the end of his notes, 'and makes the circle whole.' This triumphant cry of mastery over his materials brings us close to the heart of the exultation in the artistic process.

Reading the notes is like watching a mosaic artist selecting and arranging his pieces for his large design. James himself used a metaphor which combines cabinet-making with engineering. Each successful working-out of a relationship or a significant perception was what he called 'a joint.' 'What I want is to get my right firm *joints*,' he wrote early in the notes, 'each working on its own hinge, and forming together the play of my machine; they *are* the machine, and when each of them is settled and determined it will work as I want it' (ANS, 1010). And yet James is constantly aware, as he works, that this is only a plan for a book which is to have its own organic laws of growth. After a particularly detailed piece of designing, he adds to himself: 'I say these things after all with the sense, so founded on past experience, that, in closer quarters and the intimacy of composition, pre-noted arrangements, proportions and relations, do most uncommonly insist on making themselves different by shifts and variations, always improving, which impose themselves as one goes and keep the door open always to something *more* right and *more* related' (ANS, 1032).

The most significant example of James's open door is provided by the title he gave the novel itself. It was probably suggested by his visit to Newport and his own essay on the place in *The American Scene*. There he discusses the cosmopolites 'sacrificing openly to the ivory idol whose name is leisure' at a time when everyone else recognized only 'the great black ebony god of business ...'[5] The tower image is also a natural consequence of the isolation of his hero, Gray. There is, however, no mention of it in the notes, but it becomes an organic and essential part of the novel's design, just as the famous cracked golden bowl became the organic symbol of the earlier novel.

As in all the late works of James, the symbol is a means of organizing experience into complex artistic forms and of increasing the range of perception of the reader. Whereas a literary schema tends to set limits by providing models for figures and scenes, the organic symbol opens up a work and mediates between writer and reader in a variety of ways, especially when it is used by an artist as subtle as James. In this late development, Hawthorne probably influenced James more than any other writer. In the 1897 essay, discussed in chapter twelve, James praised Hawthorne for his ability to 'go behind' the meagre façade of New England to find the suggestive idea, the artistic motive, which were far more complex things than 'the mere eye of sense' could suspect. James found in his work the consistent stance of 'an alien everywhere ... an aesthetic solitary.' This, he concluded, 'was a faculty that gave him much more a terrible sense of human abysses than a desire rashly to sound them and rise to the surface with his report ... He never intermeddled; he was divertedly and discreetly contemplative, pausing oftenest wherever, amid prosaic aspects, there seemed most of an appeal to a sense for subtleties.' In the piece he wrote for the Hawthorne Centenary in 1904, he pointed out further that Hawthorne had made use of his New England materials with 'an artistic economy which understands *values* and uses them.'[6]

James's own stance in his later work closely resembles that which he found in his revaluation of Hawthorne. His own sense of subtleties and his fine understanding of values contribute to the remarkable detachment which is characteristic of his point-of-view technique. One of the artistic motives which James seems to have found most impressive in Hawthorne's work was his use of the comprehensive titular symbol, such as is often found in the short stories and in all the novels except *The Blithedale Romance*. From *The Sacred Fount*, published in 1901, until the end of his life, James used titular symbols for his novels and many of his short stories. These comprehensive symbols provide an organic structural element which binds together the characters and themes of the story.

The ivory tower of his last unfinished American novel is a particularly complex example of this organic function of symbolism. These are some of the ways in which it works in the fragment of the novel. In Book Second, Rosanna hands Gray a thick letter sealed in black. Her father, Mr. Gaw, a former business associate of Mr. Betterman, who is Gray's uncle, had written it on his death bed. The letter almost certainly contains a black account of how Mr. Betterman obtained his wealth. Gray himself, in the next book, indicates to Haughty that this is what he believes the letter contains. Gray does not want to open it in front of Rosanna; in fact he does not want to open it at all, and he looks around for a suitable object in which to place it. Rosanna offers him 'a gold cigar case of absurd dimensions,' but Gray rejects this obvious symbol of the tycoon. He lights at last on an ivory tower, 'a remarkable product,' James calls it, 'of some eastern, probably some Indian, patience.' He goes on to describe minutely its exquisite workmanship, its circular form, its smoothly working drawers, its carefully concealed construction with 'tiny golden rivets,' and, finally, the little golden key which secures the whole object. It is a distinguished work of art in an atmosphere, a rented mansion in Newport, otherwise singularly bare of beauty.

The ivory tower not only supplies the title; it *is*, in a rich and complex way, the projected novel itself. Its circular form resembles the intended circular form of the novel, the story of a year, in which the last chapter was to echo the first. The joints which make the drawers work so smoothly are the joints of James's action; the golden rivets are, possibly, analogous to the glittering metaphoric style of the narrative. Surely, also, there is a wistful irony in James's comment that the tower, 'its infinite neatness exhibited, proved a wonder of wasted ingenuity ...' (ANS, 936–7). Of course, the exquisite workmanship of the tower is not lost on anyone who inspects it closely, as Gray does. Remembering the critical stupidity that greeted most of James's later work on publication (not to mention subsequently), he could reasonably predict that *The Ivory Tower* would, in that sense, be wasted ingenuity too. As insurance against wasted effort, James was once again backing the quality of his art to make it outlast time. In fact in these last years of his life, James's vision was remarkably similar to that of Yeats, who, in his tower, used a similarly fraught image of a bird of 'hammered gold and gold enamelling' that is 'set upon a golden bough' to signify the durability of the work of art and the merging of the artist's personality with his own creation.

The symbol of the tower also acts as a means of characterization.

It is the choice of Gray and his own emblem. 'Doesn't living in an ivory tower just mean the most distinguished retirement?' he asks Rosanna. 'I don't want yet awhile to settle in one myself – though I've always thought it a thing I should like to come to ...' It is prophetic of what he will come to in the novel. The letter of vilification which he slips into the tower is the first of many of the 'black and merciless things' which he will try to hide away in his consciousness, where they will do their work all the same. The golden key with which he locks it and then attaches to his key ring is the key to the knowledge he possesses but which he is afraid to use.

Rosanna also reveals herself in reaction to the tower. After Gray has selected it from among her father's possessions, she pronounces herself stupid for not having anticipated this choice. She makes him a present of it, indicating that he, with his superior taste and judgment, could make a better use of his wealth than she of hers. Haughty Vint, when he sees the tower, takes the humorous view of it, congratulates Gray on his symbolic retreat, and expresses his own desire for the run of one himself. Haughty also points out that Gray wishes to mount his tower to have his fun and leave Vint outside 'in the dust and comparative darkness' to mount guard over his fortune. Gray confirms this supposition. As he tells Haughty that he wishes to insure his life and his moral consciousness with him, he caresses the sides of the tower and fiddles about with its doors. These gestures reveal his carelessness and guilelessness about money matters. Haughty tells Gray that the little golden key to the tower is the key to the wild animal's cage. When he left Gray's house, he 'fairly sprang into the shade of the shrubberies' that surrounded it (ANS, 979). The fact is that Gray simply cannot lock up all the beasts in the American jungle on the lower floors of the ivory tower of his detachment.

The part of *The Ivory Tower* that James did write shows that he had lost none of his old skill in dramatizing a theme and weaving a rich and dense texture of narrative. Although he was dedicated to the most intense economy of means, his narrative expanded as soon as he began the novel. By the beginning of the fourth book he was already exceeding his planned quota of chapters. Rosanna has left for New York, where James planned this and the next three books to take place, but Gray, who is the centre of narration again, shows no signs of leaving Newport. On the basis of this vigorous beginning, it is hard to see the justification of Matthiessen's comment that there are 'signs of great tiredness in the writing' as the novel breaks off. Oscar Cargill rightly says of this remark: 'The specifics are not given ...'[7]

The novel begins brilliantly in Newport at higher summer, as James prepares for the advent of his hero, whose first impressions are to be all of sunniness and freshness. Yet he skilfully anticipates later developments by sketching in details of the ugly architecture of the Newport 'cottages,' crowding together on the desecrated cliffs. The first of James's successive aspects is that of Rosanna Gaw, whom the reader finds awaiting Gray's arrival and restlessly wandering about the house of the dying Mr. Betterman. Her ponderous presence is symbolized by a number of images drawn from the Orient, which recalls James's interest in this exotic analogue to America as presented in *The Europeans*. She carries a vast green parasol, 'a portable pavilion from which there fluttered fringes, frills and ribbons that made it resemble the roof of some Burmese palanquin or perhaps even pagoda ...' (ANS, 867). In his later years, Rosanna's father had turned to her, James observes, 'as he might have turned, out of the glare and the noise and the harsh recognitions of the market, into some large cool dusky temple; a place where idols other than those of *his* worship vaguely loomed and gleamed ...' (ANS, 871). He is also at Betterman's house, sitting motionless in a corner of the verandah, 'like a ruffled hawk ... with his beak, which had pecked so many hearts out, visibly sharper than ever ...' (ANS, 869). He is waiting for his former colleague and present enemy, Mr. Betterman, to die so that he can find out how much he has amassed since Gaw almost ruined him years before. But Gaw himself is a sick man. Rosanna says of him later, 'He's just dying of twenty millions ... You pay by these consequences for what you have done ... The effect has been to dry up his life ... There's nothing at last left for him to pay *with*' (ANS, 933).

These two men represent a generation that has, by cunning and strength of will, piled up many of the great American fortunes. Their money is the mainspring of the novel. The rest of the characters are either its inheritors or those who batten on them. The next character to appear is Davy Bradham who calls for Rosanna at the house which she and her father have rented to take her to tea. He is a fat, self-satisfied man who 'would hang up a meaning in his large empty face as if he had swung an awful example on a gibbet ...' His hair, James observes, with a keen eye for contemporary American habits, 'is cropped close to his head after the fashion of a French schoolboy or the inmate of a jail' (ANS, 876–7). This man is 'the massive Mercury' of the 'urgent Juno' Gussy, his wife. In an extended simile describing her, James reverts to the exotic, jungle imagery that is characteristic of his late American fiction. To Rosanna's sense, her state is not human, but 'might have been that of some shining humming insect, a thing of the long-constricted waist, the minimised yet caparisoned head, the fixed disproportionate eye and tough transparent wing, gossamer guaranteed' (ANS, 890). In such humorous and ironic images of death and blight, the characters are established and the action begins.

Rosanna, surrounded by these creatures of a predatory society, has a grim vision of what she has let Gray in for by persuading his uncle to send for him. It is likely that her ultimate fate in the novel is predicted by Davey in the middle of her recital to him of her past part in and future plans for Gray's career. 'It's too splendid,' he says, 'to hear of amid our greedy wants, our timid ideas and our fishy passions. You ring out like Brünnhilde at the opera. How jolly to have pronounced his doom!' (ANS, 885–6). The operatic reference is surely not merely another comment on Rosanna's size: it suggests more serious Wagnerian parallels in, for example, her relation to her father, who is another Wotan in his love of wealth and in his grim selfishness. Rosanna's surrounding ring of fire may be her money which in its way keeps off all but the most sincere and heroic suitor. Gray, her Siegfried, might choose Cissy as Siegfried chose Gutrune, in spite of Rosanna's devotion to him. Finally, it is in the cards that Rosanna might sacrifice herself for Gray's sake in some way, as Brünnhilde did by casting herself on Siegfried's funeral pyre at the end of 'Götterdämmerung.'

The second book is told from Gray's aspect. It is James's most ambitious attempt to represent the United States from the point of view of the innocent eye. Gray feels that in America 'his cherished hope of the fresh start and the broken link would have its measure filled to the brim' (ANS, 903). His impressions are rendered with James's inimitable comic sense. 'There was,' Gray finds, 'an American way for a room to be a room, a table a table ... and a cold gush of water in a bath of a hot morning a promise of purification; and of this license all about him, in fine, he beheld the refreshing riot.' The food, he finds, is 'seasoned and sweetened, a soft, substantial coldness and richness that were at once the revelation of a world and the consecration of a fate ...' (ANS, 906). Perhaps it is the comedy of manners that most strikes him. Mr. Betterman's nurse, Miss Mumby, imperturbably sits down to lunch with Gray, and then when the doctor comes in addresses him 'rather as he had heard doctors address nurses than nurses doctors; a fact contributing offhand to his awareness, already definite, that everyone addressed everyone as he had nowhere yet heard the address perpetrated ...' He finds these democratic manners and American perceptions to be exhilarating, rather than upsetting. Indeed he feels that he would have merely to go out on the piazza to 'step straight into the chariot of the sun,' or as if he had been presented with some 'quarto page, vast and fair, ever so distinctly printed and ever so unexpectedly vignetted, of a volume of which the leaves would be turned for him one by one and with no more trouble on his own part than when a friendly service beside him at the piano, where he so often sat, relieved him, from sheet to sheet, of touching his score' (ANS, 907–8).

In presenting Gray's consciousness in terms of such abundance and richness in nature and art James is showing the reader his hero's fond innocence and laying the ground for his disillusionment. The first false note is struck by Mr. Gaw. Gray encounters him when he walks out on the verandah to find the old man in the chair still awaiting Betterman's demise. To Gray, he looks like 'a small waiting and watching, an almost crouching gnome, the neat domestic goblin of some old Germanic, some harmonised, familiarised legend ...' Gray's perception tries to fit Gaw into a cosy Europeanized schema, but this 'queer, sharp, hard particle in all the softness' refuses to be assimilated in this way. Young man and old stare at each other, and Gray at length realizes 'that he had never yet in all his life caught the prying passion so shamelessly in the act.' He begins to see that Mr. Gaw's presence and activity was the consequence of a complete unawareness of 'form.' This is the other side of the coin of democratic manners. After an approach to Gaw has elicited no response, Gray feels 'quite as if something under his tongue had suddenly turned from the sweet to the appreciably sour ...' By a close analysis of Gray's consciousness, James traces the stages of his discovery of what Gaw wants to know. The old man is assuming that since Gray has been at the house of his dying uncle all morning he knows how much he is to inherit. Therefore Gaw believes that he has a chance of finding out how effectively he had ruined Betterman in the past. From this insight, Gray 'was afterwards to date the breaking-in upon him of the general measure of the smallest vision of business a young man might self-respectingly confess to ...' Gray determines to resist this trap to his candour and, even though he has not yet seen his uncle, happily asserts to Gaw that his own presence is doing his uncle an immense amount of good and thus implies that the amount of money in the case has not yet been in question. At this news, Gaw looks quite suddenly very sick; the assertion proves in fact to be the old ruffled hawk's own death blow. The drive of his curiosity having been thwarted, his vitality diminishes, and he soon afterwards dies. Gray leaves him to be taken up to his house by the nurse, Miss Numby, and goes to see his uncle.

What follows is a scene in the great manner of James's latest phase. Mr. Betterman is propped up on pillows in 'the vast cool room' and strikes Gray as being not formidable, but like 'some weary veteran of affairs, one of the admittedly eminent whose last words would be expected to figure in history' (ANS, 914). Gray takes everything in, the apparent dignity and refinement of the invalid, the importance of the occasion and the distinction of his own role in this unfolding drama. He says: 'You yourself, uncle, affect me as the biggest and most native American impression that I can possibly be exposed to.'

In Mr. Betterman James paints a portrait of a man who has been refined by illness and reflection into rejecting the principle on which he has based his life: that of ruthlessly making money. Though on his death bed, he is an incipient Adam Verver. After looking over his nephew, he tells him: 'I've got you – without a flaw. So!' Gray has the sense that he is being regarded 'as an important "piece," an object of value picked, for finer estimation, from under containing glass' (ANS, 918). What Mr. Betterman wants Gray for soon becomes clear. He wants him for the great American public, a public which believes that 'money is their life.' Since Gray has never in his life transacted three cents worth of business, he is to symbolize to that public the diametric opposite of the business mind and the money-passion. When Gray tries to find out in more detail what his uncle requires him to do, the reply is: 'Do? The question isn't of your doing, but simply of your being.' Mr. Betterman apparently believes that Gray, simply by being himself, can prove to all the others that there is another, and better, way to live. It is clear that Mr. Betterman has confirmed his choice of Gray for an heir, as Rosanna had encouraged him to do. He is indeed happy that Gray had not come to America when he was fourteen, as Betterman had desired. The uncle realizes that if he had come then, it would have spoiled him.

After Gray leaves his uncle he wanders agitatedly about in the grounds of the house, chucking away cigarettes only a quarter smoked. He is puzzled at his own restlessness, for he thinks that the scene which he has just gone through should have left him simply captivated, as his after-sense of it 'became an impression of one of those great insistent bounties that are not of this troubled world; the anomaly expressing itself in such beauty and dignity, with all its elements conspiring together, as would have done honour to a great page of literary, of musical or pictorial art.' He thinks that the picture is perhaps too perfect, that his future fortune seems to promise him too quiet a life. It is likely that James is insinuating into Fielder's mind the suspicion that the great work of art that seems to face him is in fact only another delusion of his American experience. This reverie is broken into by Miss Mumby, who comes out to tell him, in her typically direct way, that she thinks he should go and see Rosanna Gaw. This Gray meekly does.

When Rosanna comes down to see him from the bedroom in which her father is dying, it is not with any grief, but rather with delight in what she has managed for Gray with his uncle. Gray sees in Rosanna's large form 'the amplest of mothers' – repeating the familiar pattern of James's heroes in these last stories. He seems prepared, too, to accept what she wants him to do passively, like a child. She explains to him that although Mr. Betterman's health appears to have improved after Gray's visit, it is but a temporary recovery from which he will soon lapse into death. With equal coolness she tells Gray that her own father has received his death blow from Gray's innocent

announcement that his uncle was better, even though she has assured
her father that Betterman's revival is only a temporary one. Knowing
this, she is ready to give Gray the letter that her father has written
him, which brings into play the small ivory tower.

The third book is told from the aspect of Horton Vint. He and Cissy
Foy are having a *tête à tête* on the Newport sands, secretly, for neither
wants it known that they have a passionate *liaison*. They discuss Gray
and Rosanna, and it soon becomes clear that their main concern is
getting hold of them to exploit their wealth. Haughty himself suggests
that Cissy 'fall in love' with Gray. They also debate the possibility of
Gray and Rosanna pairing off. They are surprised in the middle of
this discussion by Davy. To cover up his discovery of them and to allay
his suspicions about their relationship, they at once eagerly ask him
whether or not Gray has a moustache. Davy has recently seen Gray
but he plays with the crafty couple as one who is on to their game
and does not give a direct answer. By this point in the novel, both
Betterman and Gaw are dead, and Gray, they surmise, is sitting alone
in the house with his uncle's body. Cissy laments that this occasion,
like all others in America, is marked by a complete lack of forms. She
is sure that there are no draped hangings, no catafalque, no relays of
mourners to lend dignity to the event. Cissy then asks Davy if Gray
has asked after her. She knew Gray's stepfather well and knows also
that she has often been the subject of conversation between the two
men. Davy replies that the conversation between Gray and himself
had not taken a turn that would have included her. He maliciously
implies that since Cissy is an American girl she would naturally
assume that she would be the subject of every conversation among
people that knew her.

Cissy rounds on Davy to tell him that she has 'notoriously nothing
in common with' the American girl. She even adds, with an emphasis
of contempt for conventional limitations, 'I loathe the American girl.'

Davy points out that Cissy does 'of course brilliantly misrepresent
her.' He hastens to patch up this frankness by adding, 'We're all
unspeakably corrupt.'

Cissy denies this view, not, she puts it, as a judge of her society but
as its victim. 'I don't say we don't do our best,' she adds, 'but we're
still of an innocence, an innocence – !' (ANS, 956).

F. O. Matthiessen interprets this remark to mean that Cissy knows

that Gray will finally see through them all. In the context of the fore-
going observations the remark may imply, however, that the famous
American innocence – that James had so much capitalized on in
earlier years – is, in the hands of Cissy Foy, simply another device by
which she can beguile Gray.

Davy, however, blandly takes the remark to be without ironic intent, assumes its secondary meaning of ignorance, and replies: 'Then
perhaps ... Mr. Fielder will help us; unless he proves, by your measure,
worse than ourselves.' Cissy denies the possibility of his being worse,
and insists to Davy that Gray knows more than all of them put together. Again it seems that Cissy is being ironic and that all Gray's
knowledge will not save him from the clutches of this group.

Both Cissy and Haughty are members of the Bradham *entourage*
that symbolizes in the novel the Midas touch of American life. In *The
American Scene*, James drew his metaphor for this condition from
one of Hawthorne's short stories. He called America 'a huge Rap-
pacini-garden [sic], rank with each variety of the poison-plant of the
money-passion ...'[8] In Hawthorne's tale, the hero enters the corrupted
garden, 'the Eden of the present world,' and tries to rid Rappaccini's
daughter of the poison she has absorbed from all her years among the
envenomed plants. It is so much a part of her system, however, that
the antidote kills her. It may be that James, in *The Ivory Tower*, was
planning to have Gray attempt a similar rescue of Cissy. The effort
would certainly have been as fruitless as it was in Hawthorne's story.

In the last section of the third book, Haughty goes to see Gray in
the house that he has so recently inherited. It is after the funeral, and
Gray tells him that he has had an interview with the solicitor, Mr.
Crick, and 'almost pitifully' confesses that he appears to have been
left 'a really tremendous lot of money.' He does not know exactly how
much he has been left or even where the will now is. In effect he
throws himself and his fortune on the knowledge and business acu-
men of Haughty. Gray, as Haughty remarks, is taking his luck hard,
and is already dreading the complications he is in for. At the same
time, he wants to enjoy it, 'to get everything out of it, to the very last
drop of interest, pleasure, experience, whatever you may call it, that
such a possession can yield.' To do this, he says, he depends absolutely
on Haughty.

The latter's advice is prompt. 'Your solution is marriage to a wife at short order.' Gray does not agree that this is an immediate prospect for him. What immediately concerns him is how he can keep quiet – how he can avoid displaying the huge façade that Haughty says his new wealth has given him. Haughty is quick to point out that one of the worst threats to his peace that he now faces as a young man of wealth is the clamour of importunate women.

The ivory tower is re-introduced into the narrative at this point, and takes on additional symbolic significance. It will also represent Gray's isolation from sexual involvement. Once safely inside the tower, Haughty says, Gray can have all the fun, while Haughty takes all the trouble. Gray admits the truth of this, and also admits that he is an anachronism, a survivor from a leisured and cultivated class that has all but disappeared.

It is clear from the text that James did not intend to invest his hero only with the sentimental glory of a representative of a dying tradition. For all his intelligence and charm, Gray cannot be cleared of moral culpability when he, symbolically, enters the tower and hands over the key of his treasury to Haughty. Stephen Spender surely makes too much of James's reference to Gray as 'a happy Hamlet' when he writes: 'There is no doubt that James was trying to "do" Hamlet in modern dress.'[9] James was indicating that his hero had Hamlet's indecisiveness and his kind of sensibility, but he is happy only because he has not, so far as the novel goes at least, attained Hamlet's appalled vision of the rottenness of the state. Nor has he yet indicated that he has any consciousness of the responsibility demanded of him because of his wealth. By his uncle's bequest, he has, at least symbolically, been called to help set right a time that is out of joint. From what we see of Gray in the fragment of the novel, it seems very doubtful that he has sufficient force of character to take on the task and in so doing attain tragic stature. The Hamlet reference is, moreover, counterbalanced by several others, most notably when Haughty compares Gray to St. Francis of Assisi. The quality of innocence and of denial implied by this comparison disables a tragic sense. Gray's naïveté is demonstrated when he completely misjudges his Horatio, Haughty. This is a symptom of his inability to take account of man's capacity for evil. The character of Gray seems to be in fact a potential source of weaknesses in the novel, for, as Marius Bewley has pointed out, 'his "fineness" is hardly of a weight sufficient to balance, artistically, the

256

terrible world of gold and ruthless competition that had been opened for James.'[10]

Gray wants to renounce the responsibility that wealth brings but keep the wealth in order to live in the comfort and detachment of an ivory tower. He is content to leave the guardian of the tower in the market-place below. This plan is, of course, doomed to failure. Haughty, like Oscar Wilde and most other people, can resist everything except temptation, and is driven to use the money for his own ends. The tower, deprived of its financial foundation, will crumble into dust.

And yet, paradoxically, James is not, in this novel, condemning ivory towers as such. The tower was for James, as it was for Yeats, the place in which the artist isolated himself from society and, like the Indian craftsman, carefully and patiently constructed his edifices for eternity. Gray, by his retreat to the tower, would, presumably, have developed his finer consciousness and been enabled to evaluate and judge American society in a way that those caught up in its acquisitive processes could not. James's intention was probably to use his hero as a sharp instrument of criticism.

Whatever the outcome of the novel, it is clear from what we have that the situation of the ivory-tower dweller is fraught with moral complexities. There is a hint that Gray himself is becoming aware of this in book four. This last, unfinished section returns us again to Gray, who is alone in his inherited house. In a 'rush of nervous apprehension, a sudden determination of terror,' he restlessly paces the verandah. His attention is caught by the chair in which the silent Mr. Gaw had sat that first afternoon. He turns away from it as from an apparition, and goes out on the lawn. 'He circled round the house altogether at last,' James wrote, 'looking at it more critically than had hitherto seemed relevant, taking the measure, disconcertedly, of its unabashed ugliness, and at the end coming to regard it very much as he might have eyed some monstrous modern machine, one of those his generation was going to be expected to master, to fly in, to fight in, to take the terrible women of the future out for airings in, and that mocked at *his* incompetence in such matters while he walked round and round it and gave it, as for dread of what it might do to him, the widest berth his enclosure allowed' (ANS, 993).

The passage is a remarkable example of how James, from the very appearance of things, could extract a meaning and project it into the future. The Newport mansion not only sums up a period of vulgar and extravagant taste, but also foreshadows a world in which Le Corbusier could call a house 'a machine for living'; it looks forward to the automobile age with the affronts to taste and proportion that Detroit has produced, and lastly anticipates the age of air-warfare and transportation.

A few lines after this prophetic view, the novel breaks off. All hopes of concluding it were driven out of James's mind by the rapidly increasing ferocity of the First World War. 'My aged nerves can scarcely stand it,' he wrote to a friend, in August 1914, 'and I bear up but as I can. I dip my nose, or try to, into the inkpot as often as I can; but it's as if there were no ink there, and I take it out smelling gunpowder, smelling blood, as hard as it did before.'[11]

Percy Lubbock, in the preface to his edition of *The Ivory Tower*, writes that after the outbreak of war James 'could no longer work upon a fiction supposed to represent contemporary or recent life.' That is why, when he began to write again, he took up *The Sense of the Past* instead. And yet, *The Ivory Tower*, with its vision of implied evil, rapacity, and violence, is quite congruent with the appalling war that caught up with it.

Those critics who have most loudly denounced James's 'retreat from reality' in the later novels have conspicuously ignored *The Ivory Tower* and its voluminous notes. James's memos to himself, which sprinkle the latter, reveal that he was fully conscious of the fact that he was creating an autonomous world that was the particular expression of his own artistic personality and of his peculiar vision of evil. It is as pointless to abuse this world as a retreat from reality as it is to abuse the late quartets of Beethoven or the late etchings of Rembrandt. In each case the extraordinarily individualistic technique has created a new way of perceiving and rendering reality.

This point may be elucidated by a brief comparison of *The Ivory Tower* with the two gigantic novels of Theodore Dreiser, *The Financier* (1912) and *The Titan* (1914). Fundamentally the issues each novelist deals with are the same: the effects on individuals of the struggle for and the achievement of money and power. Dreiser, using the convention of naturalism, supplied the raw materials for the theme from an almost documentary study of the market-place and the mansion. James, on the other hand, feeling 'a total absence of business initiation,' side-stepped all the transactions and worked instead on their ultimate effects on personality and human relationships. Using again the technique of *The American Scene*, he read into the scene all he wanted, employed rich symbols of the process and allowed the reader to do the rest. Dreiser allowed for nothing in his reader, except perseverance. As James noted in one of his memos to himself in the notes: 'It isn't *centrally* a drama of fools or vulgarians; it's only circumferentially and surroundedly so – these being enormously implied and with the effect of their hovering and pressing upon the whole business from without, but seen and felt by us with that rich indirectness' (ANS, 1027). James's complex and sensitive characters carry with them the connotations of their whole society – just as chromosomes carry the characteristics of an individual.

It may be said that James painted too dark a picture of American life in the notes to and fragment of *The Ivory Tower*. Certainly the period immediately before the Progressive era in which it took place was financially irresponsible and gave rise to luxurious expenditures by the rich. But one wonders whether it was much worse than the Gilded Age after the Civil War that James had also observed.

Perhaps what appalled him most about life in America in the early twentieth century, however, was not the 'money-passion' in itself but the manners of the new age of technology that accompanied it. To him it was apparent that leisure and grace in life, or what he called the 'margin,' were rapidly being destroyed in the United States. In his view, privacy was disappearing from houses, discrimination was being eliminated from conduct and taste, and time was being divorced from space. Wealth, instead of being used as an aid to cultivated living, was being employed as a tool for an assault on sensibility. Form in manners, as well as in art and architecture, was being ruthlessly sacrificed. If *The Ivory Tower* had been completed, it might have been the artistic correlative to Thorstein Veblen's *Theory of the Leisure Class*, published in 1899. Like James, Veblen, although from a different point of view, describes a world in which 'conspicuous consumption has gained more and more on conspicuous leisure as a means of repute.'[12] James's Gussy Bradham is the very type of the modern hostess who, with indefatigable force, organizes and disposes people into combinations in order to satisfy her love of power and vanity. Gray Fielder, on the other hand, is a member of a leisure class that, as James prophetically implied, was to be wiped out by the slaughters of the war.

The Ivory Tower was James's last assay of American life; it would almost certainly have been his best. His techniques of perception and narration had been developed and refined to such a point that he could encompass and interpret American experience more satisfactorily than he had been able to do in any of his previous American fictions. As in all the late works, the primary subject is rooted in fable. This time it is 'the fairy-tale,' as James calls it, of a man who wakes up to find himself rich beyond the dreams of avarice, without any apparent responsibilities. In addition, many of the great Jamesian themes are adumbrated in the notes and the fragment. These are the international theme, the initiation theme, the fraud theme, and the acquisition theme. Even the *alter ego* theme of *The Jolly Corner* is suggested in the situation of Gray, who was supposed to come to America at the age of fourteen, and did not in fact come until he was in his early thirties. The enduring Jamesian concern for the American girl also comes in for one last look. She is represented by Cissy Foy, who has all the attributes of her predecessors from Nora Lambert of *Watch and Ward* up to Milly Theale: the beauty, the spontaneity, the grace, the flair for dress. She lacks only the quintessential quality of innocence. Hers has been compromised already, like that of her immediate predecessor, Julia Bride. This is probably symptomatic of the great reversal that took place in this novel. America is no longer the source of moral innocence it had been in all James's previous novels. Its place is taken by Europe, which sends its innocent, Gray Fielder, over to face the corruption of the new world.

The final pattern of the novel, however, was to revert to the Jamesian type. Once more the 'fresh start' in America would end in the usual rejection, and the 'broken link' with Europe would be re-forged. Once more in his art, as in his life, James's passion to create and dramatize would fall back from the power and passion of American life, with which he could never bring himself to sympathize.

❋ 17 ❋

The Obstinate
Finality

Henry James's whole *œuvre* can be regarded as a massive attempt to make a humane order out of the disorder of experience, and to give form to the multifarious impressions and ideas of conscious life. Given the rawness and disorder of American life in the late nineteenth and early twentieth centuries, it is not surprising that he became an increasingly sharp critic of the United States. We see in his work, as in that of so many American writers, the growing realization of the gulf between the ideal and the real, between the promise of American life and its achievement. Yet he never ceased to believe that he owed to America what he happened to be as a man; accordingly he believed that he must do what he could for his country as an artist.

He would no doubt have written more 'American' books if he had been able, in his early years, to accommodate his artistic schemata, so heavily English and French, to the facts of American life and to his own limited experience in the United States. His search for a tradition with which to match his perception and from which to make his writing often seems a little pathetic. The difficulties he encountered and the false steps he took meant that he had to serve a long literary apprenticeship. At least he was never misled into thinking that a career in letters was anything but arduous. He was always strenuously searching for better techniques to accommodate his vision. As Mark Schorer has said: 'Technique is the means by which the writer's experience, which is his subject matter, compels him to attend to it;

technique is the only means he has of discovering, exploring, developing his subject, of conveying its meaning, and, finally, of evaluating it.' Had James been able to discover a satisfactory tradition, and thus a technique, through which he could mould his own work early in his career, this would have been a very different book. His long search on native ground, however, led to comparative failure, but this failure may have been the prerequisite for his eventual discovery of his own techniques, a discovery that culminated in the last great novels. After the passage just quoted, Schorer goes on to say: 'The writer capable of the most exacting technical scrutiny of his subject matter will produce works with the most satisfying content, works with thickness and resonance, works which reverberate, works with maximum meaning.'[1] It is hard to think of a writer who better exemplifies this statement than Henry James.

James's expatriation enabled him quickly to find what was being done in European fiction and, paradoxically, provided him with new techniques for writing about the United States. His detachment also gave him a cool and ironic point of view from which to describe and evaluate American life. He thus provided a new dimension to American literature which, up to his time, had been largely nationalistic in its outlook. From the French, in particular, James derived a standard of professionalism in letters which separated him from the prevailing provincialism of American writers on the one hand and the amateurism of the English on the other. The lesson was not lost on a later group of expatriates that included Gertrude Stein, Ezra Pound, and T. S. Eliot.

Yet, even though he brought a new cosmopolitanism to American literature, he somehow never lost touch with an essentially American way of treating experience. He himself came to recognize that he shared his brother's pragmatic philosophy; he belonged to the tough, not the tender, minded. When he referred, then, to his 'New England conscience,' it was always with an irony. Yet the moral basis of the New England mind was an important part of his inheritance. In his book on Hawthorne, he talked about the 'absence of the off-hand element in the manner in which many Americans, and many New Englanders especially, make up their minds about the people whom they meet.' This was a reminder of 'the importance of the individual in the American world.' James went on: 'The individual counts for more, as it were, and, thanks to the absence of a variety of social types and of settled heads under which he may be easily and conveniently pigeon-holed, he is to a certain extent a wonder and a mystery.' An Englishman or a Frenchman, he maintained, judged quickly from his own social standpoint, the Englishman especially having 'a healthy mistrust of analysis,' like the prototypical Dr. Johnson.[2] Like many other things that James wrote about Hawthorne, these observations have a striking applicability to his own work. He never pigeon-holed his major characters; they are always open to experience, constantly making themselves and being moulded by others. His later works especially are mainly concerned with 'the wonder and mystery' of personality in its struggle towards freedom. They are tireless analyses into the complexities of human psychology that make this freedom so difficult to achieve.

On the other hand, James was free from those inhibiting strains of Puritanism, of the academic, and of complacency that vitiated many a New England talent in the second half of the nineteenth century. As he wrote to Mrs. Jack Gardner, he would have liked to have been 'at the head of a New York legation in Boston.' Artistically he was often just that. The New York side of his inheritance predominated over the New England, just as it did in Herman Melville. Both writers possessed an openness of mind and a sense of ambiguities that was denied to all the New England writers except Hawthorne. F. O. Matthiessen has also suggested that in this respect Henry owed a good deal to his father. Certainly a boy brought up to sample all the different forms of worship practised in New York city and to avoid 'flagrant morality' like the plague could hardly subscribe subsequently to a particular dogma. It may be added that Henry Jr. was just as sceptical about his own father's 'ideas' as about anyone else's, which is why Quentin Anderson's attempt to point out the son's indebtedness to the father often looks so strained.[3]

Henry James's mind met the supreme test of its quality, perhaps, when he encountered the corruption and extravagance of what Mark Twain dubbed the Gilded Age. Twain and James have often been used as contrasts in the study of American literature; John Curtis Underwood and Van Wyck Brooks, among others, have celebrated

Twain as the true American writer and written off James as a rene-
gade. In the perspective of time, it can easily be seen that they had in
common several attitudes towards their native land, particularly
nostalgia for the innocent pre-Civil War days and a disgust with the
rapacity and commercialism of the post-War period. Twain's disillusionment turned in the end to cynicism and despair, which partly
dammed up the rich current of his humour, whereas James remained
too detached to be either disillusioned or despairing. The spectacle of
life, even at its darkest, could always offer interest and amusement to
him, as he showed in his famous letter to Henry Adams in March
1914.[4]

The resurgence of James's nostalgia for American life after many
years of residence in England prepared the way both for his return
and the subsequent strong reaction that found its form in the complex
American fiction in the later manner. Ironic comedy, which is largely
the mode of his later work, gave him the vehicle for criticism of the
new American society, a society he believed to be at many points
inferior to the one he had known as a younger man. His return to
America in 1904 coincided with a period of immense and restless
change. He was among the first critics of American life to realize
some of the consequences.

For the first time in history there was a feeling in many people's
minds that the old American ideal of unbridled individualism plus
its modern counterpart, laissez-faire capitalism, were not working
satisfactorily. Industrialism and mass immigration had created problems that no existing machinery could deal with. In the first decade
of the twentieth century there was a rising cry for political and social
reforms. The first adequate response to the demand was made by
Theodore Roosevelt. As a contemporary writer, Herbert Croly, put
it: 'Under his leadership as President, reform began to assume the
characteristics, if not the name, of progressivism ... He was the hero
of the first moral revulsion against the abuses of the established order
...'[5] This progressivism, in a different form, was the message of Wood-
row Wilson in his New Freedom platform of 1912.

Croly, founder of the *New Republic*, which he edited until his
death in 1930, was himself the first to recognize the potential relevance of James's contribution to America's stirring conscience. In an

essay called 'Henry James and his Countrymen,' written in 1904 to welcome James back to his native land, he eloquently defended the novelist's long expatriation. 'American life,' he wrote, 'is in the making. Its social forms are confused and indefinite; its social types either local, or evasive, or impermanent. Its ideal of a democratic society in a democratic state is constantly present as an ideal, but mostly absent as a reality, offering a problem to be worked out rather than an achievement to be generalized and portrayed. Its intellectual interests are for the present subordinated to its moral, practical, and business interests. The atmosphere of its life is charged with activity and endeavor rather than with observation and reflection.' He thought that it was difficult for a novelist to write in this situation. He was in danger of becoming a patriotic orator or, as the work of Howells showed, a recorder of little more than unimportant details. James, through his expatriation, had escaped these two dangers. Although, as a result, he was separated from 'the main stream of American literary fulfillment,' his example should, Croly thought, be salutary to his fellow artists who remained in the United States. Without 'some infusion of his incorruptible artistic purpose, of his devotion to good workmanship, of his freedom from stupefying moral and social illusions,' their work would be 'at best a kind of literary journalism.' At the end of this remarkable essay, Croly looked forward to the time when American criticism would play its proper part in seeing that James's work would have its due influence on American literature.[6]

This essay was written before the publication of *The American Scene* and the later American fiction. In these works, James provided his countrymen not only with his usual artistic standards but also with proof of his stand against 'the abuses of the established order.' He cared enough about American life to pay close attention to what he thought were its failures, and he was quite willing to risk the obloquy with which patriots would greet this work. As Croly foresaw, his example has been salutary to some later American writers, while the spate of American criticism of his work in the last twenty-five years has amply testified to James's influence and effect. Yet, Jamesian criticism has continued to spawn writers who have kept up the stream of abuse that literary patriots have directed at James's work almost from his earliest publication. The latest critic in this good old tradition, Maxwell Geismar, has out-abused the rest, and taken good care to exclude James forever from the pantheon of American writers. In his conclusion to *Henry James and His Cult*, he writes: 'Compared with Melville, Whitman, Mark Twain, Dreiser – or even with Hawthorne the "romancier" whom James took such pains to dismiss from the native scene before him – Henry becomes a prodigy, yes, or some kind of exotic literary monster in truth; but a child prodigy, as we've seen, and even a childlike or childish sort of monster.'

The basis for this judgment is not only an inadequate study of James's work, as the Hawthorne reference reveals, but also a consistent misreading of the fiction and the frequent quoting of sentences and phrases out of context. Like Van Wyck Brooks before him, Geismar uses the biographical fallacy to read into the expressions of many of James's characters the views of the author. Then he takes some theories from Freud and a few hints from Jung to create a weird scissors-and-paste parody of an author who palters and prevaricates through the pages of his book. The conclusion is: 'Henry James is the most fascinating case of arrested development in the history of belles lettres. At base his whole literary world was the "pure" fantasy world of an adolescent, or preadolescent vision of how things "should be," and never were, and never could be.'[7]

The truth of the matter is quite the reverse of Geismar's view. Henry James had one of the longest and most remarkable developments in literary history. His vision remained adaptable to new schemata of perception and varieties of points of view until the very end of his life. He was continually advancing towards new grounds of experience and always taking deeper soundings of awareness. The history of American letters is marked by the decline and failure of writers in their prime. To take only the writers on Geismar's list: Melville spent his last fifteen years in literary silence; Mark Twain's work underwent a steady decline as a bitter pessimism clouded his vision; Dreiser's work was increasingly vitiated by his adherence to political programmes, and Hawthorne's last years were marred by unfinished work and a marked falling-off in imaginative power.

The causes of these failures are various, naturally; among them are failing health, weakening faith, personal tragedy, and declining audiences. The point is that Henry James, too, had to face all these difficulties, but he alone among this list of major American writers prevailed to the end and was still at work when death placed the period on the page. The sources of James's vitality in the face of adversity are ultimately unknowable, but I suggest that an important one was his ability to respond to new forms of perception and to embody these in changing forms and styles.

It is true that he did recoil from the America that he found on his return visit of 1904–5, and that this recoil is recorded in his later American fiction. He dated his identity to a period long before the rise of the new United States that he paints in *The American Scene*. As a young man he felt that American society was provincial and lacked interest and variety, but, looking back from the vantage point of his later years, he appreciated its homogeneity, its moral sense, and its democratic spirit. His later experience in his native land led him to believe that it had become wildly heterogeneous racially, that its moral sense had degenerated into money-passion, and that its democracy had created masses on the one hand and oligarchs on the other.

The explanation for his later beliefs may be partly found in the fact that he was the supreme exponent of the nineteenth-century passion for the individual point of view. In his work, he created a spectrum of seeing eyes who reported on and reacted to a variety of experience in the United States. When he returned to his native land early in the twentieth century, he found a society which had begun to break down the kind of consciousness favourable to selective points of view. As Marshall McLuhan has pointed out, modern technology, especially in communications, has gone a long way towards undercutting the autonomy of individual view-points. The telephone, the telegraph, and the mass circulation newspaper were all flourishing in the United States to which James returned in 1904. These, it seems, more than 'the working of democratic institutions,' to use James's own words, had begun to 'determine and qualify manners, feeling, communications, modes of contact and conceptions of life.' What James also called 'the will to grow' and the passion for change had set American society in rapid motion, made it so restless, impatient, acquisitive, and loud that James, fresh from years spent in his quiet, rural, domestic corner of England, could barely stand it. His response to this in life was a retreat to his 'little downward burrow' in Rye; in his fiction it was the retreat to the past or the mother symbol.

Even though America grated so much on his nerves, it did not prevent him from recording his felt experience there as accurately as he knew how. In Gray Fielder, he created an 'insanely romantic' hero who was to represent the old leisure-class society as a standard of criticism on the new, just as W. B. Yeats, about the same time, was writing about the death of romantic Ireland in 'September 1913.' In the letter to Henry Adams mentioned above, he saw himself and his old friend as 'lone survivors' from a past that was 'at the bottom of an abyss,' and his late work reflects this outlook. But that did not cause him to oversimplify the situation. He went on cultivating his consciousness for all it was worth. 'You see I still,' he continued in his letter to Adams, 'in presence of life (or of what you deny to be such,) have reactions – as many as possible – and the book I sent you [*Notes of a Son and Brother*] is the proof of them. It's, I suppose, because I am that queer monster, the artist, an obstinate finality, an inexhaustible sensibility. Hence the reactions – appearances, memories, many things, go on playing upon it with consequences that I note and "enjoy" (grim word!) noting. It all takes doing – and I *do*. I believe I shall do yet again – it is still an act of life.' He kept up the act of life until the end, thus asserting the power of the imagination over everything that worked against it. In his American writings, as in all his work, he asserted this power in presenting and criticizing reality as he intensely saw it. The perfection of the form in which he wrote, the ivory tower from which the artist spoke, was in itself the best implicit criticism of life in the United States and of the desolating transcience of human life everywhere.

Bibliographical
Note

Every student of Henry James is heavily in debt to Professor Leon
Edel for his bibliographical, biographical, and editorial work. I am
more than most. In particular his *A Bibliography of Henry James*,
edited with Dan Laurence (London, 1961), has been indispensable.
The bibliographical compilations of *PMLA* and *American Literature*
have been consulted. 'Criticism of Henry James: a Selected Check-
list,' by Maurice Beebe and William T. Stafford in the Henry James
number of *Modern Fiction Studies*, xii (Spring, 1966), gathers in a
handy form almost all the work done up to that time on James's many
works, and has proved invaluable.

To go beyond the citation of books in the footnotes, I should make
particular reference to the useful service that Professor Oscar Cargill
has rendered in his summary of Jamesian criticism in *The Novels of
Henry James* (New York, 1961). His work made it unnecessary for
me, in many cases, to refer extensively to previous discussions of
novels that I also treat. Other books on James that I have found most
helpful include Edwin T. Bowden's *The Themes of Henry James*
(New Haven, 1956), F. W. Dupee's collection, *The Question of
Henry James* (New York, 1945), Cornelia P. Kelley's *The Early
Development of Henry James* (Urbana, Illinois, 1930), Dorothea
Krook's *The Ordeal of Consciousness in Henry James* (Cambridge,
1962), F. O. Matthiessen's *Henry James: The Major Phase* (New
York, 1944), Simon Nowell-Smith's *The Legend of the Master:*

Henry James (New York, 1948), Richard Poirier's *The Comic Sense of Henry James: a Study of the Early Novels* (London, 1960), Sister M. Corona Sharp's *The Confidante in Henry James: Evolution and Moral Value of a Fictive Character* (Notre Dame, 1963), R. W. Stallman's *The Houses That James Built* (East Lansing, 1961), Krishna Baldev Vaid's *Technique in the Tales of Henry James* (Cambridge, Mass., 1964).

Books on the novel that I have found valuable or challenging for theoretical discussions include Marius Bewley's *The Complex Fate: Hawthorne, Henry James, and Some Other American Writers* (London, 1952), and his *The Eccentric Design: Form in the Classic American Novel* (London, 1959), Wayne C. Booth's *The Rhetoric of Fiction* (Chicago, 1961), Richard Chase's *The American Novel and Its Tradition* (Garden City, 1957), Northrop Frye's *Anatomy of Criticism* (Princeton, 1957), Irving Howe's *Politics and the Novel* (New York, 1957), Mark Schorer's *The World We Imagine: Selected Essays* (New York, 1968); Tony Tanner's *The Reign of Wonder: Naivety and Reality in American Literature* (Cambridge, 1965), Lionel Trilling's *The Liberal Imagination: Essays on Literature and Society* (Garden City, 1953), Dorothy Van Ghent's *The English Novel: Form and Content* (New York, 1953), and William Wasserstrom's *Heiress of All the Ages: Sex and Sentiment in the Genteel Tradition* (Minneapolis, Minn., 1959).

Abbreviations
and
Short Titles

American Essays
The American Essays of Henry James, edited with an introduction by Leon Edel, New York, 1956

ANS
The American Novels and Stories of Henry James, edited and with introduction by F. O. Matthiessen, New York, 1956

AS
Henry James, *The American Scene*, London, 1907

Autiobiog.
Henry James: Autobiography, A Small Boy and Others, Notes of a Son and Brother, The Middle Years, edited with an introduction by Frederick W. Dupee, New York, 1956

Blithedale
The Blithedale Romance in *The Complete Novels and Selected Tales of Nathaniel Hawthorne*, edited with an introduction by Norman Holmes Pearson, New York, 1937

Bewley, *Complex Fate*
Marius Bewley, *The Complex Fate: Hawthorne, Henry James, and Some Other American Writers*, London, 1952

Bewley, *Eccentric Design*
Marius Bewley, *The Eccentric Design: Form in the Classic American Novel*, London, 1959

Bowden
Edwin T. Bowden, *The Themes of Henry James*, New Haven, 1956

Cargill
Oscar Cargill, *The Novels of Henry James*, New York, 1961

271

CT
The Complete Tales of Henry James, edited with introductions by Leon Edel, 12 vols., Philadelphia, 1960–5

Dupee
F. W. Dupee, *Henry James*, New York, 1956

Edel, *Conquest of London*
Leon Edel, *Henry James, the Conquest of London, 1870–1883*, London, 1962

Edel, *Middle Years*
Leon Edel, *Henry James, The Middle Years, 1884–94*, London, 1963

Edel, *Untried Years*
Leon Edel, *Henry James, The Untried Years, 1843–70*, London, 1953

French Poets
Henry James, *French Poets and Novelists*, with an introduction by Leon Edel, New York, 1964

Future of the Novel
Henry James, *The Future of the Novel, Essays on the Art of Fiction*, edited with an introduction by Leon Edel, New York, 1956

Geismar
Maxwell Geismar, *Henry James and his Cult*, London, 1964

Harvard
The Houghton Library, Harvard University

Hawthorne
Henry James, *Hawthorne*, London, 1879

Howe
Irving Howe, *Politics and the Novel*, New York, 1957

Howells
Life in Letters of William Dean Howells, edited by Mildred Howells, 2 vols., New York, 1928

Kelley
Cornelia P. Kelley, *The Early Development of Henry James*, Urbana, Ill., 1930

Krook
Dorothea Krook, *The Ordeal of Consciousness in Henry James*, Cambridge, England, 1962

Letters
The Letters of Henry James, edited by Percy Lubbock, London, 1920

LC
Library of Congress

N & T
The Novels and Tales of Henry James, 24 vols., New York, 1906–9

NB
The Notebooks of Henry James, edited by F. O. Matthiessen and Kenneth B. Murdock, New York, 1947

Painter's Eye
Henry James, *The Painter's Eye: Notes and Essays on the Pictorial Arts*, selected and edited with an introduction by John L. Sweeney, London, 1956

Partial Portraits
Henry James, *Partial Portraits*, London, 1888

PL
Henry James, *The Portrait of a Lady*, 3 vols., London, 1883

Poirier
Richard Poirier, *The Comic Sense of Henry James*, New York, 1960

Portraits of Places
Henry James, *Portraits of Places*, Boston, 1885

Selected Letters
The Selected Letters of Henry James, edited with an introduction by Leon Edel, New York, 1961

Vaid
Krishna Baldev Vaid, *Technique in the Tales of Henry James*, Cambridge, Mass., 1964

Wasserstrom
William Wasserstrom, *Heiress of All the Ages*, Minneapolis, Minn., 1959

William James
Letters of William James, edited by Henry James, 2 vols., Boston, 1920

WW
Henry James, *Watch and Ward*, with an introduction by Leon Edel, London, 1960

Notes

CHAPTER ONE

1 This account is based on reports of the occasion in contemporary newspapers, including Wendell Phillips' anti-slavery paper *The Liberator*, and the *Boston Daily Advertiser* for 2 January 1865
2 'Emerson,' reprinted in *American Essays*, 72
3 Quoted in *Autobiog.*, 362
4 *Autobiog.*, 415
5 *Autobiog.*, 17
6 *Autobiog.*, 382–3
7 *Autobiog.*, 417–19
8 Quoted in Edel, *Untried Years*, 158
9 *Autobiog.*, 48
10 *Autobiog.*, 389
11 *Autobiog.*, 68
12 Quoted in Kelley, 53
13 Quoted in Kelley, 29–30
14 *American Essays*, 131–6
15 *Autobiog.*, 491
16 *Hawthorne*, 144

CHAPTER TWO

1 *Autobiog.*, 440

2 *Painter's Eye*, 71–2
3 E. H. Gombrich, *Art and Illusion, A Study in the Psychology of Pictorial Representation* (London, 1960), 62
4 *Painter's Eye*, 96–7
5 *Autobiog.*, 449–50
6 *Autobiog.*, 452
7 Kelley, 61
8 *Future of the Novel*, 80–9
9 *Howells*, I, 116
10 *Selected Letters*, 20–1
11 Roy Harvey Pearce, *The Continuity of American Poetry* (Princeton, 1961), 213
12 *American Essays*, 114
13 AS, 153–4
14 *Autobiog.*, 36–8
15 *Autobiog.*, 426

CHAPTER THREE

1 Nathaniel Hawthorne, *Short Stories*, edited with an Introduction by Newton Arvin (New York, 1955), 73

CHAPTER FOUR

1 *Autobiog.*, 549
2 MS Letter, 25 March 1870, Norton Papers, Harvard
3 Quoted in Edel, *Untried Years*, 339
4 Reprinted in *Portraits of Places*, 324–7
5 *Portraits of Places*, 366–7
6 AS, 222
7 See Vincent Scully, *The Shingle Style, Architectural Theory and Design from Richardson to the Origins of Wright* (New Haven, Conn., 1955), 40–1 and illustrations
8 *Portraits of Places*, 338–49
9 Nathaniel Hawthorne, *Our Old Home* (Boston, 1866), 20–1, 29
10 See particularly chaps. IX and XI of E. H. Gombrich's *Art and Illusion* (London, 1960)
11 Vaid, 35
12 *Nation*, VII (22 October 1868), 333
13 *Autobiog.*, 434

CHAPTER FIVE

1 Kelley, 125
2 Quoted in Cargill, 8–9
3 'George Sand,' in *French Poets*, 172
4 Cargill, note 15 to chap. I, 15
5 MS letter, 9 August 1871, Norton Papers, Harvard

CHAPTER SIX

1 MS letter, Norton Papers, Harvard
2 *Letters*, I, 34
3 *Letters*, I, 36–7
4 *Letters*, I, 40
5 NB, 24–5
6 N & T, XVIII, X
7 *Nation*, XX (1 January 1875), 12–13

8 N & T, I, x–xi
9 N & T, I, XV
10 'A Source for *Roderick Hudson*,' *Modern Language Notes*, CXIII (August 1948), 303–10
11 'Ivan Turgenieff' in *French Poets*, 220
12 *French Poets*, 230
13 Lerner, 35. Gilbert Phelps, *The Russian Novel in English Fiction* (London, 1956), 71–2
14 Cargill, 29
15 *French Poets*, 217
16 *Hawthorne*, 133
17 N & T, I, xvii–xviii
18 Serialized text: *Atlantic Monthly*, XXV (February 1875), 147
19 *American Essays*, 11
20 *The Marble Faun*, 591
21 *Selected Letters*, 42
22 '*Roderick Hudson* and Thomas Crawford,' *American Quarterly*, XIII (Winter, 1961), 495–504
23 Serialized text: *Atlantic Monthly*, XXXV, 12–13
24 Bowden, 25
25 *Selected Letters*, 43

CHAPTER SEVEN

1 Cargill, 67
2 *The Europeans*, with an introduction by Edward Sackville-West (London, 1952), vii
3 F. R. Leavis, 'The Novel as Dramatic Poem: *The Europeans*,' *Scrutiny*, XV, no. 3 (Summer, 1948), 215
4 *Blithedale*, 444
5 *Blithedale*, 448
6 *Blithedale*, 563
7 *The Remains of Hesiod*, trans. C. A. Elton (London, 1815), 21
8 Bowden, 49

9 Kelley, 262
10 Dupee, 88
11 Charles G. Hoffman, *The Short Novels of Henry James* (New York, 1957), 37
12 *The Europeans*, with an introduction by Edward Sackville-West, viii–x
13 Dupee, 88
14 *Washington Square, The Europeans*, with an introduction by R. P. Blackmur (New York, 1959), 9
15 Dupee, 87
16 MS letter, Harvard
17 *Washington Square, The Europeans*, with an introduction by R. P. Blackmur, 5
18 Thomas Wentworth Higginson, *Short Studies of American Authors* (Boston, 1880), 56. It is hard to resist the conjecture that this critic's middle name had something to do with his harsh attack on *The Europeans*
19 N & T, XVIII, viii
20 'Henry James: the Private Universe' in *The Lost Childhood and Other Essays* (London, 1951), 23

CHAPTER EIGHT

1 *The Autobiography of Mark Twain*, ed. Charles Neider (New York, 1959), 295
2 MS letter, Brighton, 9 October 1878, Harvard
3 *The Independent*, XXXII (6 May 1880), 1–2
4 *Letters*, I, 72
5 Poirier, 166
6 Wasserstrom, 88
7 Poirier, 178
8 PL, I, 26

9 PL, I, 37
10 *The English Novel: Form and Function* (New York, 1953), 196
11 PL, I, 66
12 *The Principles of Psychology* (New York, 1950), 11, 103
13 PL, I, 234
14 Quoted by Leon Edel in his introduction to *The Portrait of a Lady* (Boston, 1956), viii
15 PL, I, 57

CHAPTER NINE

1 NB, 23–4
2 N & T, XIV, xxi
3 *Letters*, I, 90–1
4 Typescript copy of original MS letter made by Percy Lubbock, Harvard
5 *Letters of Henry Adams*, ed. W. C. Ford (Boston, 1930), I, 333
6 NB, 40
7 *American Essays*, 68
8 Typescript letter, Lubbock, Harvard
9 Edel, *Conquest of London*, 499
10 N & T, XIV, xx
11 *Literature and Insurgency: Ten Studies in Racial Evolution* (New York, 1914), 41
12 This trilogy of tales is discussed at greater length in my article 'From Daisy Miller to Julia Bride, "A Whole Passage of Intellectual History," ' *American Quarterly*, XI (Summer, 1959), 136–46. Copyright, 1959, Trustees of the University of Pennsylvania
13 NB, 56
14 N & T, XVIII, viii–ix
15 Quoted by C. Vann Woodward in *The Burden of Southern History*

(Baton Rouge, La., 1960), 126
16 N & T, XVIII, xi
17 NB, 52
18 *Modern Language Notes*, LXV (May 1950), 317–19
19 *The Rhetoric of Fiction* (Chicago, 1961), 341
20 *Letters*, I, 99

CHAPTER TEN

1 *Howells*, I, 367
2 *The History of Impressionism* (New York, 1946), 294–5
3 'The Impressionists' in *Painter's Eye*, 114–15
4 *Alphonse Daudet* (London, 1949), 179
5 *Ibid.*, 234
6 *Letters*, I, 103
7 *Letters*, I, 104–5
8 *Partial Portraits*, 123
9 *Ibid.*, 214
10 *Ibid.*, 206
11 *Future of the Novel*, 20
12 *The Great Republic* (London, 1884), vi
13 NB, 66

CHAPTER ELEVEN

1 Bewley, *Complex Fate*, 9
2 *Autobiog.*, 144
3 NB, 47
4 Bewley, *Complex Fate*, 11
5 Cargill, 128
6 *Partial Portraits*, 199
7 *Ibid.*, 237
8 *Ibid.*, 212
9 Howe, 184
10 *Letters*, I, 116
11 *Partial Portraits*, 216

12 N & T, III, xvii
13 Howe, 191
14 Howe, 184
15 'Pragmatic Realism in *The Bostonians*' in *Henry James, Modern Judgements*, ed. Tony Tanner (London, 1968), 164
16 As quoted in NB, 49
17 *L'Evangéliste, Roman Parisien* (Paris, 1883), 264
18 *Letters*, II, 516

CHAPTER TWELVE

1 *Letters*, I, 136
2 MS letters, Norton Papers, Harvard
3 Edel, *Middle Years*, 85–6
4 N & T, V, vii–viii
5 *Modern Fiction Studies*, XII (Spring, 1966), 55
6 *The Legend of the Master*, comp. Simon Nowell-Smith (New York, 1948), 23
7 *The Reign of Wonder* (Cambridge, 1965), 11–15
8 N & T, VI, 145
9 N & T, V, xxii–xxiii
10 *Letters*, I, 143–4
11 MS letter, 25 March 1889, Norton Papers, Harvard
12 *Letters*, I, 263–5
13 *Letters*, I, 284
14 The American Letters have been reprinted by Leon Edel in *American Essays*, 197–257
15 The essay and the letter, reprinted in *American Essays*, 11–31, are discussed in my article 'Henry James on Hawthorne,' *New England Quarterly*, XXXII (June 1959), 216–21
16 *Letters*, I, 324
17 *Anatomy of Criticism* (Princeton, 1957), 305

18 *The Legend of the Master,* comp. Simon Nowell-Smith (New York, 1948), 112
19 *Letters,* I, 419
20 *William James,* II, 188–9
21 *Letters,* I, 427
22 *William James,* II, 195
23 MS letter, John Hay Papers, LC
24 MS letter, Harvard
25 MS letter, Norton Papers, Harvard
26 *Letters,* II, 23
27 MS letter, Chocorua, N.H., 14 September 1904, Yale Library
28 MS letter, 21 October 1904, George Harvey Papers, LC

CHAPTER THIRTEEN

1 *The Territory Ahead* (New York, 1957), 209
2 *American Essays,* 237
3 *Letters,* I, 420
4 Geismar, 348
5 See my article 'Aesthetics of the Skyscraper: the Views of Sullivan, James and Wright, *American Quarterly,* IX (Fall, 1957), 316–24
6 *Letters,* II, 26

CHAPTER FOURTEEN

1 James mentions this to his agent, J. B. Pinker, in a letter dated 5 December 1905, now in the Yale Library
2 MS letter (incomplete), Harvard
3 *Letters,* II, 28–9

CHAPTER FIFTEEN

1 *Letters,* I, 425
2 Krook, 350
3 It was not published until December 1908, after most of the others, but James refers to the story in a letter to Pinker dated 7 November 1906 (MS, Yale Library)
4 AS, 229
5 Geismar, 358
6 'Henry James's "The Jolly Corner," ' *Nineteenth Century Fiction,* XII (June 1957), 72–84
7 *Partisan Review,* XI (Fall, 1944), 435–55
8 'The Merciful Fraud in Three Stories by Henry James,' *The Tiger's Eye,* no. 9 (October 1949), 83–96
9 *The Confidante in Henry James* (Notre Dame, Ind., 1963), 60–1
10 Geoffery Lienhaupt, 'The Superficial Society – I,' *The Listener,* LXIV (7 July 1960), 13
11 I have collected these articles in *French Writers and American Women: Essays by Henry James* (Branford, Conn., 1960)
12 N & T, XVII, xxvi
13 Annette Kar, 'Archetypes of American Innocence: Lydia Blood and Daisy Miller,' *American Quarterly,* V (Spring, 1953), 32
14 N & T, XVIII, ix–xiii
15 AS, 192
16 Vaid, 235
17 AS, 301

CHAPTER SIXTEEN

1 AS, 237. F. O. Matthiessen first discussed the close links between *The American Scene* and *The Ivory Tower* in *Henry James: the Major Phase* (New York, 1944), chap. v. I am indebted to this perceptive study at several points
2 *Letters,* II, 22
3 This draft for the American novel

is to be found in *The Notebooks*,
343–60. This false start is also discussed by Cargill, 462–6

4 *Henry James, Man and Author* (Toronto, 1927), 90–1
5 AS, 222
6 *American Essays*, 23, 28
7 Cargill, 474
8 AS, 57
9 *The Destructive Element* (London, 1935), 100
10 Bewley, *Eccentric Design*, 257
11 *Letters*, II, 402
12 *Theory of the Leisure Class* (New York, 1911), 397

CHAPTER SEVENTEEN

1 'Technique as Discovery' in *The World We Imagine: Selected Essays* (New York, 1968), 3
2 *Hawthorne*, 50–1
3 *The American Henry James* (New Brunswick, N.J., 1957)
4 *Letters*, II, 373–4
5 *Progressive Democracy* (New York, 1915), 11
6 Reprinted in *The Question of Henry James*, ed. F. W. Dupee (New York, 1945), 28–39
7 Geismar, 434–5

Index